Catholicism and Interreligious Dialogue

Catholicism and Interreligious Dialogue

EDITED BY JAMES L. HEFT, S.M.

OXFORD
UNIVERSITY PRESS

OXFORD
UNIVERSITY PRESS

Oxford University Press, Inc., publishes works that further
Oxford University's objective of excellence
in research, scholarship, and education.

Oxford   New York
Auckland   Cape Town   Dar es Salaam   Hong Kong   Karachi
Kuala Lumpur   Madrid   Melbourne   Mexico City   Nairobi
New Delhi   Shanghai   Taipei   Toronto

With offices in
Argentina   Austria   Brazil   Chile   Czech Republic   France   Greece
Guatemala   Hungary   Italy   Japan   Poland   Portugal   Singapore
South Korea   Switzerland   Thailand   Turkey   Ukraine   Vietnam

Published by Oxford University Press, Inc.
198 Madison Avenue, New York, New York 10016
www.oup.com

Oxford is a registered trademark of Oxford University Press

Library of Congress Cataloging-in-Publication Data
Catholicism and interreligious dialogue / edited by James L. Heft.
p. cm.
Includes index.
ISBN 978-0-19-982789-3 (pbk. : alk. paper) — ISBN 978-0-19-982787-9 (hardcover : alk. paper)
1. Catholic Church--Relations. 2. Christianity and other religions. I. Heft, James.
BX1784.C42 2011
261.2—dc22   2011009506

Printed in the United States of America
on acid-free paper

CONTENTS

CONTRIBUTORS

Rachel Adler Rachel Adler is professor of modern Jewish thought and Judaism and gender at Hebrew Union College-Los Angeles. She was one of the first theologians to integrate feminist perspectives and concerns into the interpretation of Jewish texts and the renewal of Jewish law and ethics. Her essay "The Jew Who Wasn't There," first published in 1971, is generally considered the first piece of Jewish feminist theology. She is the author of *Engendering Judaism,* which won the National Jewish Book Award for Jewish Thought. She is the first female Jewish theologian to win this award. *Engendering Judaism* also won Gratz College's Tuttleman Foundation Award and the University of Southern California's Phi Lamda Phi Award for best faculty book. She is a contributor to the soon-to-be published *Jewish Women's Commentary on the Torah* and is on the editorial board of this project. Professor Adler is currently writing about the theological challenges posed by dementia.

Robert Ford Campany Robert Ford Campany earned his BA in philosophy from Davidson College in 1981. After a year at Tainan Theological College in Taiwan, he began graduate work in the history of religions program at the University of Chicago, where he completed his MA in 1983 and his PhD in 1988. He taught at Indiana University for eighteen years and at the University of Southern California for four years before joining the faculty at Vanderbilt University in 2010, where he now holds appointment as professor of Asian studies and religious studies. He has published more than two dozen articles and three books on topics in the history of religions in early medieval China and the cross-cultural study of religions, and a fourth book, *Signs from the Unseen Realm: A Study and Translation of a Collection of Buddhist Miracle Tales from Early Medieval China,* will be published in 2011.

Christopher Key Chapple Christopher Key Chapple serves as Doshi Professor of Indic and Comparative Theology at Loyola Marymount University. He has published several books, including *Karma and Creativity* (1986), a co-translation of the *Yoga Sutra of Patanjali* (1990), *Nonviolence to Animals, Earth and Self in Asian Traditions* (1993), *Hinduism and Ecology* (coedited, 2000), *Jainism and Ecology* (edited, 2002), *Reconciling Yogas: Haribhadra's Collection of Views on Yoga* (2003), and *Yoga and the Luminous* (2008). He serves on the advisory boards for the Forum on Religion and Ecology, the Ahimsa Center, the Forum on Global Ethics and Religion, and the Foundation for Indic Philosophy and Culture.

Huaiyu Chen Dr. Huaiyu Chen is an assistant professor of religious studies, specializing in East Asian Buddhism. He earned his PhD from Princeton University. His particular interests include medieval Buddhist monasticism, religious cultures on the Silk Road, Chinese intellectual history, Christian missionary Sinology, and the relationship of Buddhism to modernity in East Asia. He has published several articles on Nestorian Christianity and Buddhism in medieval China. He is the author of *The Revival of Buddhist Monasticism in Medieval China* (2007).

Francis X. Clooney, S.J. Francis X. Clooney, S.J., is the Parkman Professor of Divinity and professor of comparative theology at Harvard Divinity School. He has written widely on Hindu religious traditions and their implications for Christian theology. He taught in the Theology Department at Boston College for more than twenty years, and from 2002 to 2004 was academic director of the Centre for Hindu Studies at Oxford University. He served as the first president of the International Society for Hindu-Christian Studies and is the author of numerous books, including *Seeing through Texts* (1996), winner of the Best Book Award in Hindu-Christian Studies given by the Internatonal Society for Hindu-Christian Studies, *Hindu God, Christian God* (2001), *Divine Mother, Blessed Mother: Hindu Goddesses and the Virgin Mary* (2005), *Father Bouchet's India* (2006). Most recently, he served as editor of *Jesuit Postmodern: Scholarship, Vocation, and Identity in the Twenty-first Century* (2006). He has just completed two books, *Beyond Compare: St. Francis de Sales and Sri Vedanta Desika on Surrender* and *The Truth, the Way, and the Life: A Christian Commentary on the Three Holy Mantras of the Srivaisnavas*.

Philip A. Cunningham Philip A. Cunningham is professor of theology and director of the Institute for Jewish-Catholic Relations of Saint Joseph's University in Philadelphia. As secretary of the Council of Centers on Jewish-Christian Relations, he manages its resource Web site at http://.ccjr.us/dialogika-resources. A vice president of the International Council of Christians and Jews, he has also served as a member of the Advisory Committee on Catholic-Jewish Relations for the United States Conference of Catholic Bishops and as a delegate for the Vatican at three international conferences on Catholic-Jewish relations.

With interests in biblical studies, religious education, and theologies of Christian-Jewish relations, Dr. Cunningham is the author of numerous book and articles on these subjects. His most recent books are *A Story of Shalom: The Calling of Christians and Jews by a Covenanting God* and *Sharing the Scriptures*. He has also edited *Pondering the Passion: What's at Stake for Christians and Jews?* and coedited *The Catholic Church and the Jewish People: Recent Reflections from Rome*. He is also coeditor of *Christ Jesus and the Jewish People Today: New Explorations of Theological Interrelationships* (forthcoming).

Elliot N. Dorff Elliot N. Dorff, rabbi (Jewish Theological Seminary), PhD (Columbia), is rector and Distinguished Professor of Philosophy at the American Jewish University (formerly the University of Judaism) in Los Angeles and a visiting professor at UCLA School of Law. He has been a member of the Priest-Rabbi Dialogue, sponsored by the Archdiocese of Los Angeles and the Board of Rabbis of Southern California, since its inception in 1973 and has cochaired it since 1990, and he has taught Catholic seminary professors and seminarians in Poland in 1989 and 1996. He is also immediate past president of the Academy of Judaic, Christian, and Islamic Studies. A recipient of the *Journal of Law and Religion*'s Lifetime Achievement Award, he also holds three honorary doctorates. Author of more than 200 articles and 15 books on Jewish thought, law, and ethics, his most recent book is *The Jewish Approach to Repairing the World (Tikkun Olam): A Brief Introduction for Christians* (2008). Since 2008, Rabbi Dorff has been teaching teachers in Catholic high schools across the country in the Bearing Witness program of the Anti-Defamation League.

James L. Fredericks James L. Fredericks is a Catholic priest of the Archdiocese of San Francisco and a faculty member in the Department of Theological Studies at Loyola Marymount University. He is a specialist in interreligious dialogue, especially the dialogue between Buddhism and Christianity, and has lectured internationally in Japan, China, India, Iran, and Europe. He was a Senior Fulbright Research Scholar in Kyoto, Japan, and held the Numata Chair in Buddhism and Culture at Ryukoku University in Kyoto. For many years, he has been a member of the Los Angeles Buddhist-Catholic Dialogue Group. In addition to many articles, he is the author of *Faith among Faiths: Christian Theology and the Non-Christian Religions* and *Buddhists and Christians: Through Comparative Theology to a New Solidarity*.

James L. Heft, S.M. James L. Heft (Marianist) is a priest in the Society of Mary. He served on the board of the American Association of Catholic Colleges and Universities and chaired that board for two years. He spent many years at the University of Dayton, serving as chair of the Theology Department for six years, provost of the University for eight years, and chancellor for ten years. He left the University of Dayton in the summer of 2006 to found the Institute for Advanced

Catholic Studies at the University of Southern California in Los Angeles, where he now serves as the Alton Brooks Professor of Religion and president of the Institute for Advanced Catholic Studies. He has written and edited 12 books and written more than 170 articles and book chapters. Most recently, he edited *Passing on the Faith: Transforming Traditions for the Next Generation of Jews, Christians and Muslims* (2006) and *Intellectual Humility among Jews, Christians and Muslims* (2011), and coedited *Engineering and the Catholic University* (2011). Oxford University Press has just published his *Catholic High Schools: Facing the New Realities* (2011). Also in 2011, he received the Theodore Hesburgh Award for long and distinguished service to Catholic higher education. He is now working on a book on the nature and mission of Catholic colleges and universities.

Zayn Kassam Zayn Kassam is associate professor of religious studies at Pomona College. A graduate of McGill University, Dr. Kassam teaches courses in Islamic mysticism, philosophy, women in Islam, and contemporary Muslim literature, as well as a course on religion and the environment. She has lectured widely on gender issues in the United States, Canada, and Great Britain, and has published essays on pedagogy, ethics, gender, and violence.

Following the terrorist attacks of 9/11, Dr. Kassam felt compelled to address the public's sudden demand for information about Islam, the world's second-largest religion with 1.2 billion believers. To that end, she completed a book on Islam for the six-volume *Introduction to the World's Major Religions*. The series is meant for high school libraries and works well for a lay audience. Dr. Kassam has been honored with a Wig Award for Distinguished Teaching at Pomona College and with the American Academy of Religion 2005 *National Teacher of the Year Award*.

Daniel A. Madigan, S.J. Daniel A. Madigan, S.J., an Australian Jesuit, is an International Visiting Fellow at the Woodstock Theological Center. From 2000 through 2007 he was professor of Islamic studies and interreligious dialogue at the Pontifical Gregorian University, and founding director of its Institute for the Study of Religions and Cultures. In 2008 he became the Jeanette J. and Otto J. Ruesch Family Distinguished Jesuit Scholar and associate professor in the Department of Theology at Georgetown University. He has also studied and worked in Australia, India, Pakistan, Egypt, and Turkey.

He teaches courses on Qur'anic interpretation, classical Sufi literature, theology of religions, and the theological issues that arise between Muslims and Christians. His research is focused on the early history of the Qur'an and the nature of Qur'anic authority, on Muslim theologies of revelation, and on Christian theology in an interreligious context. He is the author of *The Qur'ân's Self-Image: Writing and Authority in Islam's Scripture.*

Anselm Kyongsuk Min Anselm Kyongsuk Min is dean and Maguire Distinguished Professor of Philosophy of Religion and Theology, the School of Religion, Claremont Graduate University, Claremont, California. He is currently engaged in writing a systematic theology of globalization that responds to the challenges of cultural difference, economic inequality, religious diversity, and ecological decline in the globalizing world. He has written on Aquinas, Hegel, postmodernism, religious pluralism, Asian theology, and liberation theology. He is the author of *The Dialectic of Salvation: Issues in Theology of Liberation*, *The Solidarity of Others in a Divided World*, and *Paths to the Triune God: An Encounter between Aquinas and Recent Theologies.*

Peter C. Phan Peter C. Phan, the Ignacio Ellacuría Chair of Catholic Social Thought at Georgetown since January 1993, has recently been named director of graduate studies for the new PhD program in theology and religious studies and brings an international reputation as an outstanding scholar to the position. He holds three doctorates: a PhD in sacred theology from the Universitas Pontificia Salesiana, Rome, and PhDs in philosophy and divinity from the University of London. He was also awarded an honorary doctor of theology degree from Chicago Theological Union. Dr. Phan began his teaching career in philosophy at the age of eighteen at Don Bosco College, Hong Kong. In the United States, he has taught at the University of Dallas; at the Catholic University of America, Washington, D.C., where he held the Warren-Blanding Chair of Religion and Culture; at Union Theological Seminary, N.Y.; at Elms College, Chicopee, Mass.; and at St. Norbert College, De Pere, Wis. He is also on the faculty of the East Asian Pastoral Institute, Manila; and Liverpool Hope University, England. He is the first non-Anglo to be elected president of Catholic Theological Society of America.

Swami Sarvadevananda Swami Sarvadevananda is a monk of the Ramakrishna Order of India, dedicated to the teaching of Vedanta. He has dedicated his life to promoting this message of harmony through spiritual ministry and social service. After joining Belur Monastery in 1965, he completed his monastic training while serving in various capacities, including working in a refugee camp during the Bangladesh War. He spent two decades at Saradapitha, a major educational and technical training institution in Calcutta, imparting Vedantic spiritual values as part of the high school and university level curriculum.

Swami Sarvadevananda became head of the Rama-krishna Mission of Sikra in 1988. There he initiated literacy and health programs for hundreds of underprivileged villagers and performed relief and rehabilitation work for the homeless.

In 1993 Swami Sarvadevananda was posted to Hollywood where he serves the Vedanta Society of Southern California as assistant minister. In addition to leading a regular schedule of classes, he addresses schools and colleges throughout Southern California. Swami continues to promote the message of harmony and respect for all traditions through participation in interfaith dialogue. He represents the Vedanta Society as a delegate on the Interreligious Council of Southern California and the Hindu-Catholic Dialogue of Los Angeles.

Jihad Turk Jihad Turk is the director of Religious Affairs at the Islamic Center of Southern California, cofounder and cochair of the Christian–Muslim Consultative Group, and president of the Wilshire Center Interfaith Council. He has dedicated himself to improving the relations between the Muslim community and other faith traditions in Southern California. He advises the president of the University of California, Mark Yudof, by serving on his Advisory Council on Campus Climate, Culture and Inclusion and has been honored for his leadership in the interfaith community by the Valley Interfaith Council, the South Coast Interfaith Council, and the U.S. Congress.

Jihad comes from an interfaith household, having been born to a Muslim–Palestinian father and a Christian–American mother in Phoenix, Arizona. He currently teaches courses on Islamic law at Southwestern Law School and is working to complete his PhD at UCLA in Islamic studies. Jihad also teaches courses in the Arabic language and the Islamic religion and culture through UCLA Extension and is now spearheading the establishment of the first American Muslim seminary and collaborating with the Claremont School of Theology and the Academy of Jewish Religion, California, to establish an interfaith seminary called the University Project.

Robin R. Wang Robin R. Wang is associate professor of philosophy and director of Asian and Pacific studies at Loyola Marymount University. She received her BA and MA in philosophy at Peking University, Beijing, China, before getting her MA in philosophy at the University of Notre Dame and PhD at the University of Wales, Cardiff. Her area of teaching and research has been Chinese philosophy, ethics, comparative philosophy, and women in Chinese culture. Her publications include the books *Chinese Philosophy in an Era of Globalization* (editor) and *Images of Women in Chinese Thought and Culture*, and essays in the journal *Philosophy East and West, Journal of Chinese Philosophy, Journal of the History of Ideas*, and the *Journal of the American Academy of Religion*. She also serves in numerous national and international academic associations and organizations.

Catholicism and Interreligious Dialogue

Catholicism and Interreligious Dialogue

JAMES L. HEFT, S.M.

Introduction

For most of recorded human history, different religions remained geographically circumscribed, except when they expanded and came in conflict with other religions. The practice of peaceful dialogue for purposes of mutual understanding between members of different religions was rare, indeed, very rare. Instead, when people of different religions met each other, they tried either to destroy or to convert the other through intimidation.

Protestant efforts at reuniting their many competing traditions began in earnest at the beginning of the twentieth century. Catholics officially signed on with the movement through the document *Unitatis redintergratio*, published by the Second Vatican Council (1962–1965). Since then, the Catholic Church has taken a leadership role in these ecumenical efforts, but not without controversies. Some leading proponents of these dialogues accuse the Vatican of dragging its feet. Others note that the results of these ecumenical efforts, carried on among academic theologians and historians, are not widely known in the churches. Remarkable degrees of consensus and even sometimes agreements achieved by theologians have yet to shape the thinking of the people in the pews.

Vatican II not only opened doors officially for ecumenical conversations, that is, conversations with other Christians, it also opened the doors to interreligious dialogues, that is, dialogues between Catholics and members of other religions. Through its document, *Nostra Aetate*, and through brief statements in other council documents, the Catholic Church can now be said to have led the way in fostering conversations with other religions, beginning with Judaism. These conversations too have encountered difficulties, and most recently have been described as running the danger of fostering relativism.

The chapters of this book provide an overview by leading Catholic scholars of the current state of interreligious dialogue between the Catholic Church and five other world religions. None of these scholars supports relativism; all of them, however, give ample evidence of the complexity, challenges, possibilities, and necessity of interreligious dialogue.

Officially Opening the Dialogue

Vatican II was the first church council to say something systematically and sympathetically about other world religions. Statements appear in several of its sixteen documents, but an important initial general statement can be found in the council's *Dogmatic Constitution on the Church* (*Lumen gentium*), paragraph 16. After devoting paragraph 15 to its relationship to various other groups of Christians, the bishops then speak of Jews and Muslims:

> Finally, those who have not yet accepted the Gospel are related to the people of God in various ways. There is, first, that people to whom the covenants and promises were made, and from whom Christ was born in the flesh (see Rom. 9:4–5), a people in virtue of their election beloved for the sake of the fathers, for God never regrets his gifts or his call (see Rom. 11:28–29). But the plan of salvation also includes those who acknowledge the Creator, first among whom are the Muslims: they profess to hold the faith of Abraham, and together with us they adore the one merciful God, who will judge humanity on the last day.[1]

Further reflection on the Catholic Church's relationship to other religions, especially Judaism, may be found in the council's *Declaration on the Relation of the Church to Non-Christian Religions* (*Nostra Aetate*). In that document, the council made clear its nondefensive understanding of the value of other religions in its famous statement that

> the Catholic Church rejects nothing of which is true and holy in these religions. It has a high regard for the manner of life and conduct, the precepts and doctrines which, although differing in many ways from its own teaching, nevertheless often reflects a ray of that truth which enlightens all men and women.[2]

Especially close to Christianity is Judaism, from which the church grew. Vatican II's clear condemnation of any prejudice against the Jews, its affirmation of the continuing validity of God's covenant with the Jews, and its recognition of the innocence of the Jews as a people for the death of Jesus have opened up the Catholic-Jewish dialogue in unprecedented ways.[3] Judaism was not just one of many world religions, but rather Christianity's "elder brother," or sister. As Pope

Benedict XVI said in an address to a delegation of the Conference of Presidents of Major American Jewish Organizations visiting the Vatican,

> Indeed, the Church draws its sustenance from the root of that good olive tree, the people of Israel, onto which have been grafted the wild olive branches of the Gentiles (cf. Rom. 11:17–24). From the earliest days of Christianity, our identity and every aspect of our life and worship have been intimately bound up with the ancient religion of our fathers in faith.[4]

The texts of Vatican II and subsequent official statements about the Jews make it clear that the Catholic Church has come to grips with it shameful history of antisemitism and is determined to open a new relationship with them.

> *Nostra Aetate* also described other world religions, but less extensively. Concerning Hinduism, the council declared that Hindus "explore the divine mystery and express it both in the limitless riches of myth and the accurately defined insights of philosophy. They seek release from the trials of the present life by ascetical practices, profound meditation, and recourse to God in confidence and love."[5]

And of Buddhism the council stated that

> Buddhism in its various forms testifies to the essential inadequacy of this changing world. It proposes a way of life by which people can, with confidence and trust, attain a state of perfect liberation and reach supreme illumination either through their own efforts or with divine help.[6]

It would be safe to say that at Vatican II, the bishops gave more thought to ecumenism than to interreligious dialogue. Ecumenism is the effort to create greater unity among Christians; interreligious dialogue is the effort to dialogue with believers in other religions, such as Christians dialoguing with Jews and Hindus. However, even though ecumenism has remained an important commitment, Pope Paul VI (1963–1978) had already established structures that located prominently the church's dialogue with other world religions. In 1964, he established the Vatican Secretariat for Non-Christians, which in 1988, Pope John Paul II (1978–2005) renamed and reorganized as the Pontifical Council for Interreligious Dialogue, precisely to focus and enhance conversations with Muslims, Hindus, and Buddhists.

In anticipation of the third millennium, John Paul II, whose long pontificate did so much to advance both human rights and interreligious dialogue,[7]
declared that

> in the climate of increased cultural and religious pluralism, which is
> expected to mark the society of the new millennium, it is obvious that
> this dialogue will be especially important in establishing a sure basis for
> peace and warding off the dread specter of those wars of religions which
> have so often bloodied human history. The name of the one God must
> become increasingly what it is: *a name of peace and a summons to peace.*[8]

In summary, then, the Catholic Church at Vatican II committed itself clearly
to both ecumenism and interreligious dialogue. Since the council, however, and
especially in the last twenty-five years, the work of interreligious dialogue has
become increasingly visible, important, and controversial.

The Purposes of Interreligious Dialogue

That the bishops of Vatican II desired to have fruitful dialogue with other
Christians and members of other religions is clear. What has remained less clear
is the purpose, or purposes, of such dialogues. Immediately following statements
of their desire to enter into dialogue with other churches and other religions, the
bishops of Vatican II regularly added statements that also made it clear that the
gospel must be preached. For example, after stating in *Lumen gentium* (par. 16)
that the church presumes that whatever truth is found in other religions should
be considered a "preparation for the Gospel," the bishops add that people are
often deceived by the Evil One and have often traded the truth for a lie (Romans
1:21). Therefore, aware of this, the church, continue the bishops, must remember the Lord's command to "proclaim the good news to all creation" (Mark
16:15, The New American Bible) and evangelize the whole world.[9] Or again,
after deploring all forms of hatred, persecution, and displays of antisemitism, the
bishops made it clear that the

> Church always held and continues to hold that Christ out of infinite
> love freely underwent suffering and death because of the sins of all, so
> that all might attain salvation. It is the duty of the Church, therefore,
> in its preaching to proclaim the cross of Christ as the sign of God's
> universal love and the source of all grace.[10]

These affirmations of the obligation to evangelize, following immediately the
church's profession of respect for other religions, raised then, and continue to

raise now, the difficult question of how to do both at the same time, that is, how to show genuine respect for those who believe in another religion and at the same time try to evangelize them. Is the purpose of theological dialogue to witness to the truth of one's faith, or is it to increase one's own understanding and deepen one's respect for Christians who are not Catholics? If a Catholic is intent on proclaiming the gospel, can she then be truly open to listen to and learn from a person who is a Protestant? Does believing that one belongs to the true church, or even the truest church, put such persons in a position of "superiority" that prevents genuine dialogue with Christians of a different church? Must successful ecumenical dialogues, then, be only friendly conversations that minimize disagreements and focus on agreements? Are ecumenical statements agreements between churches aimed mainly to find less offensive ways of saying the same things? Are they ultimately efforts to convert the other or, as was sometimes said by Catholics before Vatican II, invitations given to Protestant to "submit to Rome"?

More recently, especially in the last twenty years, interreligious dialogues in which Catholics have been involved have raised many questions, especially for some in the Vatican. Pope Benedict XVI, for example, worries, on the one hand, about relativism, but then on the other, that serious theological dialogues are avoided because they inevitably run into real disagreements. Or to pose these questions more concretely, let us consider the church's dialogue with the Jews. Since the council declared that the saving covenant God made with the Jews remains valid, should Christians still try to evangelize Jews? Or conversely, if Jesus is in some real sense still a fulfillment of the promises God made to the Jews, how can Christians not evangelize Jews? Or with Hinduism: is Catholicism mainly to learn from the ancient wisdom of the Upanishads and the Vedas, or it is also, and primarily, to evangelize Hindus? There are no easy answers to these questions. They continue to be debated.

The church has continued in its official documents to argue that interreligious dialogue has at least two components: understanding of the other and proclaiming the gospel. For example, in 1984, the Secretariat for Non-Christians, as it was then called, published a document titled "The Attitude of the Church Toward the Followers of Other Religions: Reflections on Dialogue and Mission." It stated clearly that there was to be not only dialogue but also mission to which the Catholic participants in the dialogue must remain faithful. In 1991, the Pontifical Council for Interreligious Dialogue and the *Propaganda fide* published a document, also titled with a dual focus, *Dialogue and Proclamation*, which distinguished four forms of dialogue:

> The *dialogue of life*, where people strive to live in an open and neighborly spirit, sharing their joys and sorrows, their human problems and preoccupations.

The *dialogue of action,* in which Christians and others collaborate for the integral development and liberation of people.

The *dialogue of theological exchange,* where specialists seek to deepen their understanding of their respective religious heritage, and to appreciate each other's spiritual values.

The *dialogue of religious experience,* where persons rooted in their own religious traditions share their spiritual riches, for instance with regard to prayer and contemplation, faith and ways of searching for God or the Absolute.[11]

The 1991 succinct description of the *dialogue of theological exchange* indicates that such dialogues are the province of specialists, that is, theologians and other scholars. The same document repeats the requirement that an essential part of interreligious is the proclamation of the gospel.

The tensions between some Catholic theologians committed to interreligious dialogue and the Vatican hit the headlines in the late 1990s. Fr. Jacques Dupuis, S.J., who had lived in India for nearly four decades and worked there as a theologian involved in interreligious dialogue with Hindus, published in 1997 a book[12] that summarizes what he had learned after many years of interaction and dialogue with Hindus. The publication of his book provoked the Congregation for the Doctrine of the Faith (CDF), that entity in the Vatican responsible for ensuring that the teachings of Catholic theologians are consistent with Catholic dogma, to initiate a two-and-a-half-year investigation of Dupuis's book. Initially charging Dupuis with errors, the CDF eventually mentioned only "ambiguities" in Dupuis's work, which could lead Catholics to draw mistaken conclusions about the teachings of the church on other religions. The CDF declared that "Jesus Christ . . . is the sole and universal mediator for salvation for all humanity," that it is incorrect to "suggest that the Word of God has a saving action apart from that of Jesus," that it is contrary to Catholic faith to "maintain that revelation in Christ is in any way limited or incomplete," that it is "erroneous to hold" that the "seeds of truth and goodness" in other religions "do not derive ultimately from the mediating action of Jesus Christ," and finally that it cannot be held that "other religions are complementary ways of salvation" since they "contain omissions, insufficiencies and errors about fundamental truths."[13]

In the last analysis, the CDF did not assert that Dupuis's book included errors; rather, they said, as noted above, that it contained ambiguities. Consequently, the CDF felt obliged to make clear exactly what Catholic teaching was. One of the most interesting statements of the CDF seemed significantly to qualify one its core affirmations. After stating that it was "contrary to Catholic faith to maintain that revelation in Jesus Christ . . . is limited," it immediately added that "full knowledge of divine revelation will be had only on the day of the Lord's coming in glory."[14] Perhaps the CDF had in mind an important 1973 CDF document, *Mysterium ecclesiae*, which acknowledged that even dogmatic definitions were historically conditioned in four ways: (1) due to the limited state of knowledge at the time of the definition, (2) due to the changeable conceptions and thought patterns that belong to a certain period of time, (3) due to the specific concerns that motivated the definition, and (4) due to the limited expressive power of the language used.[15]

If all dogmatic statements are inevitably historically conditioned, then perhaps theologians involved in interreligious dialogue can affirm at one and the same time that Jesus is indeed the savior of the world, but that our human grasp of that belief, even aided by faith, will always be limited. Moreover, while affirming that the revelation of God in Christ is in itself not limited or incomplete, our grasp and explication of it will always be limited and incomplete—but not for that reason simply relativized. Finally, theologians involved in interreligious dialogue have consistently pointed to John Paul II's important 1990 encyclical, *Redemptoris missio*, which insisted on the universal presence of the Holy Spirit in the world.[16] That presence, however, does not mean that "all religions are equal," but that all religions bear the impulse of the Holy Spirit, most fully found, according to Catholic teaching, in the Catholic tradition.

The Vatican has returned several times to the questions raised by theologians who are deeply involved in interreligious dialogue. The most controversial of the CDF's statements on interreligious dialogue was *Dominus Iesus*, published September 5, 2000. While breaking no new ground, that document, as noted by the bishop of Houston-Galveston, then the president of the National Conference of Catholic Bishops of the United States, "invites Catholic theologians to a continuing exploration in depth and reflection on the existence of other religions experiences, on other religious traditions which also contain elements that come from God, and on their meaning in God's salvific plan."[17] While debates over the proper way to understand the Catholic Church's relationship to other religions have continued, it should be clear that it is no longer possible for Catholics to claim baldly either that there is "no salvation outside the Catholic Church," or that all religions are equal paths to salvation.

There is good reason to be concerned, as Benedict XVI is, about relativism, which in its purest forms asserts that all beliefs are of the same value, that it is just fine to deny young women an education, that a totalitarian state is as good as a democracy, that gay men should be executed, or that what you believe is less important than being sincere. Unfairly, Benedict's critics accuse him of intolerance when, in fact, a good case can be made that what he is really doing is asking people to trust their experience and their reason to make moral judgments that make obvious that not all practices contribute to human flourishing equally.[18]

The Different Meanings of Dialogue and Evangelization

Part of the Catholic debate, then, revolves around respect for the religious other while at the same time proclaiming that Jesus is their savior. This tension could be lessened by distinguishing several meanings of each word. First, let us look at several misunderstandings of interreligious dialogue. If dialogue is equated only with tolerance of the other, such a dialogue will bear little fruit, except as an alternative to violence—an alternative, the value of which should not be minimized in our world today. In this minimalist sense of dialogue as tolerance, Kenneth Woodward, in a review of Gustav Niebuhr's *Beyond Tolerance: Searching for Interfaith Understanding in America*, wrote that "religious tolerance is a necessary but overrated virtue. Its practice comes easiest to the religiously indifferent and to the condescending."[19] Serious interreligious dialogue goes beyond tolerance to respectful engagement of the other.

Redemptorist Australian theologian and current member of the International Theological Commission Anthony Kelly described another misunderstanding of dialogue. This distortion of dialogue reduces it to "a fall-back position in just about any attempt to establish good relations." In such a case, dialogue manifests "a symptom of timidity amongst those who have lost the courage of their religious convictions, especially when the ideal of objective truth is weakened, or the positive claims of divine revelation go unrecognized." When dialogue is motivated by such timidity, it becomes "an implicit acknowledgment of common defeat, in refusal of the possibilities of a more profound reconciliation in the light of the ultimate." A loss of religious conviction and theological depth trivializes interreligious dialogue.

At the opposite end of the spectrum is an aggressive approach to dialogue—that is, a meeting during which the participants aim first and above all to convert the other. History is sadly replete with examples this form of "dialogue." An aggressive approach does not respect the other. It rarely leads to any genuine religious conversion. Vatican II's declaration on religious freedom calls all Catholics to respect people of other religious traditions and never to try to convert someone else by using coercive or aggressive tactics.

If in interreligious dialogue Catholics are to remain faithful to the mission of the church to evangelize, how should that commitment be carried out? In English, there are several words that can be used to describe proclaiming one's faith. The believer might *proselytize* (a word that has an aggressive ring to it). Or the believer might *evangelize* (which, at least in the United States, also connotes an aggressive approach—one that depends mainly on verbal testimonies to present the faith to others). Or the believer might *witness* to the faith (which sounds less aggressive). Or one might *share* one's faith (which sounds quite friendly, but is really possible only with fellow believers). Or one might offer a personal *example* of the faith (but this is more subtle, and would refer to the attitudes and behaviors that members of other religions could observe).

In the actual practice of interreligious dialogue, the participants, if they are genuinely religious themselves, do and should make clear their beliefs. What typically happens is that the dialogue then revolves around what those beliefs mean, how they are to be understood, and how best to express them. In genuine interreligious dialogue, both respect for the other religious believer and fidelity to the truth of one's own tradition find ways not only to coexist, but mutually enrich each other.

Early on, Pope Paul VI recognized that dialogue involved certain risks, but risks that he believed must be taken. In his 1964 encyclical *Ecclesiam Suam*, he wrote that "[t]he Church makes itself conversation." And to "be conversation," Christians in dialogue need to follow Christ who made himself "humbler yet, even to accepting death, death on a cross."[20] Perhaps no pope has better described the necessary attitudes for successful interreligious dialogue than Pope Paul VI, who wrote in in that same encyclical that instead of seeking "theocratic power" over the modern world, the approach of dialogue is better—a dialogue that has four qualities:

> *Clarity*: "Every angle" of one's language should be reviewed to ensure that it's "understandable, acceptable, and well-chosen."
> *Meekness*: "Dialogue is not proud, it is not bitter, it is not offensive. Its authority is intrinsic to the truth it explains, to the charity it communicates, to the example it proposes; it is not a command, it is not an imposition. It is peaceful; it avoids violent methods; it is patient; it is generous."
> *Trust*: One should have confidence "not only in the power of one's word, but also in an attitude of welcoming the trust of the interlocutor. Trust promotes confidence and friendship. It binds hearts in mutual adherence to the good which excludes all self-seeking."
> *Pedagogical prudence*: "Prudence strives to learn the sensitivities of the hearer and requires that we adapt ourselves and the manner of our presentation in a reasonable way, lest we be displeasing and incomprehensible."[21]

It is difficult to imagine how anyone who approaches interreligious dialogue with these attitudes could be thought to be without genuine respect for those who believe differently. But having addressed the danger of being overbearing in dialogue, there still remains the danger that those engaged in dialogue might still not clearly articulate the faith, or in the words of the recent Vatican decrees, proclaim the gospel.

Theological Challenges in Interreligious Dialogue

In 1996, Joseph Cardinal Ratzinger, then the head of the Congregation for the Doctrine of the Faith and later elected pope in 2005, gave an address titled "Relativism: The Central Problem for Faith Today." He was speaking to the Latin American doctrinal commissions (that is, to those theologians responsible for doctrinal orthodoxy in Latin America) and before bishops from "mission territories." Francis Clooney, the author of the chapter in this volume "Catholicism and Hinduism," succinctly summarized Ratzinger's key points as follows:

> In Ratzinger's view, too many Catholics are inclined to believe that people of all religions can contribute equally to human advancement; that truth can be known only through multiple limited expressions; that all religions reach the same transcendent goal, though by different paths; and that Christ is but one facet of ultimate reality. Tainted by this tolerant attitude, the cardinal observed, Catholics are too ready to presuppose, when they enter upon interreligious dialogue, that other religions deserve equal respect and that Christian faith is not necessarily superior to the faith articulated in other traditions. This dangerous relativism, he believes, has replaced a Marxist-influenced liberation theology as the number-one threat to the faith today.[22]

What exactly the cardinal meant by "equal respect" is not clear. And it can also be asked whether affirming that the Christian faith is "necessarily superior" is a good example of the "pedagogical prudence" that Pope Paul VI called for in interreligious dialogue. These issues, as I have already said, are complex. This much is at least clear: persons can deeply respect people while at the same time disagreeing with them. And it is also clear that Christians can believe that their faith—Christianity—represents the fullest expression of God's revelation to humanity, despite their own sinfulness and that of Christians throughout history. To speak of the fullest revelation is not, however, to assert that believers have a full grasp of that revelation, nor is it to forget that the church is still a pilgrim people, blessed indeed with a saving revelation, but a pilgrim people who only partially grasp and only inadequately live that fullest revelation of God embodied in Jesus Christ. It has been the actual experience of many of those deeply involved in interreligious dialogue that people of different religions not only come to deeply respect each other but also that they in fact assume that their own religious tradition is true, indeed, more true than that of the other. When entered into with the proper attitudes, then, dialogue and proclamation are not opposed. The chapters of this book give ample evidence of the creative interplay between respect of the other and fidelity to one's own tradition—especially since the authors of these chapters are faithful and competent Catholic theologians.

That said, it is also possible that some theologians engaged in interreligious dialogue do in fact shy away from engaging in explicitly theological issues in order to focus instead on ethical issues on which agreement can be more readily reached. Or again, it would be possible to focus on sharing religious experience (e.g., dialogues between Christian and Buddhist monks), but avoid addressing explicitly fundamental theological differences. These are legitimate concerns about interreligious dialogue. To avoid the theological issues by focusing on the consequences of religious beliefs (such as justice and peace) is, according to Pope Benedict, to sidestep seeking the truth of revelation:

> In a globalised society like the one being formed today, theologians often are challenged by public opinion to promote, above all, dialogue among religions and cultures [and] to contribute to the development of an ethics that has peace, justice and the defense of the natural environment as its natural coordinates.[23]

The pope is not dismissing the social consequences of interreligious dialogue, which he describes as "fundamental goods." Rather, his concern is that without the theological dimension, these consequences are explored apart from any theological framework.

Coming from what seems to be just the opposite direction, the question has also been raised recently, again mainly within Vatican circles, whether there can even be theological dialogue with members of other religions. Such a question presupposes that dialogue is aimed at coming up with common statements of faith—an appropriate goal for conversations among only Christians, or only Jews. If it is assumed that theological dialogue between religions is aimed at arriving at agreed-upon theological statements, then the pope has, I believe, a point. A committed Jew or Muslim, for example, is never going to agree with a committed Christian about the identity of Jesus. To assume, however, that all theological dimensions of interreligious dialogue are impossible, or ultimately end in a relativism, is to imagine the participants in these dialogues slipping into a sort of intermediate space that is no longer rooted in any particular religious tradition. But competent participants, as I referred to them earlier, in these interreligious dialogues remain rooted within their religious commitments. Understanding the reasons why there are these questions about the danger of relativism will help explain what is and is not meant by the pope's concern. In other words, we need to understand the important distinction between ecumenical and interreligious dialogues, and then we can understand better why Pope Benedict and others have worries about theologically focused interreligious dialogue.

Scholars of different faiths in the West, and especially in the United States, have long been involved in fruitful theological interreligious dialogue. Such scholars know full well that they are engaging in dialogue on a theological level. This has been most evident in the church's dialogue with Jews. And more recently, it has also become the case, as will be seen below, with Muslims. It is worth asking, then, what prompts the doubt that there can be genuine theological dialogue with other religions?

The first issue to take into consideration is the current situation of the church in Europe. There can be little doubt that the degree and aggressiveness of secularism in Europe is much higher than in the United States. What was once a cultural and institutional home of Catholicism, indeed the church as "Christendom" in Europe, no longer exists. One Catholic scholar, Robert Wilken, laments the church's institutional loss:

> There is good reason to be troubled over the supine acquiescence of Europeans today at the collapse of Christianity as a social and cultural force and over the mounting number of Muslims living in France, Germany, and Britain. Though Christianity was able to create a great civilization, it seems incapable of preventing its dissolution.[24]

The European Union Constitution makes no mentioned of Europe's historical and cultural debt to Christianity. There can be little doubt, however, that Christianity shaped European history, culture, art, and architecture for more than a millennium; whether it will ever play a similar role in the future seems highly doubtful.

Along with the weakened place of the church in European life and imagination, some secular Europeans promote "multiculturalism" as a means to prevent any religion from exercising influence on the larger culture. Building on the Enlightenment's desire to privatize religion, this form of multiculturalism removes from religion its theological basis on which it bases its convictions about to how life should be lived, not just privately, but also publicly. This privatization of religions is especially evident in France where secularism, or laïcité, seeks to proscribe any public expression of religion.

Given, then, the increasing proportion of Europe's Muslim population, and the assumptions that multiculturalism and theological dialogue extinguish important differences between religions, one can begin to understand, even if not agree with, the concern expressed by the pope and some church leaders in Europe who fear that interreligious dialogue on a theological level might actually end up papering over important theological differences between religions or privatize them. They seem to fear that theological dialogue would further weaken the church's rightful place in Europe historically and culturally. Instead, they wish to promote interreligious dialogue in nontheological areas, such as religious freedom, social justice, and common moral teachings.

As important as such cultural and ethical dialogues are, it would be a mistake, it seems to me, to bracket one's deepest religious convictions for the sake of buttressing a Christian culture in Europe. Granted, everything, including interreligious dialogue and "multiculturalism," can be distorted to the detriment of the Catholic faith. But the fears just described are based on "worst-case scenarios." For decades now, Catholic scholars have shown in their writings how interreligious dialogue does not have to lead to relativism, how respecting the other does not mean presenting oneself as personally "superior" to the other, and how the fullest revelation of God in Jesus Christ is a saving gift that remains beyond our full comprehension and faithful embodiment. At the beginning of this new millennium, such theologians continue to enrich Catholicism through interreligious dialogue. The thought of five such theologians forms the substance of this volume.

Advancing Interreligious Dialogue Today

It was in the midst of this ferment for interreligious dialogue, and the continued arguments within the Catholic community as to the purpose and scope of those dialogues, that the Institute for Advanced Catholic Studies at the University of Southern California sponsored during the 2007–2008 academic year a lecture series titled "Catholicism and Interreligious Dialogue." The institute invited five Catholic scholars, each an expert on Catholicism's relationship to another world religion, to explore the current state of the interreligious dialogue in which they were involved. For each lecture, two respondents, typically adherents of the religion being discussed, were asked to respond. In all instances, the respondents to these lectures were scholars of the religious tradition about which they spoke, even though, in some cases, they were not personally of that religious tradition. And finally, the lecturer then commented on these responses.

This book is a result of those lectures and the dialogues they initiated. At the conclusion of each chapter, the reader will find readings that the author of the chapter recommends for further study. An overview of this rich set of dialogues constitutes the rest of this introduction.

Professor Philip Cunningham contributes the first chapter on Catholicism and Judaism. More work has been done to date on this interreligious dialogue than any of the others. There are at least two reasons for this. First, Christianity has a relationship with Judaism that it has with no other world religion. To refer again to an important image from St. Paul (Romans 11:17ff.), Christianity has been grafted onto the rich root of the olive tree, which is Israel. And second, the church of Europe had to come to grips with centuries of its own antisemi-tism that, exacerbated by the pagan ideology of the Nazi regime, culminated in the destruction of six million Jews during the Shoah. Cunningham begins his lecture telling the story of an encyclical, drafted in 1938, that Pius XI (r. 1922–1939), near the end of his life, wanted to publish to condemn the Nazi racist rhetoric and policies.

The pope died before it was ready for publication. In fact, the encyclical was never published. While the authors' condemnations of the Nazis would have been welcomed, what had been written about the Jews reflected the very preju-dices that the church needed to correct. The bases for those corrections were spelled out twenty-five years later in Vatican II's *Nostra Aetate*. Since the close of the council, immense progress has been made by the Catholic Church in ridding itself, beginning with its catechisms and ordinary teachings, of its long history of antisemitism. Cunningham describes these efforts as a "dramatic transforma-tion," and offers comparisons that make that change strikingly clear, the first of which is a strong statement against "supersessionism," that is, the assumption that the coming of Christ rendered Judaism obsolete. After enumerating seven positive steps taken by *Nostra Aetate*, Cunningham reviews the fruits of the church's dialogue with the Jews over the next forty years. He ends his chapter by drawing our attention to several areas he believes require more work.

Two Jewish scholars, Elliot Dorff and Rachel Adler, express genuine apprecia-tion for the progress in the Catholic-Jewish dialogue chronicled by Cunningham. But they also raise pointed questions. In reference to Benedict XVI's concern about relativism, why not focus, asks Dorff, on "relativity" instead of the false dichotomy between absolutism and relativism? Or can Jews affirm that for Christians, but not for themselves, God reveals himself in some real way in Jesus, without coming as Jews dangerously close to believing in Jesus and thereby ceasing to be Jews? In his response, Cunningham takes the dialogue still further and reflects on the question of whether members of one religious community can imagine that believers in other religious traditions have different but none-theless "divinely willed religious encounters" with God, without becoming a member of that religious tradition.

Fr. Daniel Madigan, S.J., a specialist in Catholic-Muslim dialogue, notes that in the current geopolitical realities these conversations take place in a very diffi-cult but hardly hopeless time. He notes what is often overlooked: that religions can't dialogue; only believers can. Moreover, if, for example, someone objects to such a dialogue by claiming that no Muslim can speak for Islam, one may reply, writes Madigan, by asking whether any one Christian can speak for all of Christianity. Moreover, various Christian churches, especially since Vatican II, have carried on fruitful discussions with the Jews, even though there is no single voice that can speak for Judaism, given the diversity among religious Jews.

Why, then, could there not also be fruitful discussions with Muslims? He also explains why it is simply false to assert that Muslims do not have a history of Qur'anic interpretation, and a very sophisticated one at that. After a series of comments on Samuel Huntington's widely quoted (but not so widely read) 1996 book *The Clash of Civilizations and the Remaking of the World Order*,[25] Madigan singles out for criticism a number of bad habits that impede dialogue, including the use of labels such as "we" and "they," the ignorance of the very different political situations in which some Christians and some Muslims live, and the dubious nature of the call for "reciprocity" in dialogue. Madigan concludes his lecture by noting that both cultural and theological dialogue between Catholics and Muslims is not only possible, but is actually taking place.

Madigan's respondents, two Muslim scholars, raise further questions. Professor Kassam underscores how colonialism in general, and more specifically American foreign policy, such as that under President George W. Bush concerning the Middle East, has rendered dialogue more difficult. She also notes that genuine dialogue need not end in agreement, but that genuine disagreements can be as important as agreements. She admits that theological dialogue for Muslims is difficult, mainly because few Muslims have studied seriously Christian doctrine. Better, she writes, to address the "burning issues," the state of the Palestinians, the war in Iraq, and address honestly America's thirst for oil. Professor Turk focuses on some of the best-known texts of the Qur'an that support interreligious dialogue and religious pluralism. Despite these difficult times between Islam and the West, Turk places great hope in the recent document, *A Common Word between Us*, issued by Muslim religious leaders around the world.

Against the widespread perception in the West of Muslim responsibility for ethnic cleansing, Madigan cites statistics to the effect that the vast majority of people who died in the Bosnian War did so at the hands of Orthodox Christian Serbs. And in Rwanda, nearly a million Christians were killed by other Christians in three short months. He observed these tragic statistics are conveniently forgotten in the West, a failure of memory that makes the Christian-Muslim dialogue difficult. He also pleads that interreligious dialogues be concerned not only for the marginalized of one's own religion, but for all the marginalized of the world, regardless of religion.

When we turn to dialogue with Asian religions, it becomes immediately apparent that Christians walk an unfamiliar path, at least a less familiar path than the one they have had when dialoguing with Muslims and especially with Jews. Francis Clooney, a Jesuit and a scholar of Hinduism, provides an overview of the encounter between Catholicism and Hinduism. His method of study is comparative theology. After a personal introduction, Clooney gives a ten-point description of Hinduism that makes it difficult to reduce it simply to a key idea, a single culture or period of history, or a neat theological system. And while there is some evidence of encounters between Christians and Hindus in the first millennium, Catholics, especially Jesuit missionaries such as Francis Xavier, are known to have arrived in India only at the beginning of the sixteenth century. But even forty years after *Nostra Aetate*, the Catholic Church still gives a multiple, even if largely positive, reading of its relationship to Hinduism. Fortunately, this relationship has not been marred by a series of negative encounters, including wars over land and large Christian populations, as has been the case with Islam. While the dialogue tends to be more open and flexible, it lacks the kind of focus that certainly the Catholic-Jewish dialogue has had. Thus, after outlining ten key Hindu teachings, Clooney warns that one must not let these teachings float in a timeless space; they need to be put back into their historical contexts. The task, then, is indeed one of respecting the complexity of Hinduism in history and on the ground.

Clooney favors a comparative approach. Instead of trying to understand Hinduism in terms of Catholicism, which to some extent is impossible not to do, Clooney shows how a careful and prayerful effort to understand Hindu prayers, for example, opens up rich avenues for understanding religious practices. Visiting a Hindu temple, and looking at Hindu images provide still another rich way of entering into the religious world of Hindus. It is best, Clooney advises, to enter areas of theological and ethical disagreement, which he lists, only after acquiring a rich appreciation of some similarities. He concludes by affirming that while there needs to be "honest recognition of both theologically stated goals and on-the-street realities," the Catholic-Hindu dialogue enriches its participants in ways that are good in themselves.

Picking up on Clooney's comment that Buddhism is better known in America than Hinduism, Professor Chapple suggests than in fact Hinduism is quite well known in America where, he adds, more than fifteen million people practice Yoga on a regular basis. Chapple supports his claim with many examples, suggesting that there is already in the United States a vibrant dialogue going on with Hinduism. A second respondent, Swami Sarvadevananda of the Vedanta Society, finds much to praise in Clooney's remarks. He provides his own vision of Hinduism, stressing those advocates of the tradition who have found ways to look for harmonies with other traditions. He offers instances of Catholic saints and teachings, especially moral teachings, that find echoes in his understanding of Hinduism, an understanding that stresses not what he describes as the exclusionary theology of the Bible, nor on dogmas, but on the openness and acceptance of a trusting child of God.

While Clooney recognizes with Chapple the growing number of Americans influenced by Hinduism, he maintains that the influence of Buddhism is even greater. And while he is appreciative of the swami's comments, he notes that the swami represents only one of the many interpretations of Hinduism, that of the Ramakrishna Vedanta Society, an interpretation of Hinduism that in many ways finds areas of commonality with Christianity. Finally, Clooney notes that even though the dialogue does not have the same urgency today as that with Muslims, his respondents offer a good description of a number of the important areas that need to be addressed by the Catholic-Hindu dialogue.

The fourth chapter, by James Fredericks, a diocesan priest and specialist in the Catholic-Buddhist dialogue, is titled "Off the Map." Fredericks contends that the dialogue between Catholics and Buddhists, more than any of the other interreligious dialogues in which Catholics are involved, "drives us off our theological road map of religions." That road map, developed most extensively and authoritatively by John Paul II, may be described as an inclusive theology of religions. On the one hand, it avoids exclusivism, in that it rejects the claim that there is no salvation outside the church and, on the other hand, it avoids relativism, in that it affirms the centrality of Christ and the universality of his saving grace made available in the church through the work of the Holy Spirit. That said, Fredericks believes that even though the Catholic Church's inclusive theology of religions is "adequate to the demands of Christian orthodoxy," it is not that helpful in interreligious dialogue, at least in dialogue with Buddhists. Frederick's problem with the church's current theology of religions is twofold. First, the inclusive approach tends to domesticate differences, making it very difficult to accept differences as differences and the otherness of the other as the other. Second, it is sectarian in that it assumes ultimately that everyone should be converted to the Catholic Church. For Fredericks, the pastoral purpose of interreligious dialogue is neither conversion nor the confirmation of our theological presuppositions about other religious believers; its purpose is to establish bonds of solidarity with other religious communities. In short, Fredericks calls for less theory (theology of religions) and more actual practice of dialogue.

Fredericks's first respondent, Catholic theologian Anselm Kyongsuk Min, sharply disagrees with Fredericks not only on his criticisms of the inclusive theology of religions but also on his understanding of the purpose of interreligious dialogue. Min explains that it is incorrect to measure the adequacy of a theology of religions in terms of how adequately it serves the practice of interreligious dialogue. Fredericks's other respondent, Buddhist professor Huaiyu Chen, believes that Buddhists are at a distinct disadvantage in dialogue with Catholics because few Buddhists are schooled in Christian doctrine. Moreover, according to Chen, Catholic Christianity has enjoyed great influence in the West while Buddhism has been challenged even in its own homeland. The great diversity of Buddhist traditions poses additional challenges to a dialogue with Catholicism. Chen suggests, finally, several areas for dialogue, including the destruction of the Twin Towers of the World Trade Center and shared karma.

In response, Fredericks defends his position against the criticisms of Min, and presses Chen to consider how Christians in the West would likely differ from him in their view of the shared responsibility for the 9/11 terrorist attacks.

The final chapter, Peter Phan's exploration of both the intercultural and interreligious dialogue of Catholicism with Confucianism, begins with a brief but detailed history of the complex development and diversities of Confucian thought. Not only is it both a culture and a religion but has developed different versions and schools of Confucianism at different periods of time. Nevertheless, Phan explains that interreligious dialogues have taken place (beginning in the middle of the seventh century), and such dialogues can still bear fruit. Catholic missionaries first entered China in the late thirteenth and early fourteenth centuries, Jesuit missionaries arrived in the sixteenth century, and then members of many other Catholic religious orders arrived in the seventeenth century. The Chinese rites, forbidden by Pope Benedict XIV in 1742, were officially approved in 1939, when the Vatican decided that they were only "civil and political" rather than religious in nature.

The Marxist takeover of China caused a drastic change in the status of Confucian thought and practice, but even that revolutionary movement is now in decline, and Confucianism is experiencing something of a renaissance. Phan singles out as the most fruitful contemporary avenue for dialogue the issue of what it means to be human, followed by the place of liturgy and worship.

Picking up on Phan's invitation to discuss the meaning of being human, Professor Wang, who has studied both Western and Chinese philosophy, cites a number of classic Confucian texts to suggest several ways to pursue the dialogue. But she also notes that Confucian texts suggest that any explicit effort to articulate dimensions of transcendence is kept at a distance, preferring to focus on how one is to live in this life now. Professor Robert Campany, a historian of Chinese religion and student of comparative religions, wonders how a dialogue is possible with a very diverse tradition "for which no one in particular can speak authoritatively." Campany seriously doubts that Chinese people think that their rites are only "civil and political," and asks whether Catholicism is really open to learning from Confucianism. Phan's response to Wang underscores the value of focusing on the meaning of being human, and his response to Campany admits that in the current state of the church's dialogue with Confucianism, the church seems more ready to teach than to learn.

Conclusion

These five interreligious dialogues are not all the same. Christianity has had closer contact, even prolonged periods of conflict, with Islam and Judaism than it ever has had with the Asian religions. Moreover, Christianity's relationship to Judaism is unlike that with any other religion. Judaism is Christianity's "elder brother." The Western religions understand themselves as "revealed" in ways that Asian religions typically do not. And finally, all these dialogues, being carried on now by scholars and believers who are intent upon understanding and respecting other religionists, have begun, with rare exceptions, to take place only recently.

It is also fair to say that it has become increasingly important—sometimes a matter of life and death, of peace or war—that the religions of the world come into dialogue. It is especially important today for the Catholic Church to build bridges of trust and understanding with other religious communities. The imperative for dialogue is increasing, not diminishing, in the twenty-first century. For Catholics, *Nostra Aetate*, the church's charter for interreligious dialogue, has to be taken further, based on the many rich dialogues that have taken place since.

The essays and responses in this volume give evidence that the hopes of the bishops at Vatican II were not in vain, that the vigorous support for this dialogue by Pope Paul VI, then Pope John Paul II, and now Benedict XVI, has born fruit, and that the questions raised about interreligious dialogue by Pope Benedict have been taken seriously, if not fully resolved.

Notes

1 *Lumen gentium*, par. 16, in *Vatican Council II*, ed. Austin Flannery, O.P. (New York: Costello, 1996), 21–22.

2 *Nostra aetate*, par. 2, in Flannery, *Vatican Council II*, 570–571.

3 See especially par. 4 of *Nostra aetate*, where it states that "neither all Jews indiscriminately at that time, nor Jews today, can be charged with the crimes committed during his passion."

4 Address of His Holiness Benedict XVI to Members of the Delegation of the 'Conference of Presidents of Major American Jewish Organizations." February 12, 2009. http://www.vatican.va/holy_father/benedict_xvi/speeches/2009/february/documents/hf_ben-xvi_spe_20090212_jewish-organizations_en.html

5 *Nostra aetate*, par. 2.

6 *Nostra aetate*, par. 2. It is interesting to add here that there was no mention at all of Buddhism in the first two drafts of *Nostra aetate*. In the third draft, only *nirvana* was mentioned. In the final draft, a more positive description of Buddhism appeared (see David Grumett, "De Lubac, Christ and the Buddha," in *New Blackfriars* 89, no. 10 [March 20, 2008]: 227–228).

7 See especially in this volume James Fredericks description of John Paul II's contribution to interreligious dialogue.

8 *Novo millennio inuente*, par. 55, published in *Origins, Catholic News Service Documentary Service* 30/31 (January 18, 2001): 506.

9 *Luman gentium*, par. 16.

10 *Nostra aetate*, par. 4.

11 *Dialogue and proclamation*, par. 42. Earlier in that document (par. 9), the International Theological Commission (ITC), a group of prominent theologians appointed by the pope,

described the purpose of interreligious dialogue in this way: "In the context of religious plurality, dialogue means 'all positive and constructive interreligious relations with individuals and communities of other faiths which are directed at mutual understanding and enrichment,' in obedience to truth and respect for freedom." Note that the quotation within the quotation, taken from the ITC's 1984 document, does not underscore the need to be obedient to the truth as does the 1991 text. For an informative essay on the background and various competing positions of this document, see Jacques Dupuis, "A Theological Commentary: Dialogue and Proclamation," in *Redemption and Dialogue*, ed., William Burrows (Maryknoll, N.Y.: Orbis, 1993), 119–158.

12 Jacques Dupuis, *Toward a Christian Theology of Religious Pluralism* (Maryknoll, N.Y.: Orbis, 1997).

13 Congregation for the Doctrine of the Faith, "Notification: Father Dupuis' 'Toward a Christian Theology of Religious Pluralism,'" in *Origins* 30, no. 38 (March 8, 2001): 605–608.

14 Ibid., 607.

15 *Acta Apostolicae Sedis* 65 (1973): 402–404.

16 *Acta Apostolicae Sedis* 83 (1991): 249–340.

17 Joseph A. Fiorenza, in *Sic et Non: Encountering Dominus Iesus*, ed. Stephen J. Pope and Charles Hefling (Maryknoll, N.Y.: Orbis, 2002). This volume contains the commentary, sometimes sharply critical, of the CDF's statement.

18 See Lady (Carla) Powell, "Five Minutes with the Pope," in *The Tablet* (August 28, 2010): 12.

19 Kenneth Woodward, "Leaps of Faith," review of *Beyond Tolerance: Searching for Interfaith Understanding in America*, by Gustav Niebuhr, *The New York Times Book Review* (December 21, 2008): 21. Niebuhr's book offers a more robust understanding of the purpose of interreligious dialogue than mere tolerance.

20 *Ecclesiam Suam*, par. 81. Daniel Madigan stresses the importance of humility in his chapter on the church's dialogue with Islam.

21 *Ecclesiam Suam*, also par. 81. See also par. 78 for a description of "no coercion" in dialogue, par. 78 for the "pedagogy of dialogue," and par. 88 for warnings about dialogues that might "water down or whittle away the truth."

22 Francis Clooney, "Relativism in Perspective: Rereading Ratzinger," in *Commonweal* (Jan. 31, 1997): 9. Clooney agrees with Ratzinger that fidelity to one's own Christian commitment is required in dialogue: "We will never be free from the contingencies and limitations of human knowing, and must proceed with a certain humility; but it still can be true that God has communicated clearly and directly with the human race, and has become involved in our world, in particular ways" (10). Also see Rabbi Dorff's suggestion in this volume that the concept of "relativity" can save interreligious dialogue from the false alternatives of either absolutism or relativism.

23 "Address of His Holiness Benedict XVI to Participants at the Plenary Session of the International Theological Commission" December 5, 2008. Hall of Popes. Reported in the *Tablet* (Dec. 13, 2008): 31. http://www.vatican.va/holy_father/benedict_xvi/speeches/2008/december/documents/hf_ben-xvi_spe_20081205_teologica_en.html.

24 Robert Louis Wilken, "Christianity Face to Face with Islam," in *First Things* (Jan. 2009): 23. Also Wilken: "Memory is an integral part of Christian faith, but unattached to things it is infinitely malleable, even evanescent, like a story whose veracity is diluted as its particulars are forgotten" (ibid.). It is ironic that some European Catholic theologians welcome the increase in the Muslim population since the devout practice of Islam will, they believe, make it easier for other religious Europeans to fight Europe's aggressive forms of secularism.

25 Samuel Huntington, *The Clash of Civilizations and the Remaking of the World Order* (New York: Simon & Schuster, 1996).

The Road Behind and the Road Ahead

Catholicism and Judaism

PHILIP A. CUNNINGHAM

Introduction

On June 5, 1938, the American Jesuit John LaFarge arrived in the city of Rome as part of a journey through several European countries.[1] In the previous few weeks he had visited England, France, Germany, Czechoslovakia, and Hungary, experiencing firsthand a continent anxious about Hitler's threats to Czechoslovakia and dreading another devastating war.

To LaFarge's surprise, just over two weeks later he found himself being ushered into a private audience with Pope Pius XI, after having received a totally unexpected invitation from the pope to a private discussion on an undisclosed topic.

LaFarge was evidently known to the widely read Pius XI as the author of an important 1937 book on race relations in the United States titled *Interracial Justice*. LaFarge had insisted that all human beings, made in the image of a common Creator, equally enjoyed natural rights. He had argued on the basis of contemporary scientific research that the notion of "race," the most devastating propaganda weapon in the Nazi arsenal, was "after all an artificial concept. . . . [T]his concept cannot serve as a practical basis for any type of human relation whatever."[2]

During their conversation, Pius XI revealed his grave concern over Nazi racist rhetoric and policies. He had decided to issue a condemnatory papal letter, an encyclical, and wanted LaFarge to work with a small team to prepare a draft text. The drafters were to write under conditions of extreme secrecy because of the volatile situation in Europe.

Over that summer, LaFarge and two Jesuit colleagues, the Frenchman Gustave Desbuquois and the German Gustav Gundlach, labored in Paris on the draft of an encyclical to be titled *Humani Generis Unitas* (The Unity of the Human Race). In September 1938 the draft was submitted to Vatican officials for the pope's consideration.

The draft began with a vigorous assertion of the equality of all human beings and rejected discrimination against groups of people on the basis of racist ideologies. However, when the text turned to the subject of antisemitism, other theological principles became operative.

While rebuking circumstances in which "millions of [Jewish] persons are deprived of the most elementary rights and privileges of citizens,"[3] the draft declared that there *is* an "authentic basis of the social separation of the Jews from the rest of humanity."[4] This "authentic" reason for discrimination was not for racial but religions reasons: "The Savior . . . was rejected by that people, violently repudiated, and condemned as a criminal by the highest tribunals of the Jewish nation. . . . [However,] the very act by which the Jewish people put to death their Savior and King was . . . the salvation of the world."[5]

Having asserted that the "Jewish nation" bore a collective responsibility for the death of Jesus, the draft claimed that Jews were doomed "to perpetually wander over the face of the earth . . . [were] never allowed to perish, but have been preserved through the ages into our own time."[6] It opined that there existed "a historic enmity of the Jewish people to Christianity, creating a perpetual tension between Jew and Gentile."[7] Therefore, the church has constantly had to be on guard against "the spiritual dangers to which contact with the Jews can expose souls."[8] This danger, "not diminished in our own time"[9] of 1938, was "the authentic basis of the social separation of the Jews from the rest of humanity."[10]

In the months after the draft's submission, the situation in Europe deteriorated precipitously. In late September, the Munich Agreement began the fragmentation and eventual Nazi conquest of Czechoslovakia. On the night of November 9–10, Kristallnacht occurred, which many date as the beginning of the Shoah. Pius XI's health, which had not been robust for some years, declined to the point that toward the end of November people feared his death was imminent. He suffered a heart attack and died on February 10, 1939. It is not known whether he ever read the draft of *Humani Generis Unitas*. The project was not taken up by Pope Pius XII and the text of the draft remained hidden until decades later.

I often refer to this revealing episode because even though the drafters proceeded from the noblest of motives regarding racism, their theological stance toward Jews eviscerated their efforts. This impact of such theological conditioning is even more remarkable in someone like Fr. LaFarge, who literally devoted his entire life to improving race relations in the United States. The draft's acceptance of the "social separation of the Jews from the rest of humanity" is a goal that Hitler claimed he was merely implementing. It is fortunate indeed that the draft was never officially promulgated because this would have given authoritative expression to an anti-Jewish theology, and would probably have made all but impossible the positive theological stance expressed in the Second Vatican Council declaration *Nostra Aetate*.

With this introductory vignette, let me turn to our main subject: the road behind and the road ahead for Catholic-Jewish relations. I'll do this in four parts: 1. A Dramatic Transformation; 2. Supersessionism and *Nostra Aetate*; 3. Nearly Five Decades of Rapprochement; and 4. Challenges for the New Relationship.

A Dramatic Transformation

Even at the time of its composition, it was clear that the Second Vatican Council's "Declaration on the Relationship of the Church to Non-Christian Religions," known by its Latin title as *Nostra Aetate*, was a historic benchmark. This is true for the Catholic Church's relations to all other religions, but especially with Judaism, the focus of my remarks.

Occurring in the aftermath of the genocidal Nazi Shoah, it was the first formal ecclesiastical declaration on the church's relationship to Jews and Judaism in Christian history. That it reversed an almost two-millennia old hostility toward Judaism is evident in section 4's inability to cite any previous popes or councils. This is quite unusual in a Catholic document. In order to express a positive attitude toward Jews and Judaism, the declaration had to go all the way back to the New Testament itself, and even then was somewhat selective in its quotations.

Having had few precedents for its affirming sentiments, ever since the time of *Nostra Aetate*'s composition some have questioned whether it expressed authentic Catholic teaching.[11] In an address to the Roman curia in 2005, Pope Benedict XVI wrote that it was incorrect to regard the Second Vatican Council with a "hermeneutic of discontinuity and rupture," which "risks ending in a split between the pre-conciliar Church and the post-conciliar Church." He argued that the council should be viewed with a "hermeneutic of reform, of renewal in the continuity of the [church], which increases in time and develops, yet always remaining the same, the one subject of the journeying People of God."[12]

Nevertheless, Benedict acknowledged that after the Shoah and "a retrospective look at a long and difficult history, it was necessary to evaluate and define in a new way the relationship between the Church and the faith of Israel." This evaluation revealed "a discontinuity . . . but in which, after the various distinctions between concrete historical situations and their requirements had been made, the continuity of principles proved not to have been abandoned. It is easy to miss this fact at a first glance. It is precisely in this combination of continuity and discontinuity at different levels that the very nature of true reform consists."

It seems that Pope Benedict maintains that despite the "discontinuities" with genuine Catholicism represented by the centuries-old "teaching of contempt" for Jews, *Nostra Aetate* actually restored an essential continuity, presumably by retrieving New Testament teaching that Jews "remain beloved of God" (Romans 11:28, *Nostra Aetate*). It is thus definitively Catholic to esteem Judaism.

The transformation represented by *Nostra Aetate* can be vividly shown by contrasting some quotations from the church's patristic and medieval periods with those since Vatican II:

"Jews are slayers of the Lord, murderers of the prophets, enemies of God, haters of God, adversaries of grace, enemies of their father's faith." —Gregory of Nyssa, *Homilies on the Resurrection*, 5 (ca. 350)	"The apostle Paul maintains that the Jews remain very dear to God . . . since God does not take back the gifts he bestowed or the choice he made (cf. Rom. 11:28–29)." —Second Vatican Council, *Nostra Aetate*, 4 (1965)
"The Jews held him, the Jews insulted him, the Jews bound him, they crowned him with thorns, they dishonored him by spitting on him, they scourged him, they heaped abuses on him, they hung him on a tree, they pierced him with a lance." —Augustine of Hippo, *The Creed*, 3:10 (ca. 400)	"That cry of death, 'Crucify him!' resounds throughout history and the century now ending . . . the ashes of Auschwitz and the ice of the Gulag, water and blood of Asian rice fields, the lakes of Africa, murdered paradises. . . . Oh no, not the Jewish people, for so long crucified by us . . . but all of us, each and every one of us [have crucified Jesus] because we are all assassins of love." —Pope John Paul II, *Meditation on First Station of the Cross* (April 10, 1998)
"[When a Christian utters the Lord's Prayer, he or she] reproaches and condemns the Jews, because they not only faithlessly spurned Christ . . . but also cruelly slew him; who now cannot call the Lord 'Father,' since the Lord confounds and refutes them, saying, 'You are born of the devil as father, and you wish to do the desires of your father.'" —Cyprian, *Treatises*, 134–135 (ca. 240)	"In the Christian world . . . erroneous and unjust interpretations of the New Testament regarding the Jewish people and their alleged culpability [for the crucifixion of Jesus] have circulated for too long, engendering feelings of hostility towards this people." —Pope John Paul II, "Address to the Symposium on the Roots of Anti-Judaism" (Oct. 31, 1997).[13]

"For [the Jews] committed the most impious crime of all, when they conspired against the Savior of mankind. . . . Therefore that city where Jesus suffered these indignities had to be utterly destroyed. The Jewish nation had to be overthrown, and God's invitation to blessedness transferred to others, I mean to the Christians." —Origen, *Contra Celsum*, IV, 22 (ca. 220)	"Jews should not be spoken of as rejected or accursed as if this followed from holy scripture. Consequently, all must take care, lest in catechizing or in preaching the word of God, they teach anything which is not in accord with the truth of the Gospel message or the spirit of Christ." —Second Vatican Council, *Nostra Aetate*, 4 (1965)
"We desire to combat the enemies of God in the East, but we have under our eyes the Jews, a race more inimical to God than all the others." —an eleventh-century crusader, [Guibert of Nogent, *De Vita Sua*, III, 5]	"There can be no denial of the fact that from the time of the Emperor Constantine on, Jews were isolated and discriminated against in the Christian world. There were expulsions and forced conversions. Literature propagated stereotypes, preaching accused the Jews of every age of deicide; the ghetto which came into being in 1555 with a papal bull became in Nazi Germany the antechamber of the extermination." —Cardinal Edward I. Cassidy, "Address to the American Jewish Committee" (May 28, 1998)
"The Jews, against whom the blood of Jesus Christ calls out, although they ought not to be killed, . . . [y]et as wanderers they must remain upon the earth, until their countenance be filled with shame and they seek the name of Jesus Christ, the Lord." —Pope Innocent III (ca. 1200) [*Epistles*, 10:190]	"The Church of Christ discovers her 'bond' with Judaism by 'searching into her own mystery.' The Jewish religion is not 'extrinsic' to us, but in a certain way is 'intrinsic' to our own religion. With Judaism therefore we have a relationship which we do not have with any other religion. You are our dearly beloved brothers and, in a certain way, it could be said that you are our elder brothers." —Pope John Paul II, "Address at the Great Synagogue of Rome" (April 13, 1986), 4

The anti-Judaic concepts expressed in the left column above are not rarities or unusual, but rather represent the univocal perspective of church leaders for many centuries. They are premised on a theological idea known today as "supersessionism." This is the claim that the church has superseded Jews as God's chosen people because of their alleged guilt for the crucifixion of Jesus. It was never formally defined as Catholic doctrine by a church council, but was a part of the air Christians breathed for most of the church's history.

Supersessionism and *Nostra Aetate*

Why did these ideas arise and become dominant? The answers are not primarily theological, but sociological. In its early centuries the church was not a legal religion in the Roman Empire and was beset by internal doctrinal controversies. Subject to periodic persecutions and the insults of the imperial intelligentsia, the church felt threatened by Judaism's legal acceptance and high social status in the empire. The church's claim to understand the Hebrew scriptures better than Jews seemed silly to Roman critics who deemed Christianity to be a heretical mutation of Judaism. Especially difficult for church leaders to explain was why Christians did not have to follow the Law admittedly given by God to Moses.

In the second century, a Roman critic named Celsus pointedly asked Christians through a fictitious Jewish questioner: "Why have you, O citizens of Israel, left the law of our fathers and become slaves to the power of this [Jesus] . . .? You have been deceived. You have deserted Israel for another name."[14] He continues:

> I ask the Christians to consider further the following case: If the prophets of Yahweh, the God of the Jews, were in the habit of telling the Jews that Jesus was to be his son, then why did he give them their laws through Moses and promise them that they would become rich and famous and fill the earth? . . . Yet we are to believe that his "son," this man from Nazareth, gives an opposing set of laws: he says that a man cannot serve God properly if he is rich and famous or powerful. . . . Well, who is to be disbelieved—Moses or Jesus? Perhaps there is a simpler solution: perhaps when the Father sent Jesus he had forgotten the commandments he gave to Moses, and inadvertently condemned his own laws, or perhaps sent his messenger to give notice that he had suspended what he had previously endorsed.[15]

In addition to these challenges, church leaders were also threatened by the attraction that Jewish practices held for many Gentiles, including Christians. Recent archaeological evidence shows that many Gentiles had some affiliation with local synagogues,[16] and sometime churches were emptied when Christian congregants attended synagogue ceremonies on Jewish holy days.[17]

Church leaders responded to unflattering comparisons with Judaism by seeking to denigrate their rival. They sought to prove that the church was the true Israel, that Judaism was a pretender to that title, and that Christians need not follow the Mosaic Law—all using Jewish sources as proof-texts.

This was the context in which the constellation of anti-Jewish theological assertions that we know today as supersessionism emerged. The chart below sketches out some of its interlocking apologetic and polemical claims. As one scholar of this patristic period has concluded, "Christian beliefs are so deeply rooted in attitudes about Judaism that it is impossible to disentangle what Christians say about Christ and the Church from what they say about Judaism."[18] This anti-Jewish complex of ideas remained uncritiqued until the twentieth century. It plainly sabotaged the efforts of the drafters of *Humani Generis Unitas* in 1938. Although devised in circumstances of weakness, supersessionism would promote the social marginalization of Jews in eras when the church held political power. It was not until after the Shoah that supersessionism came under serious scrutiny. It was not until *Nostra Aetate* rejected the notion of a collective Jewish guilt for the crucifixion of Jesus and proclaimed God's love for the People of Israel that the foundations of supersession were finally overturned.

Supersessionism
and Consequent or Complementary Ideas

Basic Premise: The church has superseded Israel as God's Chosen People.
Jews are no longer in covenant with God because (A) The church fulfills Israel and so Israel is now obsolete (e.g., Justin Martyr, *Dialogue with Trypho*) and/or (B) Israel's rejection of Jesus caused God to end the divine covenant with Israel as evidenced by the destruction of the Second Temple (e.g., Melito of Sardis, *Peri pascha*).

This premise influenced Christian thought in a number of areas, including:

Judaism	**Scripture**
• Judaism prepared for Christianity and is now obsolete.	• The "Old" Testament was written to prepare for the "New" Testament.
• It was/is an imperfect and temporary religion that was/is corrupt, legalistic, and carnal.	• The Old Testament must be read "spiritually" or christologically in reference to Christ or the church in order to discern its true meaning. (Jews read it literally or carnally;
• The Pharisees, condemned by Jesus, embodied everything wrong with Judaism.	however, by preserving the Old Testament they give valuable, if unwitting, witness to the church.)

Judaism	Scripture
• "The Jews" killed their own Messiah and so were doomed by God to wander the earth without a national homeland. They bear the mark of Cain and so may not be killed. • Jews are allies of the devil.	• The prophets condemned Jewish hard-heartedness. The Torah was given to control Jewish waywardness. • The New Testament reveals the guilt of the Jews and the corruption of the Pharisees.

Jesus	The Church
• Jesus is the long-awaited Messiah of Israel who completely fulfills all of the Old Testament predictions of him, not carnally, but spiritually. • Jesus condemned corrupt Judaism. • The Jews killed Jesus. • Through his perfect sacrifice, Jesus reopened the gates of heaven. He alone brings salvation.	• The church is the New People of God, the new and perfect Israel. • The church fulfills all that was foreshadowed of it in the Old Testament. • The church does not follow the Law of Moses, even though God gave it, because Christ's universal Law of Love has replaced that temporary Law aimed at Jews. • Outside the Church there is no salvation.

Notes

1. Many of the above ideas were expressed during the patristic era in response to pagan criticisms that Christianity was a heretical mutation of Judaism and to Judaism's continuing attractiveness for both baptized and unbaptized Gentiles. The ideas tended to reinforce each other.

2. Although a Church council never formally defined supersessionism, it was an unexamined belief until the twentieth century.

3. The first relevant conciliar statement was *Nostra Aetate* (Second Vatican Council, 1965). Now that the Church teaches that God's covenant with Israel is perpetual and unrevoked, theological ideas dependent on supersessionism must be revised.

Much could be said about the difficult composition and approval process of *Nostra Aetate* at the Second Vatican Council. Here, permit me to summarize the important ideas made in its fourth section by means of seven points:

1. *Nostra Aetate* repudiated the long-standing "deicide" charge by declaring that "Jews should not be spoken of as rejected or accursed as if this followed from holy scripture."

2. *Nostra Aetate* stressed the religious bond and spiritual legacy shared by Jews and the church. It acknowledged the Jewishness of Jesus, his mother, and the apostles, and recognized Christianity's debt to biblical Israel. This has become foundational in later Catholic ecclesiastical and theological writings.

3. *Nostra Aetate* strongly implied that God and Jews abide in covenant. Citing Romans 11, the council fathers observed that "the Jews remain very dear to God, for the sake of the patriarchs, since God does not take back the gifts he bestowed or the choice he made." This was reinforced, as Eugene J. Fisher has pointed out,[19] when *Nostra Aetate* rendered an ambiguous Greek verb in Romans 9:4–5 in the present tense: "They *are* Israelites and it is for them *to be* sons and daughters, to them *belong* the glory, the covenants, the giving of the law, the worship, and the promises; to them *belong* the patriarchs, and of their race according to the flesh, is the Christ."

Nostra Aetate's implicit recognition that Israel abides in a perpetual covenantal relationship with God has subsequently been made fully explicit. John Paul II repeatedly taught that Jews are "the people of God of the Old Covenant, never revoked by God,"[20] "the present-day people of the covenant concluded with Moses,"[21] and "partners in a covenant of eternal love which was never revoked."[22]

4. *Nostra Aetate* deplored "all hatreds, persecutions, displays of antisemitism directed against the Jews at any time or from any source." While *Nostra Aetate* did not confess *Christian* antisemitism or discuss the perennial Christian teaching of contempt for Jews, subsequent documents acknowledged Christian wrongdoing and labeled antisemitism as a sin against God and humanity.

5. *Nostra Aetate* stressed the need for accurate biblical interpretation and religious education: "all must take care, lest in catechizing or in preaching the word of God, they teach anything which is not in accord with the truth of the Gospel message or the spirit of Christ." This sentence introduced a hermeneutical principle for Catholic biblical interpretation that has been further intensified in later documents.[23] Of particular note are the studies issued by the Pontifical Biblical Commission in 1993 and 2001. Especially significant is the instruction in the 1993 text that:

> Particular attention is necessary, according to the spirit of the Second Vatican Council (*Nostra Aetate*, 4), to avoid absolutely any actualization of certain texts of the New Testament which could provoke or reinforce unfavorable attitudes toward the Jewish people. The tragic events of the past must, on the contrary, impel all to keep unceasingly in mind that, according to the New Testament, the Jews remain "beloved" of God, "since the gifts and calling of God are irrevocable." (Romans 11:28–29)[24]

6. *Nostra Aetate* called for Catholics and Jews to collaborate in "biblical and theological enquiry and . . . friendly discussions." This mandate directly contradicted the prior practice of discouraging Catholics from conversing with Jews on religious matters, as expressed by the worry in the draft of *Humani Generis Unitas* about "the spiritual dangers to which contact with the Jews can expose souls."[25] This reversal has contributed to an enormous number of dialogues on all levels around the world, to the establishment in the United States alone of almost three dozen academic centers to promote Christian-Jewish studies,[26] and to many joint research initiatives among Jewish and Christian scholars.

7. *Nostra Aetate* expressed no interest in further efforts to baptize Jews, relegating the resolution of the Jewish and Christian disagreement over Jesus' significance and identity until the eschatological dawning of God's kingdom: "Together with the prophets and that same apostle, the church awaits the day, known to God alone, when all peoples will call on God with one voice and serve him shoulder to shoulder." This phrase was carefully considered during the council's deliberations, especially after controversy arose in the public media in the summer and fall of 1964.

Today, unlike some other Christian communities, the Catholic Church allocates no financial or personnel resources for the baptism of Jews. However, the theological reasons for this abandonment of previous and persistent Christian efforts have not yet achieved a definitive articulation in Catholic teaching,[27] no doubt because Catholic insight into the nature of Israel's covenanting with God is still emerging. More on this below.

Almost Five Decades of Rapprochement

Since *Nostra Aetate*'s promulgation in 1965, there have been many further documents on Christian-Jewish relations, both in the Catholic Church and other Christian communities. Of great importance for Catholics are texts of the Pontifical Commission for Religious Relations with the Jews, the Pontifical Biblical Commission, a large number of addresses by Pope John Paul II, as well as more recently by Pope Benedict XVI, and copious statements from various national conferences of Catholic bishops. I will attempt to summarize their most important teachings in these ten points:

1. Jews remain in a covenantal relationship with God. The church's "new covenant" did not replace Israel's covenantal life with God lived through the Torah.[28]

2. Anti-Judaism and antisemitism are sins against God.[29]

3. Christian preaching and teaching have contributed to antisemitism. Certain New Testament texts have regularly been misinterpreted and so have promoted hostility.[30]

4. There exists a divinely willed ongoing relationship between Judaism and Christianity. Judaism has its own distinctive "vocation" in the divine plan that goes beyond the preparation for Christianity.[31]

5. Jesus was and always remained a Galilean Jew, "an authentic son of Israel," as Pope John Paul II put it.[32] He was not opposed to the Torah or the Judaism of his day.[33]

6. Christians must respect Jewish self-understanding of their own religious experience. This includes a respect for Jewish attachment to *Eretz Yisrael* (the Land of Israel).[34]

7. Christians can learn more about God and relationship with God (and about Christianity) from the traditions of Judaism over the centuries and from the living faith of contemporary Jews.[35]

8. The Hebrew Scriptures (TaNaK) have spiritual value as revelatory texts irrespective of the church's retrospective christological reading of them.[36]

9. Christian understandings of the relationship between the "Old Testament" and the "New Testament" in terms of promise and fulfillment must be seen as still awaiting the complete fulfillment of God's designs in the coming kingdom.[37]

10. Jews and Christians both have the covenantal duty to prepare for the Age to Come.[38]

Although this listing is impressive, one should not think that all these ideas have been internalized by the entire Catholic world. That was made vividly clear a few years ago during the "culture wars" debate over the movie *The Passion of the Christ*, when, with few exceptions,[39] Catholic leaders overlooked the film's flagrant disregard of post–*Nostra Aetate* magisterial teaching. As one observer put it, "[W]hen confronted with strong mystical experiences and huge interests of a pastoral nature, and also of other types, the problem of the correct relationship with the Jews seems to be the very last thing to worry the Church."[40] Nor have all the pertinent theological questions been addressed, let alone answered. As Cardinal Walter Kasper, past president of the Pontifical Commission for Religious Relations with the Jews has said, we are still only at "the beginning of a new beginning" of a coherent Catholic theology of Judaism.[41]

Nonetheless, the repeated official Catholic appeal for interreligious dialogue with Jews has produced tremendous fruit, as is evident from the ten teachings just listed. The dialogue has been particularly rich here in the United States, because of our nation's commitment to religious pluralism, because the world's largest Jewish community resides here, and also because Jews and Catholics shared many common experiences as immigrants to these shores. It is now commonplace for Jewish and Catholic academicians to pursue research together. There are also more and more Jewish scholars of the New Testament and Christian scholars of rabbinics. Regular national and regional conversations occur among clergy of both traditions, and some local encounters have been occurring around the country for several decades. These are all historical accomplishments, and much has been learned about how the two communities approach conversation with each other.

We have learned, for instance, that Jews and Catholics generally come to dialogue with different interests, concerns, historical knowledge, and (mis)conceptions about each other. Catholics tend to want to talk "religion"—often, "why don't Jews believe in Jesus?"—while Jews are more inclined to discuss social justice issues. Jews, understandably, tend to wonder if the unprecedented Catholic overtures to dialogue are only a temporary cessation of the conversionary campaigns of the past, while Catholics, usually unfamiliar with the history of Christian oppression of Jews, can be shocked and guilt-ridden when learning of it for the first time. Catholics may find it difficult to understand the depth of Jewish fears for the survival of the State of Israel or fright over antisemitic incidents, while Jews tend to avoid expressing their general mystification over Christian claims that something called "salvation" is the result of the crucifixion of a single Jew among the thousands of Jews executed under Roman imperial rule.

Challenges for the New Relationship

While dialogue dynamics can require constant patience, certain theological and historical presuppositions, occasionally held only unconsciously, can be even more challenging. For instance, Christians come to interreligious dialogue with Jews with the presupposition that the God whom Jesus called "Abba" is the one God of Israel. Since the rejection of Marcion's contrary view in the second century, all but the most fringe Christians assume that "Jews and Christians worship the same God," as the 2000 American Jewish statement *Dabru Emet* put it. However, there are many Jews who are not comfortable with the simple equation of Judaism and Christianity as worshipping the same God, as some prominent critics of *Dabru Emet* made clear. This asymmetry can sometimes manifest itself when Jews and Catholics converse.

In addition, I think most Christians and Jews uncritically hold that something went wrong with the "parting of the ways"—the origins of Christianity and rabbinic Judaism as separate communities. Things occurred contrary to God's will. Christians can consciously or unconsciously imagine that most Jews did not accept the good news about Jesus because God "blinded" them (following Paul in Romans 11:25), or because Jews were innocently mistaken due to a misplaced myopic focus on the Torah, or less benignly, because of their obstinacy. Jews may consciously or unconsciously assume that if not Jesus, then Paul distorted the essence of Judaism and so created the fundamentally misguided Gentile church.

Both Jews and Christians can presuppose that eventually the other tradition will recognize its errors, even if only eschatologically, at the dawning of the Age to Come. This was expressed, for instance, in the pre-Vaticna II Good Friday intercession for "the conversion of the Jews," which stated:

> Let us pray also for the Jews that the Lord our God may take the veil from their hearts and that they also may acknowledge our Lord Jesus Christ. Let us pray: Almighty and everlasting God, You do not refuse Your mercy even to the Jews; hear the prayers which we offer for the blindness of that people so that they may acknowledge the light of Your truth, which is Christ, and be delivered from their darkness.[42]

A similar "something went wrong" mentality is evident in these very forthright remarks by a leading Jewish scholar at an international meeting of Catholic and Jews:

> Let us assume further that I respect believing Christians, as I do, for qualities that emerge precisely out of their Christian faith. But I believe that the worship of Jesus as God is a serious religious error displeasing to God even if the worshipper is a non-Jew, and that at the end of days Christians will come to recognize this.[43]

I suggest an alternative presupposition to "something went wrong." What if the origins of our two traditions unfolded according to God's will? Is it not possible that God would desire two covenanting communities in the world, perhaps to serve as enablers and correctors of each other? This alternative makes greater sense if divine revelation, God's self-disclosure, is understood as essentially relational in nature, so that God is perfectly free to reveal different (though not contradictory) things selectively to different people. If so, then eschatologically one side or the other will not be proved wrong in some zero-sum calculus; rather, both sides will come to understand why both were correct—a development hinted at by a certain phrase in a 2001 study of the Pontifical Biblical Commission.[44]

A third dynamic that Christians and Jews can bring to the dialogue is a tendency to retroject later developments and concepts to the time of the parting or their origins. Thus, issues or claims that later divided the communities are imagined to have been divisive at the time of Jesus. Likewise, the functioning and organization of synagogues as they later developed after rabbinic Judaism became ascendant are imagined to have existed as far back as the early Second Temple period. To give some concrete examples, the divinity of Jesus is thought by many Christians to be a subject that was debated between "Christians" and "Jews" even before the catalyzing and revelatory experience of the resurrection. Or Judaism at the time of Jesus (or worse, throughout all time) is imagined according to later Christian caricatures as legalistic and oppressive. Similarly, both Jews and Christians can assume that Christianity from its roots was antithetical to normative Judaism.

In a related fashion, both traditions would like to think of themselves as ideal types: as perfect realizations of "Judaism" and "Christianity," unalloyed by change or historical conditioning. As such, they can be thought of as isolated and uninfluenced by each other. However, as Rabbi Abraham Joshua Heschel reminded us, "No Religion Is an Island," and, in fact, our two traditions have been shaping each other—for good or for ill—throughout the past two millennia.

Those who tend to think in terms of ideal types also tend to presume that aspects of both traditions' teachings are categorically in fundamental opposition to one another. There are certainly irreducible differences between Judaism and Christianity, but a presumption that these cannot be explored impedes mutual understanding and enrichment. Actually, there is considerable joint research and conversation underway on such core topics as incarnation, trinity, and the election of Israel. Such ventures do not erase profound differences, but they do show that some subjects are not totally antithetical either.

There also forces at work that can inhibit the results of interreligious dialogue from becoming known with each community. These are the related influences of *compartmentalized speech* and the *peripheral nature* of interreligious matters for each community's daily life. By compartmentalized speech, I mean the habit of using one mode of speech for external community discourse and another for internal community discourse. For instance, sometimes one will hear Christian sermons during the season of Advent that more than smack of supersessionist understandings of biblical prophecy, and the very next day hear the prophets cited in an almost contradictory fashion in a dialogical setting.

The peripheral nature of interfaith concerns is apparent within each community's governance practices, liturgical life, educational programs, and self-understanding. Speaking for the Catholic community, I believe that we need to follow through in a consistent way with our stated commitments to Catholic-Jewish rapport. For instance, there are still hymns and prayers used regularly during worship that speak in pre–*Nostra Aetate* cadences. Similarly, there are educational issues about how we teach, even if by omission, about each other.

This brings me to a most profound set of challenges for continuing rapprochement between Jews and Christians. They are the signposts on the "road ahead." If our dialogue is not to stagnate but to deepen, then at some point it will become inevitable that participants will ask themselves if and how the other religion is authentically "of God." This is a question with enormous challenges for one's own religious self-definition, but as the past decades of unprecedented exchanges have unfolded, I believe we are now approaching a moment when such considerations cannot be postponed. I will primarily address Christian theological issues, but let me mention in passing a question that is looming for Jewish self-understanding.

In the Jewish tradition there is a laudable inclusivity in the time-honored belief that non-Jews, Gentiles, can be righteous in the sight of God if they are guided by the minimal commands known as the Noahide laws. These include prohibitions against murder and idolatry. However, the theological challenge facing Jews today regarding religious pluralism is whether it is possible to consider Jewishly the claims of Gentile *religious* traditions on their own terms. To put it another way, is it adequate to ignore the self-understanding of Christians (and Muslims) by thinking of them only generically as non-Jews, or can their contentions that they are related to the People of Israel's God be engaged in a Jewish way? There is little precedent in the rabbinic and post-rabbinic writings to draw upon because of the minority and often oppressed status of Jews in Christian and Muslim lands, but in today's world in which global interreligious understanding is crucially needed, a generic approach is surely insufficient for Judaism itself.

If Jews were to seriously grapple with a "Jewish theology of Christianity," then the particularities of the Jewish and Christian relationship will pose difficult questions, including:

- Are Christians really in covenant with the God of Israel as they claim?
- Since such a covenant could only come about if God willed it, then what are Jews to make of Jesus? In what way is he "of God"?
- How should Jews understand their historical and religious relationship to Christianity?

I hasten to add, given our history, that Christians have no ethical grounds to make any demands for Jews to address such questions. I am also aware of the importance of such topics as *avodah zarah* (strange worship) and *shituf* (permissible associations) for halakhic engagement with the particularity of Christianity. I am simply observing that logically these sorts of concerns will in and of themselves become more pressing if our dialogue progresses.

But it is more appropriate for me to discuss similarly internal Christian theological questions that demand attention. I will mention two.

First, is it possible for Christians, despite all the precedents to the contrary, to affirm theologically the centrality of *Eretz Yisrael* for Jews? Over the centuries there have been two Christian theological approaches to this. When *supersessionism* prevailed, Christians took for granted that Jews had lost any right to the Land of Israel as part of the divine curse for the crucifixion of Jesus. A later approach, *restorationism*, was a product of post-Reformation era ways of reading the Bible. It anticipated a Jewish ingathering to their ancestral homeland prior to the return of Jesus as sovereign Lord. Restorationism has historically not been as influential in Roman Catholicism as in certain strains of Evangelical Protestantism. Instead, until the Second Vatican Council, Catholic attitudes had been dominated by supersessionism.

Neither supersessionism nor restorationism is adequate for Catholic theologizing about *Eretz Yisrael* today. I cannot explore the possibilities now, other than to note an interesting suggestion made some years ago by Philip Culbertson. He proposed that the Christian category of "sacramentality" be the lens through which Christians view the importance of the Land of Israel for Jews.[45] Just as sacraments mediate the presence of God to the church, so the land mediates the covenantal presence of God among the Jewish people. This strikes me as an especially appealing approach for Catholics, but the relationship between the sacramental *Eretz Yisrael* and the political *Medinat Yisrael* (State of Israel) would need careful exploration.[46]

I would like to devote a bit more time to another theological question facing the post–*Nostra Aetate* church: how might the church understand its doctrine that Jesus Christ is the savior of all humanity, given its recent recognition that Israel lives in eternal (and presumably "saving") covenant with God? This question touches on the central nervous system of Christian self-identity and has numerous pastoral implications, including whether Christians should seek or even hope for the baptism of Jews. Cardinal Kasper has framed the problem this way: "How can the thesis of the continuing covenant be reconciled with the uniqueness and universality of Christ Jesus, which are constitutive for the Christian understanding of the new covenant?"[47]

A few years ago, I assisted in organizing a major international conference at the Pontifical Gregorian University in Rome to mark the fortieth anniversary of *Nostra Aetate*. A number of papers focused on the theological implications of that declaration appeared to converge in interesting ways, suggesting that a scholarly consensus on some issues might be within reach. Under the sponsorship of four Catholic universities, about two dozen academicians from six countries met near Rome in October 2006 for intense conversation, which for a portion of the time included Cardinal Kasper, in a consultation called "Christ and the Jewish People." This was followed by a smaller gathering at the Catholic University of Leuven in Belgium. The results of our work have recently been published in a collection of essays.[48] My contribution with Didier Pollefeyt offers these general orientations:[49]

1. "Salvation" is multifaceted. It involves relationship with God both as individuals and communities that leads toward the Reign of God or Age to Come, that ultimate reality which is both "already" and "not yet."

2. For Christians and Jews, this relationship with God is "covenantal"—a sharing in life with mutual responsibilities. Israel and the church walk in covenant with God through distinctive experiences of covenantal life. Israel's experience is Torah shaped; the church's experience is Christ shaped.

3. *From a Christian perspective,* Israel and the church both live in covenant with the One God who is Triune. The Jewish people are, therefore, in relationship with God's divine Word, whose every activity is now done in unity with the glorified humanity of Jesus. God has not chosen to reveal to the church what this might mean to Israel's own way of walking in covenant with God. The church and the Jewish people can resonate with and be enriched by each other's experiences of God, but there is ultimately a distinctive integrity to each community's covenantal life that, while related, cannot be shared with or embraced by the other.

Time will tell whether these approaches will be helpful in shaping a coherent Catholic theology of Judaism. Meanwhile, let me bring these reflections to a close by observing that although the road behind has been harrowing and the road ahead difficult, we Jews and Christians can be a sign to the whole world of the possibility of reconciliation between religious communities long hostile to each other. As John Paul II expressed it, "As Christians and Jews, following the example of the faith of Abraham, we are called to be a blessing for the world. This is the common task awaiting us. It is therefore necessary for us, Christians and Jews, to first be a blessing to each other."[50]

Notes

1 This introduction is based upon Georges Passelecq and Bernard Suchecky, *The Hidden Encyclical of Pius XI,* trans. Steven Rendall (New York: Harcourt, Brace, 1997).

2 John LaFarge, *Interracial Justice* (New York: America Press, 1937), 12, 14, cited in Passelecq and Suchecky, 26.

3 Passelecq and Suchecky, 246.

4 Ibid., 247.

5 Ibid., 248–249.

6 Ibid., 249.

7 Ibid., 251–252.

8 Ibid., 252.

9 Ibid.

10 Ibid., 247.

11 For example, three days before the Second Vatican Council's vote on *Nostra Aetate* a self-designated "International Association of Bishops" urged rejection of the declaration.

Signed by Bishop Luigi Carli, Archbishop Maurice Mathieu Louis Rigaud, and the later excommunicated Archbishop Marcel Lefèbvre, their letter among other things protested that it was "unworthy of the Council" to have framed "the future conversion of Israel" so as to preclude proselytizing of Jews. See John M. Oesterreicher, *The New Encounter between Christians and Jews* (New York: Philosophical Library, 1986), 272, 274.

12 Pope Benedict XVI, "Address to the Roman Curia," (Rome, December 22, 2005), http://www.vatican.va/holy_father/benedict_xvi/speeches/2005/december/documents/hf_ben_xvi_spe_20051222_roman-curia_en.html.

13 Pope John Paul II, "Address to the Symposium on the Roots of Anti-Judaism" (Vatican City, Oct. 31, 1997). http://www.ccjr.us/dialogika-resources/documents-and-statements/roman-catholic/pope-john-paul-ii/321-jp2-97oct31.

14 Celsus, "On True Doctrine," III; R. Joseph Hoffmann, *Celsus on the True Doctrine: A Discourse against the Christians* (New York: Oxford University Press, 1987), 60.

15 Ibid., IX; Hoffmann, 108–109.

16 See, e.g., Joyce Reynolds and Robert Tannenbaum, *Jews and God-fearers at Aphrodisias: Greek Inscriptions with Commentary* (Cambridge: Cambridge Philological Society, 1987).

17 See, e.g., Robert L. Wilken, *John Chrysostom and the Jews: Rhetoric and Reality in the Late Fourth Century* (Berkeley and Los Angeles: University of California Press, 1983).

18 Robert L. Wilken, *Judaism and the Early Christian Mind: A Study of Cyril of Alexandria's Exegesis and Theology* (New Haven, Conn.: Yale University Press, 1971), 229.

19 Eugene J. Fisher, "Official Roman Catholic Teaching on Jews and Judaism: Commentary and Context," in *In Our Time: The Flowering of Jewish-Catholic Dialogue*, ed. Eugene J. Fisher and Leon Klenicki (New York: Paulist, 1990), 6.

20 John Paul II, "Address to the Jewish Community in Mainz, West Germany" (Mainz, West Germany, November 17, 1980). Available in *Spiritual Pilgrimage: Pope John Paul II, Texts on Jews and Judaism 1979–1995*, ed. Eugene J. Fisher and Leon Klenicki (New York: Crossroad, 1995), 13–16.

21 Ibid.

22 John Paul II, "Address to Jewish Leaders in Miami" (Miami, September 11, 1987). Available in John Paul II, *Spiritual Pilgrimage*, 105–108.

23 Fisher, "Official Roman Catholic Teaching," 7.

24 Pontifical Biblical Commission, "The Interpretation of the Bible in the Church" (1993), IV, A, 3.

25 Passelecq and Suchecky, *Hidden Encyclical*, 252.

26 Visit the Web pages of the Council of Centers for Jewish-Christian Relations (CCJR) at www.ccjr.us.

27 Though see the text and discussion of the 2002 dialogue document of delegates of the U.S. Bishops Committee on Ecumenical and Interreligious Affairs and the National Council of Synagogues, "Reflections on Covenant and Mission," http://www.ccjr.us/dialogika-resources/documents-and-statements/interreligious/517-ncs-bceia02aug12. More recently, Pope Benedict XVI affirmatively quoted Hildegard Brem as follows: "In the light of Romans 11:25, the Church must not concern herself with the conversion of the Jews, since she must wait for the time fixed for this by God, 'until the full number of the Gentiles come in' (Rom. 11:25) (JESUS OF NAZARETH, Part Two, HOLY WEEK: FROM THE ENTRANCE INTO JERUSALEM TO THE RESURRECTION (San Francisco: Ignatius Press, 2011), p. 45.)

28 See notes 19–21; Commission for Religious Relations with the Jews, "Notes on the Correct Way to Present Jews and Judaism in Preaching and Teaching in the Roman Catholic Church," 1985, I, 3.

29 John Paul II, "Address to the Jewish Leaders in Bucharest" (Bucharest, August 18, 1993); John Paul II, *Spiritual Pilgrimage*, 155–158.

30 John Paul II, "Address to the Symposium on the Roots of Anti-Judaism," (Vatican City, October 31, 1997, 1.

31 John Paul II, "Address at the Great Synagogue of Rome" (Rome, April 13, 1986), 4, in John Paul II, *Spiritual Pilgrimage*, 60–66; John Paul II, "Address to Jewish Leaders in Warsaw" (Warsaw, June 14, 1987), in John Paul II, *Spiritual Pilgrimage*, 98–100; John Paul II, "Address to the Jewish Community in Mainz, West Germany" (Mainz, West Germany, November 17, 1980), in John Paul II, *Spiritual Pilgrimage*, 14–16; Commission for Religious Relations with the Jews, "Notes," II, 6; VI, 25.

32 John Paul II, "Address to the Pontifical Biblical Commission," April 11, 1997, 3.

33 Commission for Religious Relations with the Jews, "Notes," III (1985).

34 Commission for Religious Relations with the Jews, "Guidelines and Suggestions for Implementing the Conciliar Declaration, Nostra Aetate, 4," 1974, Prologue; CRRJ, "Notes," VI, 25.

35 John Paul II, "Address to Experts Gathered by the Commission for Religious Relations with the Jews," March 6, 1982, in John Paul II, *Spiritual Pilgrimage*, 17–20; Benedict XIV, "Address at the Roonstrasse Synagogue of Cologne," August 19, 2005.

36 Commission for Religious Relations with the Jews, "Notes" (1985), II, 6; Pontifical Biblical Commission, *The Jewish People and Their Sacred Scriptures in the Christian Bible* (2001), II, A, 6–7.

37 Commission for Religious Relations with the Jews, "Notes," II, 8–10; Pontifical Biblical Commission, "*Jewish People*," (2001), II, A, 5.

38 Commission for Religious Relations with the Jews, "Notes," II, 11.

39 Two notable exceptions were Bishop Richard J. Sklba, "The Passion of the Lord Revisited," *Milwaukee Catholic Herald*, April 8, 2004; and French Bishops' Conference, "Position du Comité permanent pour l'information et la communication sur le film 'La Passion du Christ' de Mel Gibson" [Position of the Standing Committee for Information and Communication on the Mel Gibson film *The Passion of the Christ*], March 30, 2004, http://www.cef.fr/catho/espacepresse/communiques/2004/commu20040330_passionduchrist.php.

40 Riccardo Di Segni, "Progress and Issues of the Dialogue from a Jewish Viewpoint," in *The Catholic Church and the Jewish People: Recent Reflections from Rome*, ed. Philip A. Cunningham, Norbert J. Hofmann, and Joseph Sievers (New York: Fordham University Press, 2007), 17.

41 Walter Kasper, "Christians, Jews and the Thorny Question of Mission," *Origins* 32, no. 28 (December 19, 2002): 457–466.

42 From the 1963 Roman Missal; translation courtesy of Maxwell Johnson.

43 David Berger, "On *Dominus Iesus* and the Jews" (paper delivered at the seventeenth meeting of the International Catholic-Jewish Liaison Committee, New York, May 1, 2001).

44 Pontifical Biblical Commission, "Jewish People" (2001), II, A, 5:

> What has already been accomplished in Christ must yet be accomplished in us and in the world. The definitive fulfillment will be at the end with the resurrection of the dead, a new heaven and a new earth. Jewish messianic expectation is not in vain. It can become for us Christians a powerful stimulant to keep alive the eschatological dimension of our faith. Like them, we too live in expectation. The difference is that for us the One who is to come will have the traits of the Jesus who has already come and is already present and active among us.

45 Philip Culbertson, "Eretz Israel: Sacred Space, Icon, Sign, or Sacrament?" *Shofar* 6, no. 3 (Spring 1988): 9–17.

46 See Commission for Religious Relations with the Jews, "Notes" (1985), VI, 25:

> Christians are invited to understand this religious attachment [to the Land] which finds its roots in Biblical tradition, without however making their own any particular religious interpretation of this relationship (cf. *Declaration* of the US Conference of Catholic Bishops, November 20, 1975). The existence of the State of Israel and its political options should be envisaged not in a perspective which is in itself religious,

but in their reference to the common principles of international law. The permanence of Israel (while so many ancient peoples have disappeared without trace) is a historic fact and a sign to be interpreted within God's design.

47 Walter Kasper, "The Relationship of the Old and the New Covenant as One of the Central Issues in Jewish-Christian Dialogue" (address delivered at Cambridge University, Cambridge, England, December 6, 2004).

48 Philip A. Cunningham, Joseph Sievers, Mary C. Boys, Hans Hermann Henrix, and Jesper Svartvik, eds., Christ Jesus and the Jewish People Today: New Explorations of Theological Interrelationships (Grand Rapids, Mich.: Eerdmans, 2011).

49 Philip A. Cunningham and Didier Pollefeyt, "The Triune One, the Incarnate Logos, and Israel's Covenantal Life" in Cunningham, et al, eds., Christ Jesus and the Jewish People Today, 183–201.

50 John Paul II, "Address on the Fiftieth Anniversary of the Warsaw Ghetto Uprising," (Vatican City, April 6, 1993) in John Paul II, Spiritual Pilgrimage, 168–169.

A Response to Philip A. Cunningham

ELLIOT N. DORFF

This is a wonderful essay—thorough, clear, honest, probing, and *very* suggestive. Even though I have had long and extensive experience in interfaith dialogue between Jews and Catholics, I learned a great deal. I am going to make a few brief comments on four specific parts of Cunningham's essay and then proceed to two of my own suggestions about how to carry his theological project forward.

Comments

First and foremost, Dr. Cunningham is clearly right in asserting that *Nostra Aetate* itself, and his list of ten new Catholic positions on Jewish matters that the church has affirmed since then, have been truly remarkable and absolutely wonderful in changing the entire landscape of the relationship between the Catholic and Jewish communities. My father, who was born in Poland in 1908 and who suffered from a lot of antisemitism there, could never have dreamed of these developments. As he would say in Yiddish, this is really "Mashiahzeit"— Messianic times (and with no reference to Jesus).

As Dr. Cunningham also notes, though, much has yet to be done to educate Catholics about these developments. I have twice been to Poland to teach Catholic seminary professors and seminarians there, and the very first question a seminarian asked me in Crakow was "Why did the Jews kill Jesus?" He had no clue about *Nostra Aetate*, let alone anything that has happened since, so this rabbi had to teach him and his classmates what his own church says about that. Changes of this nature take time and a lot of effort to trickle down, and I was glad to be part of that effort in Poland. I am also glad that the curriculum that my wife, Marlynn, wrote on behalf of the Jewish Federation Council of Los Angeles for teaching about Israel in Catholic high schools is now being used in many more schools here as well as other parts of the country, and that other curricula about the Holocaust and the beliefs and practices of Judaism have been developed by the Anti-Defamation League and the American Jewish Committee, respectively.

We Jews now have to do much more in teaching our youth and adults—and, for that matter, our rabbinical students—about these developments in Catholic-Jewish relations.

As a Zionist Jew living in the Diaspora, I fully appreciate Dr. Cunningham's effort to formulate a Catholic theology of Israel in sacramental terms, with Israel mediating the covenantal presence of God among the Jewish people. I think, though, that the majority of Israelis, who are not religious, would be both surprised and irritated to think of their homeland that way. Conversely, where does that leave religious Jews who live outside of Israel? Israel is clearly meaningful for us, but we also have other ways of approaching God—or else the religious among us would all move there. I can offer Professor Cunningham some comfort on this issue, though: Jews are no more at one in their theories of Israel and Zionism than Christians are. So welcome to the fray!

In any human transformation like this, there will inevitably be bumps along the road, and Dr. Cunningham mentions the tepid Catholic reaction to Mel Gibson's movie and the recent papal endorsement of the Tridentine rite as two of them. *Dominus Jesus* was another, and there will undoubtedly be others as the church tries to work out its theology of how it can at the same time claim to be the right way for Christians and all other people to approach God and yet also maintain that Jews can do that within Judaism. As a Jew, I understand fully how hard it will be for Catholics to work out a coherent Catholic theology on Judaism and the Jews that affirms both of these tenets in a coherent way.

Toward that end, let me suggest two things, one from my background as a Jew and the other from my training as a philosopher.

First, I wish to comment on Pope Benedict XVI's assertion that it is incorrect to regard the Second Vatican Council with a "hermeneutic of discontinuity and rupture" that "risks ending in a split between the pre-conciliar Church and the post-conciliar Church."[1] The pope's statement sounds very familiar to me as a Jew, but it should sound familiar to Catholics too. Both of our traditions have a rich tradition of, and great respect for, the process of what we Jews call "*midrash,*" of hermeneutics. We Jews and Catholics both know that no text can be read without interpretation, and that interpretations vary with changes in individuals, in time, and in circumstances. Some interpretations hew fairly close to the text, and some stretch texts and the traditions built on them quite far. The important thing to note, though, is that every living tradition is critically based not only on its constitutional texts—its holy scriptures—but, even more important, on the ongoing interpretations, limitations, and expansions of those texts over time, together with the changes in practice that accompany such interpretive changes. In choosing to focus on Romans 11 to change radically Catholic doctrines about Judaism and the Jews, the church is both bringing about admittedly large changes in its views and practices and also linking those changes to some of the texts of its past. To use a metaphor that Robert Cover and Ronald Dworkin developed in legal thought, our modern continuations of our communal and religious narratives may change their meaning radically, but they are still recognizably ours if they have some linkage to the past. Other links might be stronger—maybe even much stronger—but it is the duty of a tradition's modern interpreters to shape it in the best way they know how to make its modern expression as true to the tradition's values and as relevant to modern times as possible. So I say bravo to Pope Benedict!

Dominus Jesus, it seems to me, foundered on an important philosophical point—namely, the difference between relativism and relativity. In denouncing relativism, where individuals or groups decide the truth for themselves, it assumed that the only other option was absolutism, where there is only one truth. In fact, however, there is an option in between those two alternatives—namely, relativity, in which we assert that there is only one truth although we recognize that any human being can know it only from his or her vantage point. This means that what Catholics believe to be the truth may be different from what Jews believe to be the truth, but that does not mean that we are talking about completely different things; we just have different starting and viewing points, which makes the truth look different to us. We both need to have a large dose of epistemological humility in asserting what we do, even if we deeply believe what we affirm and maybe are even willing to risk our lives for it. In my book *To Do the Right and the Good*, I develop a theory of pluralism based on this philosophical point as well as a historical point (namely, that our traditions have changed over time and so no one can claim that the present version of even one's own tradition is the only possible one) and a theological one (namely, that God, in Jewish texts, *wants* people to be different).[2] I would suggest, then, that these points can form the basis for developing both a Jewish and a Catholic *theology* of the other.

Moreover, as the immediate past president of Jewish Family Service of Los Angeles, I learned a great deal about, and came to deeply appreciate, all the good that is being done by Catholic Social Services. I would suggest that our common efforts to make this a better world, based on the theological foundations in Judaism that I describe in my book *The Way into Tikkun Olam (Fixing the World)*,[3] can serve as the basis of a Jewish and a Catholic theory of practice with regard to the other. Taken together, my hope is that an enriched theology and theory of practice of how we relate to each other can carry us farther in both thought and action in the direction that *Nostra Aetate* began.

Notes

1 "Remarks on Interpreting the Second Vatican Council" by Pope Benedict XVI, an address given to the Roman Curia December 22nd, 2005, may be found as an Appendix in "The Crisis of Authority in CatholicModernity," edited by Michael Lacey and Francis Oakley (Oxford University Press, 2011), p. 358.

2 Elliot N. Dorff, *To Do the Right and the Good: A Jewish Approach to Modern Social Ethics* (Philadelphia: Jewish Publication Society, 2002), chapter 3. See also chapter 8, which discusses a question that emerged in the Priest-Rabbi Dialogue sponsored by the Los Angeles Archdiocese and the Board of Rabbis of Southern California—namely, what it would mean for Jews to forgive Catholics for what they did and did not do during the Holocaust.

3 Elliot N. Dorff, *The Way into Tikkun Olam (Fixing the World)* (Woodstock, Vt.: Jewish Lights, 2005).

A Response to Philip A. Cunningham

Catholicism and the Paths of Righteousness

RACHEL ADLER

Changing a time-honored theological position is a difficult enterprise, as Dr. Cunningham demonstrates in this lucid analysis of *Nostra Aetate* and the Catholic Church's change in its teachings about Jews and Judaism. Theologies have real consequences in history, sometimes bloody consequences, enacted on the bodies of unbelievers or heretics or demonized races. A conscientious religious tradition must own these consequences, make sense of them, and, insofar as it is possible, atone for them. To change requires enduring the pain of discontinuity with the past, and on the point, a Jewish scholar can well understand the concern of Pope Benedict XVI. One will never again be able to read certain texts of the past without feeling separate from them and perhaps uncomfortable with them. One will never again be able to pray certain pieces of liturgy without recalling how they called some to injustice and violence. Most of all, change challenges us theologically: it requires us to admit that the supposedly eternal and immutable truth of our tradition is not whole but partial and subject to the influence of time and culture.

What, then, motivates a religious tradition to take on the stressful task of changing its theology as the Catholic Church has in the past fifty years? As an outsider invested in the church's progress, I would like to venture a few guesses. One reason might be integrity. If members of the tradition see the problematic theology as inimical to their true identity as a holy body, they cannot be the church they are meant to be without addressing the problem. The perception of a law, a tenet, or a narrative as problematic constitutes a revelation of sorts, and like revelation, it will not leave us alone. This is the complaint of the prophet Jeremiah, handed a most unwelcome prophecy:

> I thought, "I will not mention Him,
> No more will I speak His name"—

But it was a raging fire in my heart,
Shut up in my bones;
I could not hold it in. (Jeremiah 20:9)[1]

We change, in other words, because we are so uncomfortable we just can't stand not changing.

Another possible reason for change is that the relatively new discipline of historiography and its critical readings of texts have exposed cherished beliefs and assumptions as inaccurate. Only last week I was teaching my rabbinical students that the great liturgical poem for the Days of Awe, *U'netaneh Tokef*, was not created by an eleventh-century rabbi martyred by a cruel Christian ruler, as legend has it. It cannot have been, because a version of *U'netaneh Tokef* has been unearthed in the Cairo Geniza that well predates the eleventh century. Moreover, rather than memorializing Jewish resistance to Christian coercion, this liturgical classic turns out to share strong parallels with the Catholic *Dies Irae*, traceable in both poems to a fifth- or sixth-century Byzantine poem by a Christian liturgical poet named Romanus. This is another example of the historical point Dr. Cunningham makes that Jews and Christians had extremely porous boundaries until as late as the fifth century. A theology—Catholic or Jewish—that distorts historical fact is not credible, and any tradition with intellectual values must rethink its assumptions in the light of new information.

A third reason for theological change could be, as Dr. Cunningham observes, that as Americans, Catholics and Jews are not inhabiting sealed, homogeneous communities. We live out our faith commitments in the presence of the Other. Will the Other understand our faith? Respect it? What can we learn about the faith and praxis of the Other? Through the news media and the Internet, as well as through the forging of political and social alliances, this Other who is our neighbor comes to appear accessible, possibly knowable. We are lured into dialogue hoping that we can make comprehensible or at least less opaque our beliefs and commitments, maybe even the inarticulate, unsystematizable texture of our traditions—the smells, the sounds, the tastes, the feelings that cling to our observance, and matter ultimately so much more than reasons.

Finally, then, building upon the forty years of rapprochement between the Catholic Church and the Jews, Dr. Cunningham comes to the kind of change that requires the highest degree of mutual trust: the change we catalyze in one another through genuine theological encounter. As the theologian David Tracy remarks, dialogue is only possible if both partners acknowledge that their version of the truth is incomplete. Otherwise there is no reason for dialogue. But this kind of dialogue goes far beyond the usual "you show me yours and I'll show you mine" exchange that passes for dialogue. What kind of impact will we let the Other have on us? I am usually theologically far from David Berger, the Judaic scholar who believes that worshipping Jesus is a Christian mistake, but can I believe that God disclosed Godself to Christians as Jesus of Nazareth? You must understand that for me to acknowledge Jesus of Nazareth as my God is a violation of my covenant so serious that, eight hundred years ago, when Catholic-Jewish dialogue consisted of forcible conversion to Christianity, Jews died rather than concur. Indeed if some spooky retro-Catholic group kidnapped me and made a similar demand, I too would have to die for my Jewish integrity. So Dr. Cunningham's challenge leaves me feeling squeamish. I know how God disclosed Godself to me at Sinai. At the same time, it is also true that I am unable to predict how God is likely to present Godself in other situations. A God who reveals to the prophet Ezekiel the semblance of a human being whose lower half is all fire seated on the semblance of a mobile chariot-throne amid a court of four-faced angels and wheel-shaped creatures covered with eyes is a little difficult to second-guess. What would make such a dialogue feel safer to me are the points Dr. Cunningham distills from Catholic insights into the fundamentals of Jewish beliefs and understandings.

At the very beginning of the twentieth century, the Jewish philosopher Franz Rosenzweig published a treatise called *The Star of Redemption*, which argued that Jewish and Christian traditions both work out Divine redemption for the world and for God's creatures. Like the Catholic Church's efforts to overcome centuries of distortion and enmity, it is a starting point. There is much more work to do if, in contrast to those Christians who believe that the Rapture is going to lift them right out of this global mess, we become convinced that, on the contrary, our redemption is tied to the redemption of the Other.

Note

1 Jewish Publication Society, 1999, Philadelphia, the Hebrew-English Tanakh.

Philip A. Cunningham Continues the Dialogue

I would like to express my gratitude to Professors Adler and Dorff for their kind words and very interesting observations. It is an honor to engage in a stimulating exchange with two such esteemed scholars. I only wish time had permitted a longer conversation!

I thank Elliot Dorff for his helpful reminders in regard to developing a Catholic theological appreciation of the centrality of *Eretz Yisrael* for Jews. At the risk of offering some inadequate possibilities, perhaps it might be that for secular Jews living in Israel that the Land's mediating power is latent or potential, just as long-disregarded sacraments may suddenly become meaningful for non-churchgoing Catholics during important life events. Diaspora Jews have other "sacramental" encounters with God, such as the veneration of the Torah, but the Land as religiously important for Jews surely operates from afar and may exert its full "sacramental" potency only during visits there.

I appreciate very much his two suggestions for advancing the Christian-Jewish theological conversation. It is certainly true for Catholics that all authoritative texts are necessarily *interpreted* texts. To be sure, Jews and Catholics have different traditions of interpretation of their respective normative writings, but as living traditions each community is committed to maintaining continuity with the past while growing through its encounters with present and future realities. This is an important commonality between Catholicism and Judaism that deserves further investigation.

Rabbi Dorff also provides, I think, an extremely helpful distinction between relativism and relativity in his reference to *Dominus Iesus*. That Jews and Christians have legitimate though differing perspectives in their relationships with God has been asserted quite explicitly in the 2001 study of the Pontifical Biblical Commission, *The Jewish People and Their Sacred Scriptures in the Christian Bible*:

> Christians can and ought to admit that the Jewish reading of the Bible
> is a possible one, in continuity with the Jewish Sacred Scriptures from

the Second Temple period, a reading analogous to the Christian reading which developed in parallel fashion. Each of these two readings is part of the vision of each respective faith of which it is a product and an expression. Consequently, they cannot be reduced one into the other.[1]

This clearly calls for epistemological humility, as Rabbi Dorff rightly observes. Regrettably, this has not been a prominent institutional virtue of the Catholic community over the centuries, and it remains a challenge today. The recognition that mortal engagement with transcendent Truth is unavoidably limited, and hence admits of relativity, avoids the extremes of relativism or absolutism, but it seems that Catholic theological praxis has yet to internalize this insight.

I am very grateful for Rachel Adler's appreciation of the difficulties confronting a religious community that seeks to recraft its theological self-understanding in relation to others. I fully concur that "theologies have real consequences in history." It is the undeniable truth that the Second Vatican Council was motivated to confront Christian anti-Jewish teachings and practices primarily because of the horrors of the Shoah. Thus, *Nostra Aetate* was the beginning of a grappling with the sinful acts of Christians in history, but Catholic theology is still in the process of pursuing this ethical obligation. She is certainly correct in positing that any theology "that distorts historical fact is not credible."

The historical fact that the Jewish and Christian communities have been interacting for good or for ill for centuries also means that rapprochement is only possible, as Professor Adler notes, through "the change we catalyze in one another through genuine theological encounter." I believe that the past decades of dialogue have now brought to the forefront her crucial question, "What kind of impact will we let the Other have on us?"

In this regard, let me clarify a point I attempted to make when I asked in the context of a potential Jewish "theology" of Christian particularity, "What are Jews to make of Jesus? In what way is he 'of God'?" Professor Adler wonders, "Can I believe that God disclosed Godself to Christians as Jesus of Nazareth? . . . [F]or me to acknowledge Jesus of Nazareth as my God is [an extremely serious] violation of my covenant."

Once again, Professor Adler has put her finger on a key issue whose complexity would take another book in order to begin to discuss with any adequacy. I offered some fuller thoughts in an article on this topic a few years ago,[2] but here let me tentatively suggest that for Jews to entertain the possibility that Christians encounter God's self-disclosure in Jesus of Nazareth is not the same as to embrace Jesus "as *my* God." This would clearly be a violation of normative Jewish self-understanding.

Rather, I would ask if it is possible for members of one religious community to acknowledge that the Other may have a different but nonetheless divinely willed religious encounter with the One God that leads to a distinct, evolving tradition in which the outsider does not participate and possibly includes aspects that the outsider would reject.

This approach is predicated on an understanding of revelation as a relational engagement between God and humans. Thus, Christians can acknowledge that the rabbinic project was truly "of God," even though they do not participate in that living rabbinic tradition. They do not encounter God through the rabbinic grappling with the Torah, a process somewhat opaque to Christian eyes, and do not take on Torah observance. Might it be possible for Jews to categorize Christian attachment to Jesus as a "revelatory process" in which Jews do not participate? Jews do not encounter God in the person of Jesus and Christian claims derived from their "revelation" are somewhat opaque to Jews.

I realize there are difficulties here in several respects, not the least of which is the history of Christian supersessionism toward Judaism. Such difficulties may become more apparent to Christians if they tried to think similarly of Islam or even perhaps of the Church of Latter-day Saints. Theologically, is it possible for Christians to imagine that these traditions are somehow "of God" since they claim revelations that in one way or another supersede the New Testament?

These questions obviously are part of the future interreligious agenda. As Professor Adler points out, they require "the highest degree of mutual trust" in order to be pursued. Otherwise, these topics feel "unsafe," especially to the minority community. I am not sure when, if ever, a totally unthreatening environment in which to explore such fundamental topics can be attained. But that is clearly one goal of substantive interreligious dialogue. A prerequisite for Catholics is a more thoroughgoing internalization of post–*Nostra Aetate* teachings than is presently the case. Nevertheless, I believe that Pope John Paul II's prayer at the Western Wall (reiterated twice by his successor Pope Benedict XVI) has committed or recommitted the Catholic Church to following that path.

> God of our fathers,
> you chose Abraham and his descendants
> to bring your Name to the Nations:
> we are deeply saddened by the behavior of those
> who in the course of history
> have caused these children of yours to suffer,
> and asking your forgiveness we wish to commit ourselves
> to genuine brotherhood
> with the people of the Covenant.
> We ask this through Christ our Lord.[3]

Notes

1 Pontifical Biblical Commission, The Jewish People and Their Sacred Scriptures in the Christian Bible (2001), II, A, 7.

2 "Reflections from a Roman Catholic on a Reform Theology of Christianity," *CCAR Journal— A Reform Jewish Quarterly* (Spring 2005): 61–73.

3 http://www.ccjr.us/dialogika-resources/documents-and-statements/roman-catholic/pope-john-paul-ii/338-jp2-00mar26. See also Benedict XVI, "Address at the Great Synagogue of Rome" at http://www.ccjr.us/dialogika-resources/documents-and-statements/roman-catholic/pope-benedict-xvi/660-b1610jan17, and "Address to Delegates of the Conference of Presidents of Major American Jewish Organizations" at http://www.ccjr.us/dialogika-resources/documents-and-statements/roman-catholic/pope-benedict-xvi/471-b1609feb12.

SUGGESTIONS FOR FURTHER READING

1. Mary C. Boys, *Has God Only One Blessing?: Judaism as a Source of Christian Self-Understanding* (New York: Paulist, 2000). This book provides both an ideological foundation for dialogue and suggestions for church practice, emphasizing the Catholic experience. The author offers a schematic description of how Christianity became distinct from Judaism and makes suggestions for Catholic liturgy about bridging the gap by changing how certain scriptures are read during the church calendar. Uniquely offering scholarship on many complex questions in one source, Mary Boys sensitizes Christians to how their worship might be very differently perceived by Jewish guests.

2. Mary C. Boys, ed., *Seeing Judaism Anew: Christianity's Sacred Obligation* (Lanham, Md.: Rowman & Littlefield, 2005). In September 2002, twenty-one prominent Catholic and Protestant scholars released the groundbreaking document "A Sacred Obligation," which includes ten statements about Jewish-Christian dialogue focused around a guiding claim: "Revising Christian teaching about Jews and Judaism is a central and indispensable obligation of theology in our time."

3. Philip A. Cunningham, Norbert J. Hofmann, S.D.B., and Joseph Sievers, eds., *The Catholic Church and the Jewish People: Recent Reflections from Rome* (New York: Fordham University Press, 2007). This book makes available in English important essays that mark the fortieth anniversary of the Second Vatican Council's "Declaration on the Relationship of the Church to Non-Christian Religions," *Nostra Aetate*. Featuring essays by Vatican officials, leading rabbis, diplomats, and Catholic and Jewish scholars, the book discusses the nature of Christian-Jewish relations and the need to remember their conflicted and often tragic history, aspects of a Christian theology of Judaism, the Catholic-Jewish dialogue since the Shoah, and the establishment of formal diplomatic relations between the Holy See and Israel.

4. Philip A. Cunningham, Joseph Sievers, Mary C. Boys, Hans Hermann Henrix, and Jesper Svartvik, eds., *Christ Jesus and the Jewish People Today: New Explorations of Theological Interrelationships* (Grand Rapids, Mich.: Eerdmans, 2011). Sponsored by universities in Europe and North America and encouraged by Cardinal Walter Kasper, president of the Pontifical Commission for Religious Relations with the Jews, an international team of scholars, beginning in 2005, devoted sustained research and discussion to a crucial question: how might we Christians in our time reaffirm our faith claim that Jesus Christ is the Savior of all humanity, even as we affirm the Jewish people's covenantal life with God?

5. Edward Kessler, *An Introduction to Jewish-Christian Relations* (Cambridge: Cambridge University Press, 2010). Relations between Christians and Jews over the past two thousand years have been characterized to a great extent by mutual distrust and by Christian discrimination and violence against Jews. In recent decades, however, a new spirit of dialogue has been emerging, beginning with an awakening among Christians to the Jewish origins of Christianity, and encouraging scholars of both traditions to work together. This book sheds fresh light on this ongoing interfaith encounter, exploring key writings and themes in Jewish-Christian history from New Testament times until today.

3

Muslim-Christian Dialogue in Difficult Times

DANIEL A. MADIGAN, S.J.

These are difficult times for dialogue. An increasing number of voices within the Catholic Church are skeptical about, or even hostile to, Muslim-Christian dialogue, and there seems a real risk that many of the gains of recent decades will be lost in this hardening of positions. In this article I would like to examine some of the factors in this increasing polarization and propose ways of interpreting Muslim-Christian relationships that might offer more hope.

I will begin by using "Catholic" in the widest possible sense in this first section since at the time of the rise of Islam the term was not used to distinguish particularly the Church of Rome, and of course there were no Protestants. Islam did not, indeed does not, present itself as a new religion, but rather as the reestablishment of the original religion that has existed from the beginning, of which Judaism and Christianity are examples—even if Islam holds that they have needed to be purified of certain extraneous elements. It could be seen as a reform movement within the Judeo-Christian world of its time, a movement that proposes a substantial rereading of the Abrahamic, Mosaic, Christian tradition that had developed in biblical and postbiblical literature and practice. For believing Muslims, it is not simply a human reform movement, but God's reform. Precisely because of this the faith of Muslims has a very particular claim on the theological attention of both Christians and Jews. Just as most Jews have come to accept gracefully the idea that Christianity, with its radically alternative reading of the biblical tradition, is not going to fade away, so also we Christians may have to accommodate ourselves to the idea not only that Islam as a religion is not going to fade away, but that it will remain a lively challenger of our reading of the Jesus event, and will call us to an ever clearer expression of our faith.

The most important common belief the Abrahamic traditions share is that the Word of God—the eternal divine word that is of the very nature of God—has been spoken in our world. One might say that the thing that distinguishes our three traditions from one another is the place we believe we can hear most definitively that Word of God. For a Jew, the Word of God has been spoken in a privileged way at Sinai and thus in the Torah, understood not only as the Five Books of Moses, but as the whole edifice of rabbinic reflection and study right up until our own day. For the Muslim, God has spoken his word in Arabic in the Qur'an—and indeed in other earlier scriptures. For Christians, God's Word is spoken not primarily in words but in the flesh—in "body language" as it were. The words of scripture are not simply the words of God, but words written by believers to put us in touch with the capital-W Word that they had experienced in the flesh. For Christians, scripture is not revelation itself. It is the witness to revelation.

Although Muslims see Jesus and the gospel as being parallel to Muhammad and the Qur'an, Christians do not see things this way. What Jesus is for the Christian, the Qur'an (not Muhammad) is for Muslims. What Muhammad is for Muslims (the human channel through which the Word of God entered the world), Mary is for Christians. Of course, that Mary role does not exhaust the reality of who Muhammad is for Muslims. He is also a Moses figure as the leader of the community and its lawgiver. He is like Constantine in having united religious and political authority in his own person.

Singular and Plural

I deliberately use the plural "relationships" because one of the characteristics of the current negative discourse is that it tends to use the singular "Islam" rather than the plural "Muslims" and thus tends to ignore the extraordinary variety of views and types of people represented in the Muslim community. The skeptics are right to think that it is difficult, if not impossible, to dialogue with Islam—not just about religion, but about anything at all. That is because Islam is to a large extent an abstraction. There are many Islams—many ways of being Muslim in this world. Indeed, there are many ways of living one's willing submission to God even within a particular Muslim-majority culture. This is stating no more than the obvious, yet it is a fact that seems to escape so many skeptical commentators. A moment's reflection on the Christian parallel would make it clear to them. Can one dialogue with Christianity? Is Christianity able to speak? And if not, who really speaks for it? Even within the Catholic Church, which has a unique authority structure, there is not uniformity of opinion, not even on some serious moral questions. When Pope John Paul II stood resolutely against the death penalty or the Bush doctrine of preemptive war, for example, not a few of his fellow bishops and many others quietly but nonetheless publicly distanced themselves from his positions, dismissing them as "prudential judgments" rather than authoritative teachings.

The fact that it is difficult to dialogue with "Islam" does not mean, however, that the same difficulty applies to Muslims. They are anything but an abstraction. They are actual people, and like all people they are individuals of very different types, with varying political and religious opinions, of many different cultures and experiences.

Again the skeptics raise their voices to lament that there is no common doctrinal magisterium among Muslims and that we can only dialogue with individuals or with groups who cannot represent the whole. This is a profoundly unjust criticism. The Catholic Church is the only religious body in the world to have such a structure of authority. No other religion has developed structures of this kind, and it is not clear that they ever will or should. Still, we carry on dialogue, for example, with Jews and with Buddhists, even though this involves dealing with individuals and select groups who can neither claim to speak for all their fellow believers, nor enter into binding agreements on their behalf. Why, then, should we disqualify Muslims on these grounds?

Looked at from the other side, members of other religious traditions are usually glad to find an authoritative interlocutor in the Catholic Church. However, they also often discover that on a local and individual level the authoritative central policy—for example, *Nostra Aetate's* crucial statement that the Church "esteems" Muslims—is either not known or not respected.

Dialogue does not take place between religions, but between believers, and so it is of necessity a complex and often untidy process. It rarely results in neatly drafted agreements and shared resolutions. It is the long, patient work of creating relationships and transforming hearts.

The injustice done to Muslims in dismissing them as dialogue partners because they do not have a central authority structure goes hand in hand with another injustice—one that Muslims also tend to perpetrate against Christians—that is, disqualifying the positive voices as being unrepresentative, or worse, as being disingenuous. Negative, aggressive, prejudiced voices are not hard to find in these polarized and conflictual times, and they have a wide media audience only too ready to give them credence, and to believe that they represent the truth about their religion. More moderate, less antagonistic voices are not only ignored; they are often accused of bad faith and duplicity, of hiding or denying the truth about their respective religions. Instead of encouraging those who find in their religious traditions the grounds for peaceful mutual respect, the skeptics dismiss their interpretations as false, and quote Qur'an or Bible against them.

Text and Interpretation

Dismissing others' interpretations is easily done, of course. It is simple enough to quote other traditions' scriptures against them, but it shows a profound ignorance of the way scriptures actually function in a faith tradition. Take, for example, the Christian scriptures. Here are some lines from the Psalms, the book that forms the backbone of Christian and Jewish daily worship: "O daughter of Babylon, you devastator! A blessing on the one who treats you as you have treated us. A blessing on him who takes your babies and dashes them against the rocks!" (Psalm 137:8–9). "The righteous will rejoice when they see vengeance done; they will bathe their feet in the blood of the wicked" (Psalm 58:10). We cannot deny the presence of these verses in our scripture and worship, yet we do not think of them as in any way defining the Christian attitude to enemies. Nor would Jews think that they are bound by God's command to slaughter those who change religion, not just individuals but whole cities, their cattle included (Deuteronomy 13:6–15). Moses had led the way in this at the time of the incident of the golden calf: "He said to them, 'Thus says the Lord, the God of Israel, 'Gird on your sword, each of you! Go back and forth from gate to gate throughout the camp, and each of you kill your brother, your friend, and your neighbour'" (Exodus 32:27). Even the New Testament is not without verses open to a violent interpretation:

> Do not think that I have come to bring peace to the earth; I have not come to bring peace, but a sword. For I have come to set a man against his father, and a daughter against her mother, and a daughter-in-law against her mother-in-law; and one's foes will be members of one's own household. (Matthew 10:34–36)

> If you have no sword, sell your cloak and buy one. (Luke 22:36)

The point of quoting these texts is not to claim that Christianity and Judaism are inherently violent religions, but rather to offer proof that scriptures that apparently justify, and at times even glorify, violence do not necessarily make for a violent religion. Christians and Jews have ways of reading their scriptures that allow them to maintain the sacredness of those texts without at the same time considering large parts of them normative for behavior or attitudes. Muslims have traditionally used similar methods of interpretation. It is simply false to say that Muslims cannot or do not interpret the Qur'an. It is regrettable that such a position is repeated by church leaders in order to back up the equally egregious assertion that Muslims are incapable of theological dialogue. First there is the obvious linguistic issue: the vast majority of Muslims do not know

Arabic and therefore depend for their reading on dictionaries, commentaries, and translations—all of which are forms and instruments of interpretation. Even among Arab Muslims, very few are at home with the vocabulary and style of Qur'anic Arabic, and so they rely on interpretations and glosses to understand it.

Second, it is clear philosophically that any reading of a text, even for someone who knows the language, is not simply the reacquisition of the author's original thought, but that it is in itself an interpretive activity. The decision that a particular verse is relevant to a certain question or situation is a further act of interpretation. A major element in Qur'anic interpretation has always been to try to understand the context in which the verse was revealed, and therefore its applicability or otherwise to various questions of law and ethics. Since the Qur'an itself rarely indicates the context of its *logia*, and never in a precise manner, the tradition has felt free to propose multiple contexts even for a single verse. This opens the possibility of multiple interpretations.

Third, the Qur'an itself indicates that it requires interpretation, distinguishing among the different types of verses it contains: "It is He who has sent down to you the scripture, some of whose verses are decisive—they are the essence [*umm*, lit., "mother"] of the scripture—and others whose meanings are not straightforward" (Q 3:7). In this famously controversial passage the Qur'an distinguishes between those verses that are considered *muhkamāt* (defined, fixed, firm, decisive, straightforward) and those that are *mutashābihāt* (lit., "resembling one another" possibly meaning doubtful, ambiguous, allegorical, or metaphorical). Since the Qur'an does not specify which verses are which, this pair of terms has been interpreted in many different ways.[1] It is the *muhkamāt* that are said to constitute the essence or substance of the scripture. Qur'anic commentators often understand this to mean that such verses lay down the principles of Islam; they contain the basics of creed and law; they outline all the duties, punishments, and commandments that are essential to the religion. The *muhkamāt* are sometimes thought to be the abrogating verses because they remain firm and fixed whereas the *mutashābihāt*, although they *resemble* the others, are in fact without legal force due to their having been abrogated. Other commentators would distinguish between the *muhkamāt*, those verses that can stand alone and so require little or no interpretation, and the *mutashābihāt*, those that can only be fully understood in relationship to other verses treating the same or related matters.

This important verse goes on to explain the danger of interpretation—that people with dishonest motives deliberately choose to interpret the less straightforward verses of the Qur'an in a way that will divide the community. The interpretation (*ta'wīl*) of these verses is not open to all, the verse tells us. Certainly God knows the true meaning, but it may also be known by scholars. That depends on how we read and punctuate the verse, and Muslim commentators have done so in differing ways. It could be translated as "No one knows its interpretation except God. And those who are well grounded in knowledge say, 'We believe in all of it.'" Or we might read it "No one knows its interpretation except God and those who are well grounded in knowledge. They say, 'We believe in all of it.'" The Arabic original allows both possibilities. Thus the verse that speaks about the possibility and risk of interpreting the Qur'an itself contains various points that require, and have historically received, considerable interpretive attention.

It is true that many Muslims will themselves deny that they are interpreting the Qur'an when they read and apply it. To them it may seem straightforward and univocal. Yet they are in fact interpreting it, as becomes clear to them when they encounter another Muslim with a different "straightforward" reading. What the Islamic tradition wants to avoid, and justly so, is what we might call "interpreting away" the Qur'an—that is, reading it in such a way as to avoid its authoritative claim on the believer and to empty it of any real significance as scripture.

Thus, both in fact and by tradition Muslims do indeed interpret their scriptures. It seems to me nonsense, then, for non-Muslims to tell Muslims that, since they believe the Qur'an to be a revealed text rather than simply an inspired text, Muslims therefore cannot interpret it. This mistake is gaining more and more currency these days in church circles. Worse still, we sometimes reject Muslim interpretations and offer our own more literal reading as authoritative—that is, we claim that what we are proposing is what the Qur'an "really" says. That word, *really*, suggests that we believe a text has a single, objectively verifiable meaning. Yet when texts speak, they speak to particular people in particular circumstances. The Qur'an's meaning, as Wilfred Cantwell Smith has pointed out, is the history of its meanings.[2] That is true in both an internal and an external sense. First, the Qur'an reflects the history of its own development over the more than twenty years of its address to a varied audience. Second, since the time of its canonization it has been read by a very diverse community of faith in widely different historical contexts.

If a twenty-first-century Western Muslim tells us that the words "There is no compulsion in religion" (Q 2:256) mean that the Qur'an defends religious freedom, why would we want to deny her interpretation? Yet that is what is frequently done. Preference is given to those who would interpret that verse in a narrower sense, or who would claim that it has been abrogated by other less accommodating verses. It may be true that, historically speaking, most of those who have offered formal interpretations of this verse had little conception of religious liberty, which is, after all, a very modern idea only recently accepted even in the Catholic Church. However, the weight of that history—whether Catholic or Muslim—does not necessarily condemn us to simply repeat it.

Contemporary questions of religious liberty, the secular state, and public and private religion are elements of a discussion that must go on among Muslims. It cannot be prejudged by Christians. One might have expected Christians to have encouraged Muslims who are trying to find a way of living their Islam that is fully compatible with life in a modern pluralist environment. The skeptics, however, often privilege more medieval voices in order to deny any possibility of change and dialogue. The effect of all this is to increase the polarization that already characterizes Muslim-Christian relations.

The Clash of Civilizations?

The authority often appealed to in order to defend the idea that this polarization is a permanent and unavoidable facet of our world is Samuel P. Huntington. The idea of the "clash of civilizations" first enunciated eighteen years ago by Huntington has become a commonplace of conventional wisdom.[3] Yet most people have only a vague notion of the theory, and know little of the caveats and qualifications that his article carried. Huntington has lamented that so many people had entirely ignored the question mark in the title, and have presumed that he was predicting or describing such a clash rather than posing the question of whether "civilization" might be a more helpful interpretive category than "nation-state" for understanding global politics after the Cold War.[4] There is not space here to deal comprehensively with this important work—especially with the fuller treatment he gave in his book three years later. However, it is important to address some opinions that claim to be based on Huntington, but that are an oversimplification and a misunderstanding of his positions.

The people of different civilizations, Huntington tells us, have different views on the relations between God and humanity, individual and group, citizen and state, parents and children, husband and wife. They also have differing views of the relative importance of rights and responsibilities, liberty and authority, equality and hierarchy. These civilizational differences are real, fundamental, and enduring, more so than ideological or political differences. However, Huntington also notes that differences are not the same as conflicts; and even if differences become a source of conflict, those conflicts are not necessarily violent.[5] This is an extremely important point, often overlooked. The message most commentators have taken from Huntington (or from reports about him) is that we are condemned to a future of increasingly violent conflict between irreducibly different civilizational blocs. Although he discusses nine major civilizations, many think of his theory as applying basically to two blocs—Islam and the West.

Huntington's project is not, as some of those who appeal to him would have it, offering some apocalyptic vision of the violent, Hobbesian future that awaits us. He rather wants to identify the likely sites, causes, and aggravating factors of future conflicts in order to understand and perhaps avoid them, or at least to aid in their resolution. He did recommend in his article that the West try to maintain its military and economic power to protect its interests in the face of other competing interests,[6] but he does not advocate what some of his acolytes do—a West closed in on itself and armed against an inimical, largely Muslim, world.

Though he is often invoked by the skeptics as offering a social scientist's empirical proof of the futility of dialogue, here and there in Huntington's work we find some key insights that could contribute substantially to the development of dialogue.

"People can and do redefine their identities," Huntington reminds us, "and, as a result, the composition and boundaries of civilizations change."[7] It is often forgotten that civilizations are dynamic, and so are not simply rigid masses that will inevitably collide with one another until one or another shatters. Our nightmare of ceaseless conflict seems to presume that anyone who bears the title "Muslim" belongs to a different, irreducibly other, civilization. Yet actual experience gives the lie to such essentializing discourse, and leaves us unconvinced that many of the world's 1.2 billion Muslims actually belong to the Islamic civilization of our fears. If the puritanical and fanatical Wahhabis of Saudi Arabia and Afghanistan's warlords and Taliban belong to it, then how can an urbane and thoughtful British professor, or a skillful and compassionate Malaysian doctor be said to belong to the same "civilization"? Huntington's valuable observations about the ways in which people identify themselves with civilizations must not be allowed to obscure the fact that identity is more complex than simply identification with one group. If it is the potential for conflict between civilizations that makes dialogue indispensable, it is the flexibility and dynamism of civilizational identities that renders dialogue possible and offers hope of success.

The Grammar of Dialogue

Huntington defines a civilization with admirable simplicity when he writes, "Civilizations are the biggest 'we' within which we feel culturally at home as distinguished from all the other 'thems' out there." Here he has put his finger on a key issue for dialogue—our grammar, the way in which we use the first-person plural: we, us, our. There are three basic ways of constructing our "we." The first relies on an excluded third-person: "our" identity is, in a sense, negative and probably unstable because it relies more on the fact that "we" are not "them" than on anything we might positively have in common. The second is a constructed "we" that fails to recognize the diversity of "you." "You" are not recognized in your particularity and difference but are reduced to just another example of "me." Such a grammar does not recognize, and so ultimately does not permit, difference. Each of these constructed first-person plurals is inimical to real dialogue, either by absolutizing otherness, assuring us that it can never be overcome, or by disregarding it, failing to acknowledge and respect uniqueness.

The third grammar of the first-person plural is quite different. From experience we know that our personal identity is constituted by multiple belongings. Each "I" belongs contemporaneously to many different "we's": to particular friendships and relationships, family, nation, religion, church, class, language group, and so on. We recognize that human maturity consists in the ability to negotiate this multiple belonging without losing a coherent sense of self. We also recognize that our identity is not threatened, but rather enriched and expanded by developing new relationships, learning new languages, and exploring unfamiliar cultures. At the personal level we shape and construct the self through dialogue and in relationship; we do not first construct a self-contained identity and only then enter into relationships. This is no less true at the level of religious communities. The Christian identity was formed initially in dialogue with the various religious strands of Second Temple Judaism and with Hellenistic culture; and it has continued to interact with other "selves," shaping its theology and proclamation—which are its self-understanding—in conversation with interlocutors such as Aristotelian philosophy, Renaissance humanism, the Enlightenment, atheism, and Marxism. For most of Western Christian theology Islam has been, if at all, only a minor interlocutor. In the Eastern churches slightly more attention has been paid to it, yet after the first few centuries relatively little theological progress has been made in developing a dialogical theology. As a religious vision that emerged as a critique of the Christianity and Judaism of its day, and that proposes a radical rereading of the Abrahamic, Judaic, Christian tradition that had developed in biblical and postbiblical literature and practice, the faith of Muslims has a very particular claim on the theological attention of Christians and Jews. This is especially true now that we are increasingly in contact with one another.

In dialogue, therefore, the task is to construct a new first-person plural, one neither based simply on the rejection of "them," nor on a too-easy affirmation of similarity, but rather on a preparedness to question and to be questioned. This new "we" is built only gradually and with sustained commitment. Muslim students I had the privilege of working with in Rome establish strong links with their Catholic, Orthodox, and Hindu companions; they develop friendships with their Jewish professors. Gradually a new "we" is created that does not cancel difference but learns to live it richly.

What emerges from dialogue is not a negotiated settlement of differences that eventually creates a single faith and a single culture. Huntington is surely right to maintain that the idea of a universal civilization is untenable.[8] He has little comfort to offer those who believe that Western civilization is destined to become universal. Indeed, he is less than sanguine about the very possibility that it will survive in the long term—not because it is under attack from outside, but because it is crumbling from the inside. Even if it succeeds in dealing with its internal weaknesses, Western civilization, he argues, is particular and is not generalizable, at least not without domination based on violence and oppression. Huntington calls not for a world civilization, but for a world of civilizations in dialogue. Quoting Lester Pearson writing in the 1950s, he agrees that we are moving into

> an age when different civilizations will have to learn to live side by side in peaceful interchange, learning from each other, studying each other's history and ideals and art and culture, mutually enriching each other's lives. The alternative in this overcrowded little world is misunderstanding, tension, clash and catastrophe.[9]

History and Destiny

Huntington is certainly skilled in analyzing history, especially recent history. Yet he does not see history as destiny, and this is a most important distinction. Even if it might be true that relations between Muslims and the West have often been conflictual, that does not mean they are forever condemned to being so. Huntington's analysis, while scarcely optimistic, is certainly not fatalistic. His work is a call for dialogue, not a dismissal of it in favor of dogged defensiveness. The question we face in dialogue is not primarily what Christians have been, but what we intend to be in the future, not what Muslims have been, but what they want to be.

One weakness in Huntington's analysis, and a point in which his predictions have not proved true in the years since his book-length treatment of the theme, is the question of intra-civilizational conflicts. He claims that conflicts within civilizations will tend to be less violent and less intractable.[10] Yet such has not been the experience of recent decades or even centuries. Huntington passes over with a single vague reference[11] the genocidal rage that devastated Rwanda in 1994, which saw an estimated 800,000 people massacred in a matter of weeks, for the most part by their fellow Christians. He obviously had nothing to say about the long-standing civil war that has cost an estimated four million lives in the Democratic Republic of the Congo since 1998. Going further back, we need to recognize the long history of warfare in Christian Europe, whose internal conflicts in the last century twice embroiled the whole world in war. Similarly among Muslims there is a long and continuing history of internecine warfare—much more extensive and bloody, it might be argued, than the conflicts with non-Muslims. In our own time it is easily verifiable that the number of Muslims killed by their coreligionists in Iraq, Pakistan, and Sudan is much greater than the number of victims of the attacks in New York, London, Madrid, and Bali. The history of the Muslim community, no less than that of the West, has been marked by internal struggles that taken altogether dwarf the wars against other civilizational blocs.

This is a key element to recall in dialogue, because an honest encounter must be based on a realistic self-image. There is always a gap, sometimes a very large one, between the ideals we profess and the reality we manage to live—between the vision we have of society and the actual state of our cities and countries. Many attempts at Muslim-Christian dialogue founder at precisely this point—each partner has a strong tendency to compare his own ideals with the reality of the other. The result is that each assumes the moral high ground, and with a sense of superiority speaks down to the other. We claim to be speaking the truth, and so we are, but only about the failures of the other party, not about our own. The frustrating and dispiriting result is what has sometimes been described as a "dialogue of the deaf."

Huntington cannot be much help to us here, except in his realistic presentation of the internal problems of Western civilization. He is proposing not a specifically Christian approach to the current world situation, but rather a pragmatic political and cultural solution. Christians do not enter into dialogue simply on pragmatic grounds, calculating the risks to be run and the advantages to be had. To be in dialogue with the world in which we live is an integral part of our being church. "La Chiesa si fa colloquio," wrote Pope Paul VI in *Ecclesiam suam* (#67), "The Church makes itself conversation."[12] To enter into such honest dialogue requires great humility, and such humility is always risky, because it can easily be misinterpreted as weakness. Yet this is a risk we cannot avoid, since we are followers of the Christ who made himself "humbler yet, even to accepting death, death on a cross" (Philippians 2:8). There is no other choice for Christians in dialogue but to trust that the way of the humble Christ is the way to the truth.[13]

An element of great complexity in the question of dialogue is that the very Christians who have for centuries had the closest contact with Muslims have been living in a minority situation, and find themselves very often politically, and sometimes also socially and economically, disadvantaged. It is all too easy for Western Christians to speak about openness and dialogue, but such openness is much more difficult in a situation where one's survival is at stake. These are people who live on what Huntington calls the fault lines between civilizations, and who therefore are more likely to be in a situation of conflict, even if it is not always or even often violent. Those who, on the one hand, have the greatest opportunities for dialogue, and perhaps also language and culture in common with Muslims, on the other hand, also run the greatest risk of losing further ground politically and socially because of the attitudes that are required of a Christian in dialogue. The local churches in Muslim-majority countries have a most demanding and unenviable vocation. Their situations are very diverse and it is important to recognize the particularities of their positions: Algeria is not Pakistan; Indonesia is not Lebanon. It is also important to recognize that the bitter experience of, for example, Middle Eastern Christians is not simply generalizable to Europe. Arab Christians can speak with authority about their experience of living as minorities and the difficulties that that may involve, and their experience is not to be denied. However, they are not necessarily the best guides for those who have to develop relations with Muslims in Europe, North America, or Australia. Their heightened experience of conflict at the fault lines is not a reliable basis for developing a new and constructive relationship between Muslims and Christians in the heartland of Western civilization.

Each country will have its own particular issues in dialogue depending on many factors: for example, the cultural background and sophistication of the Muslim immigrants; the history of Muslim immigration and the social and economic integration of successive generations; the political context and also the religious makeup of the country. A dialogue relationship in New York will probably be very different from what it would be in Amsterdam. It will be different again in Marseille or Sydney. Within each of those cities the relationships will vary with much more personal factors about the people involved.

Reciprocity?

We have begun to hear much more in recent times about reciprocity as an important principle in Muslim-Christian dialogue. This seems to me a very dubious development that requires clarification. There is a world of difference between reciprocity as a *condition* for dialogue, and reciprocity as a hoped-for *outcome* of dialogue. However, the distinction tends to be blurred, especially in press reporting of Vatican policy, but also among some theologians.

Reciprocity is not a Christian value. Gratuity is. The teaching of Jesus could not be more explicit on this subject:

> You have heard that it was said, "An eye for an eye and a tooth for a tooth." But I say to you, Do not resist an evildoer. Rather, if anyone

strikes you on the right cheek, turn the other also; and if anyone wants to sue you and take your coat, give your cloak as well; and if anyone forces you to go one mile, go also the second mile. Give to everyone who begs from you, and do not refuse anyone who wants to borrow from you. You have heard that it was said, "You shall love your neighbour and hate your enemy." But I say to you, Love your enemies and pray for those who persecute you, so that you may be children of your Father in heaven; for he makes his sun rise on the evil and on the good, and sends rain on the righteous and on the unrighteous. For if you love those who love you, what reward do you have? Do not even the tax collectors do the same? And if you greet only your brothers and sisters, what more are you doing than others? Do not even the Gentiles do the same? (Matthew 5:39–47)

We give without hope of return and we open our tables especially to those who will not repay our hospitality (Luke 14:12–14). There is absolutely no question of setting conditions to our dialogue with others. If we were to do so, we would be betraying our faith, not defending it. Of course we hope that our openness and honesty will be reciprocated, but if it is not, still we persevere. Pope Paul VI taught in *Ecclesiam Suam* that we begin dialogue not by talking, but rather by listening: "Before speaking, we must take great care to *listen* not only to what men say, but more especially to what they have it in their hearts to say" (*ES* 87). Even if we are not listened to, we continue to listen with infinite patience.

Talk of reciprocity is common not only in what we might think of specifically as dialogue but also in relation to laws, rights, and freedoms. There are many calls in Europe to restrict the rights of Muslim citizens and immigrants until full and equal rights are accorded to Christians in Muslim-majority countries—Saudi Arabia is the case usually cited because it is the most flagrant violator of the rights and freedoms of non-Muslims. Some commentators have wanted to see in the Holy See's references to reciprocity a concern and a demand for reciprocal rights as a condition of further dialogue, and an encouragement for Western governments to use Muslim citizens' rights and freedoms as leverage to achieve reforms.

Such a strategy can be reconciled neither with the gospel, nor with explicit Catholic teaching about the basis of religious freedom in the dignity of each person. We must accord equal rights and freedoms to Muslims in the West, even if such recognition is not reciprocated by the governments of Muslim-majority countries. We may not repay one wrong with another. If we were serious about our concern for the fate of the oppressed, then we might refuse to trade with oppressor countries—refuse, for example, to sell arms to Saudi Arabia[14] or to buy oil from it, until it reforms its laws to recognize the human rights of non-Muslims. However, this would require more sacrifice than most people are prepared to make, and so we propose to force the poor Muslim citizen or immigrant to pay the price. This is tantamount to hostage-taking: we will oppress "theirs" until they stop oppressing "ours." Most of these Muslims have come to live in Western countries precisely because they do not accept the laws, customs, and regimes of their own countries. In any case, their fate is of little concern to the likes of the Saudi royal family.

None of this is to suggest that the correct Christian attitude is one of supine acquiescence in the injustices perpetrated by dictatorial regimes. The voice we are obliged to raise against injustice will, however, have more force and coherence if it speaks not only for our fellow Christians, but for all the oppressed. And it will be more convincing if it is evenhanded in denouncing wrong not only abroad but at home as well.

Is Theological Dialogue Dead?

A sound case can be made for the idea that justice and peace, rather than theology and doctrine, should be the central focus of our dialogue with Muslims, especially in situations of conflict. However, we may find that it is a more demanding dialogue than we expected. While the injustices and acts of violence perpetrated by Muslims are regularly identified and reported, Christians are inclined to distance themselves from the failures and injustices of the West, because we claim that religion and politics are separate. Such sleight of hand will not be convincing in an honest dialogue, and we will be forced to admit first the failure of the Christian message successfully to shape the West's economic and political vision, and second the acquiescence of avowedly Christian politicians and businesspeople in the injustices attributable to Western policies.

It seems to be this kind of dialogue about justice and politics that people have in mind when they speak of a shift in the Holy See's policy away from theological dialogue with Muslims toward a dialogue of cultures or civilizations. Four observations need to made about this, albeit briefly. First, such a dialogue cannot simply be an opportunity to denounce Muslim injustices and discuss the means of redressing them. It will be much more demanding for the Christian side than some might expect. Second, if it is a dialogue of culture or civilization, then who will be able to speak with any authority? Do the proponents of this change of approach imagine that the Holy See can speak for the West? Third, most of the formal dialogues undertaken with Muslims by the Pontifical Council for Interreligious Dialogue were already on themes that would be considered cultural rather than theological. For example, in the annual dialogues with Al-Azhar

University, themes have included religious extremism, the war in Iraq, the necessity for self-criticism in religions, and the dangers of stereotyping and generalization. From the Muslim side there has often been an explicit option to avoid theological issues lest the dialogue seem to be a negotiation to arrive at a common position on disputed doctrines. So if indeed there has been a change of policy—and it is far from clear that there has been—it will merely reflect rather than affect long-standing practice by both parties.

The fourth observation is more serious. I have long argued that the term "interreligious dialogue" often gives rise to misunderstandings: first that dialogue takes place between religions; in fact, only people can dialogue. For this reason I prefer to speak of the dialogue of believers. The second misunderstanding it causes is that these dialoguing believers should be talking about religion. On the contrary, we should be talking about whatever is really on our minds; and more often than not this will be questions of justice, human rights, public policy, world affairs, or more local practical issues. However, there is in Catholic circles an increasingly skeptical voice being raised against the possibility or value of any real theological dialogue with Muslims, and this skepticism needs to be addressed.

There has been no lack of frustrations and disappointments in attempts by Muslims and Christians to engage in serious theological dialogue, and there are certainly many elements that make it particularly difficult. Not least of these is that Islam began in part as a critique of Christianity, and so Muslims often find difficulty in moving beyond the rather peculiar presentation of Christianity found in the Qur'an, and its condemnation of important elements of Christian faith, even though it is hard to say how well those Christian positions are understood. To comprehend the parallel case for a Christian, imagine a Pharisee wanting to enter into dialogue with us. The figure of the Pharisee is very negative in the New Testament—synonymous with oppressive legalism and hypocrisy—and the teaching of Jesus, as well as the letters of Paul, seem to us to be the definitive word about Pharisees and their religiosity. Therefore, it would be extremely difficult to enter into that kind of dialogue with real openness—indeed some people find it difficult to open themselves to dialogue with Jews for just that reason. Of course, Jews also often find it difficult to get Christians to listen to what they are saying because the Christians presume they know all they need to know about Jews from the New Testament.

These attempts at theological dialogue are made more difficult by the fact that very often the Christian participants have studied Islam, often in great depth, whereas still relatively few Muslims have made a serious theological study of Christianity. The resulting lack of balance in the dialogue is very disappointing. However, we cannot afford to let disappointment lead to despair. Those who would argue that Muslim-Christian theological dialogue is impossible must logically prove that it has never taken place at all. Anecdotal evidence of their own disappointments is proof not of the impossibility of such a dialogue, but only of its difficulty. Those who, like myself, would maintain that it is indeed possible, have logically only to show that it has taken place at least once. Anecdotal evidence is in this case sufficient to demonstrate the feasibility of such an encounter. It has been my privilege in recent years of teaching to take part from time to time in what I would consider a truly theological dialogue. The context has been academic, yet the involvement has been more than simply intellectual. Theological dialogue takes place when, as a first step, we have been able to take one another seriously as believers, as people who are listening for the Word of God, who believe that God is working to guide them to the truth.[15]

The second essential element in this dialogue is the ability to use the theological language, methods, and authorities of the other tradition, to feel the weight of the other tradition's theological questions, and so to engage with the other on his or her home ground. This requires not only sustained study but also a kind of mutual hospitality—a preparedness to help someone who does not belong to my tradition make herself "at home" in my theological conversation. Hospitality is at its best when both host and guest are sensitive enough to each other to be able to share the same space with delight. To carry further the metaphor of hospitality, much of our experience as Christians has been that Muslims have barged into our theological "home" uninvited, complained about the decoration, reorganized the furniture, and even claimed ownership! The Jews might want to say the same of Christians. However, there are Muslims who are making great efforts to enter seriously into this relationship of mutual theological hospitality. This is not the time to abandon the effort on our part, and so settle for being theological strangers to one another.

If our faith and, hence, our theology are precious to us, then we cannot rule out theological dialogue with Muslims. Indeed, we need that dialogue because, if anything is clear from the persistence of Islam, it is that Christians have not yet found a convincing way to express and proclaim their faith to that substantial percentage of the world's population who already believe in the one God of Abraham. I would identify four particular areas where an attention to the Muslim questioning of Christian theology is beneficial for refining and sharpening that theology: trinity, Christology, sin and redemption, and the theology of revelation. These are all areas in which there is much to be gained from taking seriously Muslim perplexity about our doctrines or about the language in which we express them. We do this not in order to find a compromise—our theological "home" is not for sale or lease—but rather to find a more satisfying, perhaps even more convincing, expression of them. These key Christian doctrines are neither simply theological hurdles for testing our faith, nor for maintaining the distinctions between religions. They have a central role in our relationship with the divine, and so it is not an option simply to say that they are not open to exploration and discussion.

Dialogue is never merely a strategy or a pragmatic calculation of advantages to be had. It is an integral part of the mission of the Christian community to foster love, unity, and peace among people (*ES* 94). As such, it is an act of love. Like every act of love it is costly, and so not for the fainthearted. Let us allow Paul VI the final word: "Today, every day, should see a renewal of our dialogue. We, rather than those to whom it is directed, should take the initiative" (*ES* 77).

Notes

1 An enlightening survey of the way these terms were used and understood in medieval Muslim exegesis is given in Leah Kinberg, "*Muhkamāt* and *Mutashābihāt* (Koran 3/7): Implication of a Koranic Pair of Terms in Medieval Exegesis," *Arabica* 35 (1988): 143–72. See also Michel Lagarde, "De l'Ambiguïté (*mutashābih*) dans le Coran: Tentatives d'explication des exégètes musulmans," *Quaderni di studi arabi* 3 (1985): 45–62.

2 Wilfred C. Smith, "The True Meaning of Scripture: An Empirical Historian's Nonreductionist Interpretation of the Qur'ān," *International Journal of Middle East Studies* 11 (1980): 504.

3 Samuel P. Huntington, "The Clash of Civilizations?" in *Foreign Affairs* (Summer 1993), 22–49.

4 Samuel P. Huntington, *The Clash of Civilizations and the Remaking of the World Order* (New York: Simon & Schuster, 1996), 13. Henceforth, when *Clash* is italicized in citations, I am referring to the book; when not italicized and followed by a question mark, I am referring to Huntington's article.

5 Huntington, "Clash?" 25.

6 Ibid., 49.

7 Ibid., 24.

8 Huntington, *Clash*, 301–321.

9 Lester Pearson, *Democracy in World Politics* (Princeton: Princeton University Press, 1955), 83–84, quoted by Huntington, *Clash*, 301–321.

10 Huntington, "Clash?" 38.

11 Huntington, *Clash*, 28.

12 The English translation is much weaker: "The Church has something to communicate" (*Ecclesiam Suam* [*ES*] 65). For some reason the paragraphs are numbered differently in the English version. Other references here are to that version.

13 Again Paul VI puts this elegantly:

> Our dialogue must be accompanied by that meekness which Christ bade us learn from Himself: "Learn of me, for I am meek and humble of heart." . . . Our dialogue . . . makes no demands. It is peaceful, has no use for extreme methods, is patient under contradiction and inclines towards generosity. (*ES* 81)

14 On July 22, 2006, for example, the George W. Bush administration announced a $6 billion arms sale to Saudi Arabia.

15 A good example of substantive theological dialogue among an international group of Jews, Christians, and Muslims may be found in the book *Learned Ignorance: Intellectual Humility among Jews, Christian and Muslims*, ed. James L. Heft, S.M., Reuven Firestone, and Omid Safi (New York: Oxford University Press, 2011).

A Response to Daniel A. Madigan

ZAYN KASSAM

I would like to comment on two considerations Fr. Madigan brings to the table: the need for dialogue on "what is really on our minds" and the need for dialogue on "theological" matters. Concerning the first, some of the most pressing issues for Muslims and Catholic Christians go unattended, and, as a consequence, undermine the conversation. They are like the proverbial elephants in the room that are too difficult to talk about. For example, Middle Eastern and Asian Catholic Christians who live in Muslim societies may not be accorded the respect and tolerance that should be due to them as taxpaying citizens in those countries. This lack of respect and tolerance is sometimes due to the legacy of colonization that stereotypes Christians as suspect citizens who advance Western economic and ideological interests, or at other times is embedded in the fear that such minorities will actively proselytize and try to convert Muslims to Christianity. This fear comes to the forefront also in Iraq with the entrance of Christian missionaries who, while providing aid, are also perceived as attempting to exploit the opportunity of a U.S. military presence in Iraq to extend the reach of Christianity.

A second example is the Israeli treatment of Palestinians, in which Palestinian Christians find that they are not always in agreement with the material and ideological support given by American and European Christians to the State of Israel when the latter translates that support into policies that are perceived as punitive by Palestinians, among whom are included Christians, even if their numbers are small.

A third example is the situation in Iraq, and looming in Iran, against which Christians need to consider how they may speak out against injustice in the form of wars ostensibly targeted at regime change and the fear of weapons of mass destruction but which, as Michael Klare, a Five Colleges professor of Peace and World Security Studies argues in his 2004 book, "Blood and Oil: The Danger and Consequences of America's Growing Dependency on Imported Petroleum" (Metropolitan Books), may in fact be wars undertaken to feed the American thirst for oil. If the latter is indeed the case, then dialogue is essential among American Catholics and Muslims as both are included in the complicity of the average American citizen, regardless of persuasion, who engages in a lifestyle that contributes both to escalating resource wars and increased global warming from the burning of fossil fuels.

On the theological front, there is no question, as Fr. Madigan points out, that serious theological dialogue occurs best when the dialogue partners are well acquainted with the Other's key theological doctrines, thinkers, and hermeneutical principles. Indeed, reading one religious tradition from the perspective of the Other often opens up interesting and enriching questions that may, in turn, be asked of one's own religious tradition, questions that would not have come into view until such a comparative lens is brought into the conversation. Opening up such dialogue to believers rather than to official spokespersons for the religious tradition in question—something that is difficult but not impossible to do in the case of Islam and Muslims, provided no one Muslim group is given the privilege to speak for all others—also allows for multiple conversations to take place. For instance, the question of how the divine inhabits the material or corporeal or embodied realm may spark very different conversations when undertaken with South Asian Muslims who are well acquainted, from their own cultural and geographical location, with the notion of the *avatara*, the Hindu deity that takes on a corporeal form in order to save the world, or with some Sufi Muslims who place equal emphasis on immanence as they do on transcendence, than with those Muslims who maintain a strict boundary of separation between the Creator and the created. As always, the danger of such theological conversations is the sometimes implicit agenda in such dialogues that takes the form of "if you understand me (that is, this concept), then why don't you agree with me (that is, convert to my clearly superior religion)?" Clearly, the purpose of such theologically oriented conversations might be clarified from the outset: (1) increasing mutual understanding for its own sake, without attaching the agenda of conversion or cultural hegemony; and (2) clarifying the ends to which such mutual understanding could be applied—ends that would be in accordance with the most profound values of each tradition.

Thus, if mutual understanding of the Other, undertaken empathically and from the Other's perspective (and not from a defensive perspective) is one of the purposes of theological dialogue, that is, understanding for its own sake, then I would suggest that we enrich the conversation through an additional perspective to those spelled out for us by Fr. Madigan. Julius Lipner has used the word *resonances* in his comparative work, and here it might be salient to point out that our theological differences are what make each of us different from the Other, give us something of a unique stamp, and are not to be feared, because sameness of theological doctrine does not necessarily translate into commonality of action, interpretation, or even commonly shared values.[1] However, strangely, sometimes the more different we appear in our theological creeds, the more we might find interesting points of commonality, especially when we begin to examine the force of the theological principle away from having to defend it at all cost to how it is applied and understood. For instance, a soldier in Iraq was removed from duty for handing out coins that invoked John 3:16, "God so loved the world that he gave his only Son, that whoever believes in him may not die, but may have eternal life" (New American Bible). What if we were to ask how God shows love for the world to Muslims (for instance, in Islamic scripture, thought, and recommended courses of action)? Or if we were to ask how Muslims struggle to attain everlasting life? The possible responses might surprise us with the resonances that emerge: that Christianity is not the only world religious tradition to subscribe to the notion that God loves creation, nor is the hope and possibility of eternal life restricted to one set of believers to the exclusion of all others. And we might just discover that compassion is not found only in the Buddhist quarter, or mercy only in the Muslim quarter, or healing the world only in the Jewish quarter. We might all become the richer for what such conversations might add to our theological understanding.

I also consider it essential, in addition to holding separate conversations about "speaking our minds" and "theological dialogue," to link theological dialogue to addressing common social justice issues. So, for instance, understanding the notion of gratuity in both traditions and how it appears in foundational narratives and practices may open the way for concerted actions on the part of members of both faith traditions to address as a joint effort the question of mistreatment of religious minorities in both European and Muslim societies. Discussions of the ways in which the persons of both Jesus and Muhammad are privileged in different ways, respectively, in Catholic Christian and Islamic traditions, may enable fruitful discussions on how the imitation of qualities such as the heightened social conscience embodied by both figures could translate into conversations and programs of action with respect to how to treat the marginalized in our societies and what kinds of concerted actions could be undertaken on behalf of the many who are underprivileged. In this respect, theological dialogue and address the real issues on our minds, when linked, may prove to be just the kind of force for positive social change that our present historical moment calls upon engaged religious persons to mobilize. I thank Fr. Madigan for generating such a critically relevant discussion.

Note

1 Julius Lipner, *Hindus: Their Religious Beliefs and Practices* (London and New York: Routledge, 1994).

A Response to Daniel A. Madigan

JIHAD TURK

There should be no doubt about Fr. Madigan's statement that Muslim-Christian dialogue faces many challenges in today's world. As he rightly indicates, both sides have skeptics who point to a number of cultural, political, theological, and even practical considerations that either pose as real obstacles to dialogue or create a pretense for avoiding engagement with the Other. In his essay, Fr. Madigan suggests ways to navigate around these obstacles.

The first most important step, however, is to clearly identify the goals of and motivations for any such dialogue. From the Muslim point of view, there is a Qur'anic imperative to get to know the "Other."

> O mankind! We created you from a single (pair) of a male and a female, and made you into nations and tribes, that ye may know each other (not that ye may despise each other). Verily the most honoured of you in the sight of God is (he who is) the most righteous of you. And God has full knowledge and is well acquainted (with all things). (Qur'an 49:13)[1]

At the very basic level, comparing and contrasting oneself with the "Other" (race, tribe, religion, nationality, culture, etc.) helps to define more clearly one's own identity.

While a deeper self-understanding results from truly fruitful exchanges, many still shy away from serious inquiry into the "Other's" faith, and this for a couple of reasons. There are those who feel threatened by the diversity of belief; that is, they feel that anyone who holds differing understandings of God is by definition negating and challenging his or her own understanding. Such challenges cause discomfort. The Qur'an speaks about this discomfort by redirecting the focus of the dialogue to acts of virtue and away from theological disputation.

> [T]o each among you have we prescribed a law and an open way. If God had so willed, He would have made you a single people,

but (His plan is) to test you in what He hath given you: so strive as in a race in all virtues. The goal of you all is to God. It is He that will show you the truth of the matters in which you dispute. (Qur'an 5:48)

From the Islamic point of view, it is God's will that there be diversity. This diversity should make us question our assumptions and preconceived notions. It is through this intellectual and soul-searching process and in the coming together to seek the common grounds of virtuous acts that faith becomes strengthened.

Yet some see no point in dialogue as they hold judgment over (i.e., condemn) the "Other." They simply want to persuade or impose their belief system upon others. But if it is God's will that there be diversity, who then are we to impose uniformity or conformity? The oft-repeated Qur'anic instruction to the Prophet of Islam, "Your duty is only to convey the message," should serve as a guiding principle for Muslims who chose to engage in dialogue with Christians or other peoples of faith.

From the Christian point of view, the teaching to "love thy neighbor" sets a very high bar for the Christian interlocutor. This mandate implies that one faithful to Christianity should get to know not only the neighbor (and here I join with those Christians who interpret this mandate broadly to include the "Other") but also come to appreciate him or her to the point of gaining genuine respect and even love for the essence of who he or she is. One could argue and make a strong case that the greatest display of love for other people is to want ultimate salvation for them. While this might be true, we should also not forget that loving our neighbors would also entail treating them now in this life with dignity, as Fr. Madigan points out. Loving our neighbor means respecting their free will and right to practice religion according to their beliefs.

All of this then should inform both the motivation for Christians and Muslims to engage in dialogue as well as the approach that should be taken. The motivation is to discharge one's duty to God by getting to know and love each other; the approach is to engage in theological dialogue to understand each other and to work together in acts of virtue, that is, acts of social justice, defense of human rights, and the protection of religious freedom.

One of the obstacles to meeting these goals is, as Fr. Madigan points out, the complex way in which we form our identities, religious and beyond. At the cultural and civilizational level, Fr. Madigan addressed at some length the arguments of Samuel Huntington, exploring the relevance of the larger paradigm of the Muslim and Western civilization to the Muslim-Christian dialogue. Identity is no doubt complex and, yes, religion often plays some role in that identity formation. However, when we are talking about a serious dialogue between religious groups, one would hope that whatever the framework, commitment to religion and religious principles would be primary. The civilizational level is not very useful then as an interpretive category for interfaith dialogue given that most people in a civilization are more motivated by culture than religion, even if a given civilization is identifiable as being strongly influenced by or belonging to a certain faith tradition.

I suspect that Fr. Madigan discusses the impact of civilization in order to make the relevance of the dialogue extend beyond simply the religious communities. The conflicts around the world without question do give us a sense of urgency; we feel compelled to find solutions. Nevertheless, it is my contention that these conflicts are not really motivated by religion; rather, they are in fact contrary to the teachings of each faith tradition. If this is true, then the work of the faithful from both sides should be to strive not only to moderate extremism and hawkishness in their own societies but also to forge alliances with peace loving moderate-minded faithful people from the other side of the divide. The real struggle, therefore, is not between Christians and Muslims, but between moderates and extremists/militants of both faith traditions.

That times are difficult for Christian-Muslim dialogue is not new. At every age there have been significant challenges and major misunderstandings among adherents to both traditions. And although one might notice these days a change in tone coming from the highest office of the Catholic Church, a tone that can be characterized as "losing gains" previously made—and I speak as one who is both engaged at the academic level as well as at the grassroots level in interreligious dialogue—the momentum seems to be building for greater engagement in dialogue. I am encouraged not only by the discourse that is taking place locally in the United States but also by what is going on worldwide. It is often the most difficult times that produce the best results. It was in response to Pope Benedict XVI's Regensburg address of September 13, 2006, that a group of scholars, representing all of the major Islamic schools of thought and denominations, produced a document titled "A Common Word"[2]—a document intended to highlight both the commonalities between Islam and Christianity, and the need to agree to differ respectfully. The verse from the Qur'an upon which the document is based reads:

Say: 'O People of the Scripture! Come to a common word between us and you: That we shall worship none but God, That we associate no partners with Him, That we erect not, from among ourselves, lords and patrons other than God.' If then they turn back, say ye: 'Bear witness that we (at least) are Muslims bowing to God's Will). (Qur'an 3:64)

The impact of this document continues to be felt today. In the United States, Yale University has taken the initiative to host the dialogue.

Notes

1 'Ali, Abdullah Yusuf. "The Meaning of the Holy Qur'an" 11th ed. Amana Publications, Beltsville 2004
2 See http://www.acommonword.com/.

Daniel A. Madigan Continues the Dialogue

The responses of Dr. Kassam and Imam Turk, indeed all our interactions in this process, are an illustration of the point made by the latter in his piece, that the civilizational divide, if it exists in our world, is not between Christianity and Islam. Rather it is between those who are prepared to listen to the Other and those who are not. We encounter such people in every religious tradition and among those who have no religious affiliation. From experience, I can say that I have felt more at home with some Muslims than with some Christians; to use Huntington's terms, I find it easier to consider myself part of the same "we" with many Muslims I know than I do with certain types of Christians. I won't name names. Our civilizational links—the things that make us think of ourselves as "us"—are intertwined and overlapping. As academics, we three are part of an international culture with shared rituals, languages, hierarchies, structures, and interests. As residents of the United States we are part of other cultural structures that define us as "us." Gender, race, marital status, employment, age, abilities, and disabilities—all these things make us part of various identity groups. Any clash of civilizations à la Huntington can only arise from the gradual breakdown of each of these intertwined identities and their replacement, against all the evidence to the contrary, by one single identity defined by religious affiliation.

We have seen such things happen even in the relatively recent past. An example would be the Balkans, a tragic situation raised by one of the questioners after my lecture. Referring to a member of her family who was from the former Yugoslavia, a woman asked how it was possible to trust Muslims when they had shown themselves to be mass murderers there? It is strange, but also very significant, that she had this perception, seeing that a CIA report concluded in 1995 that 90 percent of the acts of "ethnic cleansing" were carried out by the Orthodox Christian Serbs.[1] Ethnic cleansing generally describes the practice, common in the Bosnian War, of killing, forcibly evicting, and persecuting ethnic groups other than one's own. All parties acknowledge that the more than three-quarters of the estimated 40,000 civilian casualties in the conflict were Muslims.

However, in spite of the extensive coverage of the Balkan War and the media attention given to the concentration camps, the massacres, and the mass graves, there is a strong public tendency to remember, quite wrongly, the Muslims as the aggressors and the perpetrators of war crimes. Yet only about 7 percent of those convicted by the International Criminal Tribunal for the former Yugoslavia were Bosniaks. The vast majority have been Serbs, and their indictments and arrests continue. A Western public finds it difficult to imagine that its fellow Christians were the perpetrators of "ethnic cleansing" and even the inventors of that chilling euphemism. "We" don't do that kind of thing, do we? It must have been "them."

So a clash of civilizations, if such there were to be, would be the result of the degeneration and breakdown of our richly complex, intertwined identities. It would not be the inevitable result of some rigid identities we are already presumed to have.

Among the many valuable points Dr. Kassam raises about theological dialogue is the idea of Jesus and Muhammad as moral exemplars in our respective traditions, and the possibility this opens up for a dialogue about justice for the marginalized. There are two comments I would like to make about this. The first is that I recognize that in my laying out of the theological schema that places Jesus and the Qur'an in the same category because each is seen in its own tradition as *the* revelation in history of God's eternal Word—and I insist this is crucial to our understanding of each other—I risk losing sight of the fact that Jesus and Muhammad play parallel roles from an ethical point of view. I also risk undervaluing the strong strand in the Islamic tradition that sees Muhammad as himself somehow God's primordial expression, and on earth an embodiment—not in exactly the same sense as the Christian notion of incarnation—of the Qur'anic word.

The second is this: our concern for the marginalized is often present in what Dr. Kassam calls the "speaking our minds" kind of dialogue. Yet it is often *our own* marginalized, or ourselves as marginalized, that we are concerned for, rather than the marginalized *tout court*. Our calls for justice would have more force if they were made on behalf of all those who suffer unjustly. This might have the advantage also of turning our attention beyond its sometimes obsessive focus on Muslim-Christian relations to a broader appreciation of the world's needy, many of whom are completely extraneous to our vexed relationship, yet whose suffering is greater because of our failure to see them. When we are so engaged in facing off against one another, we are unable to stand shoulder to shoulder and face the world that cries out to us for mercy and for justice.

I thank my colleagues for their observations and their commitment in this process. The way we have been able to engage one another should be a sign of hope for those who have asked themselves if dialogue is just going through a difficult time or if it was just an overoptimistic dream like so many others from the 1960s.

Note

1 Roger Cohen, "C.I.A. Report on Bosnia Blames Serbs for 90% of the War Crimes," *The New York Times*, March 9, 1995.

SUGGESTIONS FOR FURTHER READING

1. Mahmoud Ayoub, A *Muslim View of Christianity: Essays on Dialogue*, ed. Irfan A. Omar. (Maryknoll, N.Y.: Orbis, 2007). A valuable collection of the essays of Ayoub, a Muslim scholar who has distinguished himself by the sophistication of his grasp of the history of Christian theology. The third part of the collection is devoted to Muslim perspectives on christological issues.

2. Maurice Borrmans, *Guidelines for Dialogue between Christians and Muslims*, Pontifical Council for Interreligious Dialogue, prepared by Maurice Borrmans, trans. R. Marston Speight (New York: Paulist , 1990). Still the standard official guidelines for dialogue in the Catholic Church, though rather in need of updating, given the changed world situation.

3. Kenneth Cragg, *The Call of the Minaret*, 3rd ed. (Oxford: Oneworld, 2000). Cragg has been the most prolific and insightful interpreter of Islam to an English-speaking readership. Although he has sometimes been accused of Christianizing Islam in his reading of it, he shows a profound sensibility for the particularity of each tradition, which nonetheless does not preclude dialogue.

4. Sidney H. Griffith, "The Bible and the 'People of the Book,'"*Bulletin Dei Verbum* 79/80 (2006): 22–30, http://www.deiverbum2005.org/Paper/Panels/Griffith_e.pdf. An introduction to the various questions connected with Muslim-Christian relations by a master in the field. Though the article is introductory, it is sophisticated and rich in insights.

5. Thomas F. Michel, *A Christian View of Islam: Essays on Dialogue*, ed. Irfan A. Omar (Maryknoll, N.Y.: Orbis, 2010). This compendium (a companion volume to Ayoub's, above) is organized into three parts: (1) various approaches to interreligious dialogue; (2) five comparative studies; and (3) a section in which Michel addresses a number of issues, including Islam as the "Other," Islamic nonviolence, holiness and ethics in Islam, and a Qur'anic approach to ecology.

4

Learning Our Way

*Some Catholic Reflections on the
Catholic-Hindu Encounter*

FRANCIS X. CLOONEY, S. J.

Religions, however, that are bound up with an advanced culture have struggled to answer the same questions by means of more refined concepts and a more developed language. Thus in Hinduism, men contemplate the divine mystery and express it through an inexhaustible abundance of myths and through searching philosophical inquiry. They seek freedom from the anguish of our human condition either through ascetical practices or, profound meditation, or a flight to God with love and trust... The Catholic Church rejects nothing that is true and holy in these religions. She regards with sincere reverence those ways of conduct and of life, those precepts and teachings which, though differing in many aspects from the ones she holds and sets forth, nonetheless often reflect a ray of that Truth which that enlightens all men. Indeed, she proclaims, and ever must proclaim Christ "the way, the truth, and the life" (John 14:6), in whom men may find the fullness of religious life, in whom God has reconciled all things to Himself (*Nostra Aetate*, 2).

I. Getting Started: Encountering Hinduism

The question before us today is the relationship of Catholicism to Hindu traditions, particularly here in the United States; we need to consider how a Catholic is to think about Hindu traditions in a fruitful way, so as to remove misunderstandings, and make clear the way to better relationships among Catholics and Hindus. We can rightly imagine ourselves contributing to this

learning in various ways, ranging from official dialogues and official pronouncements by Catholic and Hindu leaders, to longer-term committed conversations
among individuals who learn to understand one another and (possibly) become
friends, to more or less systematic theological reflections. At every level, learning
is required, since nothing is accomplished in ignorance or by bland approval. In
this essay, I wish to trace features of the path by which the required learning on
the part of Catholics can occur.[1]

In focusing not only or even primarily on the content of Catholic and Hindu
traditions and more on our way of learning and its necessary dimensions, I am
heeding what I have learned in thirty-five years of thinking about Hindu traditions, its potential and actual place in my own life. After college, I spent two years
teaching in a Jesuit high school in Kathmandu, Nepal, where my students were
all Hindus and Buddhists. As a teacher there, I learned to learn from these students and the traditions that they lived, and I received more than I gave in my
teaching. I learned on multiple levels, and recognized early on that just as the
ideas and great texts of the Hindu tradition are interesting and impressive, so too
the lived devotion is real and persuasive, the practices most often inviting. I have
learned too that to recognize connections and decipher their meaning also
requires us to reflect on what we learn in practice, with a vulnerable openness
that makes learning possible.[2]

What Is Hinduism? Some Starting Points

While it is counterproductive to use the word *Hindu* with overconfidence, as if it
marks off some single entity, it is not helpful to reject the word entirely, as if we
clarify things by referring more vaguely to "the vast array of religious beliefs and
practices across the Indus River, that is, in India." While it is very hard to define
"Hinduism," it is preferable to alternatives, particularly if we use it with a sense of
its necessarily fluid boundaries. In its unity-in-difference—seemingly infinite
variety that seems often enough to point to a deeper oneness—it differs from
Buddhism and other religions east and west. So it is worthwhile finding a viable
way of speaking of the "Hinduism" that is in contact with "Catholicism."

But what then is Hinduism, or what can we say about it? The following list
provides a succinct overview of Hinduism—in one page—as a starting point. I
offer this here in that tightly condensed form, since to expand it properly would
turn it into a book—that would be added to the many books that already exist as
introductions to Hindu traditions.[3] Here, for the sake of our discussion, are my
ten points:

(1) *"Hinduism" is a set of human, cultural, and religious energies* developing,
complexifying, adjusting over time, beginning with the indigenous (and largely

pre–documentable records) religious traditions of India, probably including the cult of multiple local Gods and Goddesses, belief in rebirth, the practice of yoga,

(2) *plus the linguistic, social, cultural, ritual, religious, and polytheistic heritage* of the Indus Valley and Indo-European civilization (taking shape around 3000 B.C.E.);

(3) *together, these many sources contribute to forming the Vedic tradition of ancient India,* the Vedas (1200 B.C.E.); the Upanishads (after 1000 B.C.E.); the accompanying array of rites, social structures, texts, theoretical developments such as Vedanta theology, plus other developing intellectual systems such as grammar and logic,

(4) *all of which is in turn regularized as the Brahminical heritage* in the theory and practice of orthodoxy—the dharma—a heritage that proves to be enormously resourceful, elastic, and inclusive for millennia, and

(5) in turn, *this orthodoxy is critiqued* by Buddhism (ca. 500 B.C.E.), Jainism (before 500 B.C.E.), and other ascetical alternatives such as yoga, and many emerging popular movements,

(6) *and thus an array of changes and challenges* leading to the reformation and expansion of the Vedic, Brahminical tradition into what many of us tend to call "Hinduism,"

(7) *a Hinduism that thus combines* the complex indigenous and Vedic heritage, Brahminical orthodoxy, and ascetical extensions and alternatives; epics such as the Ramayana and Mahabharata plus other important texts and practices; devotion to new, popular Gods such as Shiva, Vishnu, Rama, Krishna; leading to the formulation (particularly in Brahminical discourses) of major theistic traditions, plus an array of holy places, images, pilgrimages, and so forth, connected with devotion—some traditions being dedicated to one supreme Deity or Reality,

(8) *and all this flourishes as a complex Hinduism constantly and continually enriched and challenged by further input* from the indigenous traditions, the cults of new, local deities who become widely popular, particularly Goddesses such as Sarasvati, Sri Laksmi, Devi, and Kali, plus new, renewed systems of practice such as the tantra that draws on yoga, vernacular literatures, the perspectives of marginal and excluded communities,

(9) *and so we might now speak more accurately of "Hinduisms,"* but even so, all this is further transformed by the arrival of Islam (around and after 1000 C.E.), the rise of Sikhism (fifteenth century), the arrival of the European colonial powers (1498 C.E.), and then the colonial scholarship and representations of the meaning of Hinduism,

(10) *and this complex set of Hindu traditions continues to change today* in light of new social, economic, and political realities in India and globally, learning

from Indian Hindus abroad and from converts to Hindu traditions, by learning from previously marginalized voices and from scholars and students globally constructing new intellectual discourses stepping beyond the colonial heritage; by paying attention to gender studies, and new social, political, and religious analyses; and from studying revived older Hindu traditions; and all of this in relation to other religions—which also keep changing, in a changing world.[4]

It is crucial, if not particularly comforting, to realize that any engagement with Hindu images, ideas, and practices ends up being complicated, since Hinduism itself marks this complex set of possibilities displayed over long periods of time and vast spaces too. But the immediate consequence is a plea for learning; only when we know what we are talking about, in some detail (and yet still well short of the expert knowledge Indological scholars might have) should we venture to reflect further on the Catholic relation to Hindu traditions.

II. Acknowledging a History

When we think about our Catholic-Hindu encounter, we need to remember that we are not at its beginning, by any means. There has been a long history of interactions that, like most histories, is both a resource and burden today. In the early Christian era, we find mention of encounters with Indian ascetics and sages, even the visits of such figures to the Mediterranean world. Tradition holds that St. Thomas the apostle preached the gospel in South India. Christian communities, in the Orthodox traditions of the Syriac Church, were certainly established in India in the first millennium C.E. The modern encounter began with the opening of the European colonial period, and the arrival of the Roman Catholic Portuguese on the west coast of India in 1498. From then on, the religious interactions of Hindus and these newly arrived Christians became more intense and complex, inextricably intertwined with economic and political calculations; in controversy and debate, specifically religious factors have sometimes seemed secondary to various communal, political, and social issues at work on both sides.

Early missionaries such as Francis Xavier (1506–1552) knew little about the Hindu traditions, and had little opportunity to learn of its traditions in detail. Later missionaries, for example, Jesuits such as Roberto de Nobili (1577–1656), Jean Venance Bouchet (1655–1732), and G. L. Coeurdoux (1691–1779), developed more sophisticated notions of culture and religion, and argued that the Catholic engagement with India, with the goal of evangelization and conversion, would be best grounded in detailed knowledge of Hindu traditions. A long tradition of the West's coming to learn from India, even while reshaping the meanings of Hinduism, begins in and follows upon the work of these

foreign missionary scholars, whose successors worked in India even until very recently.[5]

There were many other ways, beyond the engagement of intellectuals who wrote books, of course, in which Hindus and Catholics met in India. Over the centuries, innumerable Hindus have studied in Catholic schools, and everywhere there have been medical services and hospitals run by Catholic and other Christian groups. Similarly, many, perhaps most, Indian Catholics have had Hindu relatives and neighbors, and there have been myriad more narrowly defined interrelationships on the village level. We would be misguided if we imagine "Hinduism" and "Catholicism" as two entirely separate entities brought into contact simply by the work of leaders and intellectuals; in addition to the disciplined intentional encounters that attract attention from scholars, creative and fruitful encounter has always happened informally, in unplanned living encounters.[6]

As we look at this history, we ought not be naively cheerful. For many Hindus, the first experience of Christianity was by way of colonial power and colonial intrusion, be it Portuguese, Dutch, French, or, most notably, British. The church, however it sought to distinguish itself, was in fact the religion of foreign powers that exercised brutal force when deemed necessary. Even the most sincere and spiritual of missionaries most often worked in contexts where Christian colonialists were ruling over Hindu subjects, and there is no reason why Hindus should simply forget the dark period of foreign rule.[7]

In the past sixty years, after Indian independence and as the age of the foreign missionary engagement in India waned, Catholic interest in Hindu traditions has remained vital. The scholarly traditions of learning have continued, often now in the setting of colleges and universities in the West. Yoga and other practices closely connected with Hinduism have flourished greatly in the United States, as teachers have brought various forms of Hindu spirituality and practice to life in our towns and cities, where the possibilities of learning have increased so greatly as to mark a new moment in our shared histories. Here I can add a personal note: it would have been most unlikely for me even to have met an Indian when growing up in the 1950s and 1960s in Staten Island, New York, but now there is a flourishing Hindu temple several miles from my family's home. Much Catholic-Hindu relationship occurs "on the ground," and our more academic work in reflecting on its meaning and possibilities is best thought of as in complement to and illumination of that living evolution.

The sheer fact of this long and yet living history—which I cannot detail here—should awaken us and chasten us to remember our past, with an awareness that we are unlikely to break entirely new ground, are not innocent of that past, and unlikely also to avoid its errors; and yet, we can still argue that there was great positive gain for Catholics in the centuries of encounter, and more also to come.[8]

III.   The Contours of a Catholic "Starting" Point

But even as we deepen our sense of our history, we must also attune ourselves to the possibilities defining the present moment, more than forty years after *Nostra Aetate*. I cited a key passage from that document at the beginning of this chapter, a text that marked out a new path of greater openness. We know that the last forty years have seen great effort in the work of enacting the meaning of this invitation for Catholics in engagement with Hindus, both in India and the West, and even in the context of Vatican concerns. It would be yet another large project to trace the contours of the church's experience and teaching on religions, and here too we offer an abbreviation, simply by calling attention to several paragraphs of a recent Vatican document. "A Doctrinal Note on Some Aspects of Evangelization," issued by the Congregation for the Doctrine of the Faith (CDF) in December 2007, shares something of the insight and spirit of the Second Vatican Council, even as it is also inscribed with the worries about the limits of openness so evident in recent decades.[9] Preaching the gospel is described in several ways, but most important with reference to the supreme value simply of knowing Jesus:

> Although non-Christians can be saved through the grace which God bestows in "ways known to him," the Church cannot fail to recognize that such persons are lacking a tremendous benefit in this world: to know the true face of God and the friendship of Jesus Christ, God-with-us. Indeed "there is nothing more beautiful than to be surprised by the Gospel, by the encounter with Christ. There is nothing more beautiful than to know him and to speak to others of our friendship with him."[10]

The document goes on to say that at the core of the process lie acts of listening, friendship, and empathy:

> Evangelization also involves a sincere dialogue that seeks to understand the reasons and feelings of others. Indeed, the heart of another person can only be approached in freedom, in love and in dialogue, in such a manner that the word which is spoken is not simply offered, but also truly witnessed in the hearts of those to whom it is addressed. This requires taking into account the hopes, sufferings and concrete situations of those with whom one is in dialogue. Precisely in this way, people of good will open their hearts more freely and share their spiritual and religious experiences in all sincerity. This experience of sharing, a characteristic of true friendship, is a valuable occasion for witnessing and for Christian proclamation.[11]

The CDF likewise admits that the process has failed in the past, and so that our era in particular requires that Catholics—and not just others—support the human right to make free choices regarding religious belonging:

> As in any other field of human activity, so too in dialogue on religious matters, sin can enter in. It may sometimes happen that such a dialogue is not guided by its natural purpose, but gives way instead to deception, selfish motives or arrogance, thus failing in respect for the dignity and religious freedom of the partners in dialogue. For this reason, "the Church severely prohibits forcing people to embrace the faith or leading or enticing them by improper techniques; by the same token, she also strongly defends the right that no one be deterred from the faith by deplorable ill treatment."[12]

Once we take to heart the truth that evangelization cannot tolerate a less than serious commitment to dialogue, there is mutual learning of people of different religious traditions:

> Evangelization does not only entail the possibility of enrichment for those who are evangelized; it is also an enrichment for the one who does the evangelizing, as well as for the entire Church. . . . Beyond its intrinsic anthropological value, every encounter with another person or culture is capable of revealing potentialities of the Gospel which hitherto may not have been fully explicit and which will enrich the life of Christians and the Church. Thanks to this dynamism, "tradition, which comes from the Apostles, makes progress in the Church by the help of the Holy Spirit."[13]

Mutual openness and genuine desire to share are also set in a doctrinal atmosphere that we can illustrate by returning to the passage cited above, but now quoting a bit more of it. For it not only links necessary knowing the truth to knowing Jesus and entering the church—a sequence Hindus would generally not recognize as necessary—but also to chillier intimations about those who live in darkness without the truths about ultimate questions[14]:

> Although non-Christians can be saved through the grace that God bestows in "ways known to him," the church cannot fail to recognize that such persons are lacking a tremendous benefit in this world: to know the true face of God and the friendship of Jesus Christ, God-with-us. Indeed, "there is nothing more beautiful than to be surprised by the Gospel, by the encounter with Christ. There is nothing more beautiful than to know him and to speak to others of our friendship

with him." The revelation of the fundamental truths about God, about the human person and the world, is a great good for every human person, *while living in darkness without the truths about ultimate questions is an evil and is often at the root of suffering and slavery which can at times be grievous.*[15]

The document does not name those living in darkness, but it suggests that our non-Christian partners in dialogue are in darkness even as we are engaging them in dialogue.

There is no way around the fact of multiple, mixed messages inscribed in this largely positive document. There will be no Catholic encounter with Hindu traditions that omits the desire to make Jesus Christ known; no intelligent and religiously vital evangelization can render Catholics immune to learning from Hindus and Hindu traditions. On the whole, this official view opens up the possibility of dialogue in a rather sober fashion that is preferable to views that would pass over in silence the problems that accompany Catholics into dialogue, and that face those who would agree to dialogue with Catholics.[16] This creates a situation where learning is important, so let us now consider more closely how we might learn from Hinduism.

IV.   Hinduism and the Catholic Imagination

Hinduism and Catholicism have much in common, and important differences too, so nothing is determined simply by paying attention to doctrines and institutional views. Likewise, our long history of interactions seems not to be decisive in fixing Hindu and Catholic attitudes toward each other. We are advised to be careful in making the dialogue work, but there seem to be no historical issues so grave as to prevent dialogue entirely. We therefore have to chart an only partly defined path, and have a need for religious and theological imagination in our learning from Hindu traditions: Catholics and Hindus share a real history and real theological connections that are nonetheless incomplete, underdetermined, still open, and demanding of our creativity and imagination.

As I have suggested earlier, Hinduism is a rich theological tradition, or set of traditions, with distinctive teachings and characteristic strengths, including its decentered cohesion, myriad possibilities nurtured over millennia, and an acute sensitivity to the needs and capacities of individuals. None of the Hindu traditions is without structure, none is exactly comparable to any specific Catholic analogue, and all are capable of adapting to the perspectives of the observer. There is no single set of issues predetermining a Catholic-Hindu agenda, and none of us can be merely spectators, or merely definitive in our judgments about what the encounter is supposed to mean. A Catholic engagement with Hindu traditions is, accordingly, distinctive, neither an imitation of our encounters with Judaism or Islam, nor to be slighted as a diminished version of those. As I have suggested, there is a long history, but nothing in this history has fixed the Catholic-Hindu encounter in a definite mold; there are no key moments that have irrevocably defined our relationship.

While Hinduism's fluidity-within-boundaries means that no encounter is neat and utterly clear, and may frustrate those seeking a straight path to the resolution of religious and theological differences, its very diversity puts a premium on inventiveness and multiple strategies of engagement. The Catholic-Hindu encounter is for the imaginative, and those willing to enter upon an encounter that has not been predictably fixed by history or doctrine. All of this indicates a creative site for theological exchange with no one in a position to determine where exactly the theological exchange is to go or to declare unilaterally that it is complete.

Without a particularly defined history or current crisis, there is no urgency to clarify, heal, or resolve the relationship (tensions and misunderstandings notwithstanding); the myriad possibilities for exchange can liberate and enliven the Catholic theological imagination, as innumerable starting points in text, ritual, and practice present themselves. In the following sections, I explore some of these ways of encounter.

V. Ways of Learning from Hindu Traditions

One obvious way for a Catholic to learn from Hinduism is to study great ideas of the Hindu tradition; there are many such ideas worthy of our consideration, and they may be profitably thought through, learned, and then compared and contrasted with ideas from Catholic theology and doctrine. While I have stressed that this kind of study never encompasses the entirety of the exchange, it is important, basic, and worthy of illustration here. The following expressions of Hindu wisdom worthy of our consideration are by no means all professed by all Hindus—they are select, formulated in a way that is geared to the great intellectual traditions, open to other formulations—but they do help map out the theological "frame" in which much more technical Hindu thinking has occurred. Here, for the sake of discussion, are ten points:

1. The Self is not a body, but is always in some relation to matter; over multiple lives, it inhabits a series of bodies—plant, animal, human, and God.

2. Ignorance, not sin, is the greatest of evils; and yet, our minds and imaginations can guide us.

3. The divine can be imagined and related to in multiple ways, and by meditation upon divine names and forms we are led to understand God—and Self.

4. There are multiple great divinities; supreme, gracious Gods and Goddesses; or simply a Reality beyond images. These deities have a substantive reality for most Hindus, and should not be condescendingly termed "representations of the One."

5. Living beings are always already one with God, Ultimate Reality, and indeed are materially and spiritual generated from that Being.

6. Ultimately, there is no single way to understand Self and God; no one is in a position to decide such matters.

7. Religious practice matters more than specific doctrine; one acts according to the possibilities one is born to.

8. In the end, all will reach enlightenment—however many lives it takes.

9. These and other truths are enunciated in sacred texts and passed down in Tradition; to learn them properly requires humility, docility before one's teachers, and a willingness to enact and live what we learn.

10. All of the preceding, and whatever else might be learned, is received in accord with the capacities of the knower, who need not strive beyond what makes sense to her or him at any given point—even over a lifetime or lifetimes.

Such a list is not timeless, and does not float in space; rather, it is representative of the kind of learning that might ground a truly thoughtful and intelligently explored Catholic-Hindu relationship. But this starting point makes possible a deeper reflection on the basis of which we, as Catholics today, can go about learning from and with Hindu traditions. The point of this merely suggestive list is to indicate that we share common ground while yet holding theological positions differing in important ways. Even for nonspecialists, judgments about the two religions in their proximity can be differentiated in light of the "What is Hinduism?" summation earlier in this essay, now melded with this "What Hindu Theology Teaches" list.

There is a temptation to engage detached ideas, allowing them to stand in for a richer religious encounter. It is at least necessary to put the ideas back in some context—a move we may take for granted with respect to many ideas of the Catholic tradition, but which is necessary with respect to ideas from an unfamiliar religious and cultural setting.[17] We might, for instance, locate any of the above ideas in specific textual frameworks, and then too, if possible, examine them in light of earlier and later development in the Hindu history of ideas. Yet all of this, of course, marks a demanding and long course.

Learning to Read the Hindu Classics

Fruitful too is the study of Hindu texts, since by full texts we can begin to put doctrinal positions and claims into specific contexts where they make more sense. By reading texts and their commentaries with an eye toward Catholic parallels in light of the distinctiveness of each tradition, all kinds of fruitful exchanges are made possible. My own work falls largely in this area, and my projects have included a close and lengthy study of South Indian devotional poetry, such as the great devotional classic "Tiruvaymoli" (Holy Word of Mouth); hymns dedicated to Goddesses, such as the "Srigunaratnakosa" (Treasury of the Jewels That Are Sri's Qualities), "Saundaryalahari" (Wave of Beauty), and "Abhirami Antati" (Linked Verses for the Beautiful One), and commentaries on those hymns; a Hindu "Summa theologiae," the medieval theologian Vedanta Desika's "Srimadrahasyatrayasara" (Auspicious Essence of the Three Mysteries), focused ultimately on the spiritual value of abandonment before God; the practice of yoga as theorized in the classic *Yoga Sutras* of Patanjali.[18]

For each project I have chosen an analogue—chosen in accord with my own familiarity, my own intuition—from the Catholic tradition, and so we have:

Complete devotion, lyrically expressed	"*Tiruvaymoli*" of Satakopan	a series of Christian mystical texts
On the Supreme Female	Hindu Goddess hymns	select Marian hymns
On Loving Surrender to God	*Essence of the Three Mysteries*	Francis de Sales's *Treatise on the Love of God*
On the intersection of theology, spirituality, practice	*The Yoga Sutras*	*Spiritual Exercises* of Ignatius Loyola

One can read the full texts or, as I have often done, one might simply read together a pair of short excerpts, such as these prayers from, respectively,

Vedanta Desika's *Essence of the Three Mysteries* and Francis de Sales's *Treatise on the Love of God*:

Nadadur Ammal, twelfth century, cited by Vedanta Desika	St. Francis de Sales, (*Treatise on the Love of God* IX)
I have been wandering about this world from time without beginning, doing what does not please You, my God. From this day forward, I must do what pleases You, and I must cease what displeases You. But my hands are empty, I cannot attain You, my God; I see that You alone are the means. You must be my means! Hereafter, in the removal of what is not desirable or in the attainment of what is desirable—could anything be a burden to me?	But mark, I pray you, Theotimus, that even as our Savior, after he had made his prayer of resignation in the garden of Olives, and after he was taken, left himself to be handled and dragged about at the will of them that crucified him, by an admirable surrender made of his body and life into their hands, so did he resign up his soul and will by a most perfect indifference into his Eternal Father's hands. For when he cries out: *My God, my God, why have You forsaken me?* this was to let us understand the reality of the anguish and bitterness of his soul, and not to detract from the state of most holy indifference in which he was. This he showed very soon afterwards, concluding all his life and his passion with those incomparable words: *Father, into Your hands I commend my spirit.*

For a still easier starting point, one might simply choose to read an easily accessible Hindu text, such as the classic *Bhagavad Gita*, some abbreviated version of the great religious epic known as the *Ramayana*, or, in more modern times, Rabindranath Tagore's lovely songs in *Gitanjali*, or Gandhi's autobiographical *Story of My Experiments with Truth*.[19]

Of course, no matter how productive reading is, we can begin to learn from Hinduism in a rich variety of other ways too. The Hindu traditions are visually very rich tradition and, as is rightly said, one picture can be worth a thousand words. Great progress in learning the Hindu traditions can be made simply by looking at Hindu imagery, either sculpture, classic paintings, or popular images and posters. The simple act of seeing is a powerful point of entry. It has turned out to be impossible in this context to reproduce the thirty images I showed in the lecture on which this presentation is based, so I wish simply to stress that *seeing* must remain a primary way of engaging Hinduism. While of course the Internet provides us with innumerable images—one needs only to search the name of any particular deity and images will be appear in abundance—library art sections provide many books of images with which to begin a visual encounter with Hindu traditions.

So too, hearing chant and devotional singing, for instance, will also be effective, as well as ritual contexts wherein smells and tastes are accentuated. As already implied, visiting places of worship also promises to be a powerful resource for those open to learning from the Hindu traditions. Learning from texts and now too from images and through the other senses is a rich and promising process; it is also slow, and with results never quite predictable. Yet the effort is worthwhile as it opens up, fruitfully and with pleasure, the possibility of an engagement in the Hindu traditions that is considerably deeper than a merely notional observation. And again, simply meeting one another as neighbors and friends will be a most promising starting point.

Learning Also to Pray

Since attentive reading inevitably engages the reader, it opens the way for more intimate forms of personal reflection. In another recent book,[20] for instance, I studied three sacred mantras, prayers and words of divine speech, of the Srivaisnava South Indian tradition: the Tiru Mantra (Aum, obeisance to Narayana); the Dvaya Mantra (I approach for refuge the feet of Narayana with Sri, obeisance to Narayana with Sri), and the Carama Sloka (Having completely given up all *dharma*s, to Me alone come for refuge; from all sins I will make you free. Do not grieve). I suggested that at a chosen level of intentional engagement, one might enrich recitation of Christian texts—biblical in this case—with Hindu counterparts that, though in no way identical with or in replacement of the Christian texts, resemble them closely and open possibilities for theological and spiritual connection. Thus I suggested that specific biblical texts could be probably pondered—richly, spiritually—alongside the mantras:

	The Three Holy Mantras	Christian Prayers
a	Aum, obeisance to Narayana (*Tiru Mantra*).	Abba, Father.
b	Having completely given up all *dharma*s, to Me alone come for refuge . . .[21]	If you want to be perfect, go, sell your possessions and give the proceeds to the poor.
c	I approach for refuge the feet of Narayana with Sri, obeisance to Narayana with Sri.	Father, into Thy hands I commend My spirit.
d	From all sins I will make you free.	and you will have treasure in heaven.
e	Do not grieve.[22]	Then come, follow Me.[23]

Since both openness and attentiveness are at stake when we venture to pray so near to the Hindu realm, we will do well to avoid confusing the knowledge and piety of the one tradition with that of the other. Indeed, as we reflect on the roots of our own prayer and knowledge of God, we who are Catholic will almost surely not be able to bring the same intuition and openness to bear in pondering the words of the mantras. Yet practice in reading back and forth, with a prayerful attitude, can open up a particularly rich avenue of Catholic-Hindu connection, as we might recite, proximate to one another, "Abba, Father" and "Aum, obeisance to Narayana," or hear, one after the other, "If you want to be perfect, go, sell your possessions and give the proceeds to the poor ." and "Having completely given up all dharmas, to Me alone come for refuge." Such instances, if carefully crafted, give us much to talk about and pray about.

While these are just examples of the kinds of reflective, prayerful practice we might undertake, it seems that an encounter that is authentically Catholic requires some practice of this sort; an exchange that shuns spiritual commingling will be mere talk that fails to live up to the ideals of either tradition.[24]

Or, but again with care, prayer may be easier in specific holy places. A Catholic interested in encountering Hindu traditions and thinking about their implications for Christianity might simply visit Hindu temples and observe with empathy and openness the practices of Hindus frequenting their temple for ordinary worship or on some special occasion. Ideally, if such visits are repeated frequently enough that the routines of ritual can begin to feel commonplace rather than exotic, they will provide deeper and more habitual insights—and, as a not inconsiderable bonus, they may also bring that person acquaintances and friendships in the Hindu community—Catholic and Hindu seeing each other in holy places, getting to know each other through sharing important sacred moments, even if each in her or his own way.

Whether it is possible or advisable in specific places for Catholics to move this dynamic into a public realm, taking the lead in arranging opportunities for Hindus and Catholics to pray together remains a debated issue;[25] but it is clear that when intelligent and spiritually engaged Catholics—individuals, communities, churches—learn of the Hindu traditions, study the sacred texts of one or more Hindu traditions, visit holy sites, and take to heart on many levels what can be learned of and from Hinduism, it then becomes exceedingly odd to imagine that prayer would not be affected, or that the influence on individuals should not "overflow" into a sense of how a Catholic community prays, either by itself, or with some Hindu community. If this infusion of the grace of the prayerful spirit of a Hindu ritual or mantra is unexpected and not easily interpreted, we must nonetheless finds ways to be open to the possibility and to learn from it wisely and carefully.

VI. When Can We Argue?

Only at a mature stage in our learning—after we have acquired knowledge of Hindu traditions, sifted through our shared (yet underdetermined) history, and engaged in spiritual and imaginative learning—ought we venture into more sensitive areas that might challenge our Hindu neighbors in honest dispute. Once we know who we and our neighbors are, and know what we are talking about, we can be more forthright in thinking of specific areas where Catholics are unlikely to agree with Hindus, but rather may hold very different views.[26]

Easiest to anticipate would be theological disagreements since, if we have sufficient knowledge, we will find grounds for argument and the means to engage in it usefully. From a Catholic perspective, it is easy to notice points clearly hard to reconcile with Catholic doctrine. Some may be teased out of previous sections of this essay, but others too come to mind: polytheism and the reality of multiple deities not reducible to a single Ultimate Reality or taken as merely symbolic; the flourishing of Goddesses as divine persons at various hierarchical levels including even a Goddess's status as the supreme deity; rebirth, taken for granted as a fact of reality that is intricately woven into a wide variety of Hindu beliefs and practices; and Jesus as a true but not unique divine embodiment.

While I prefer to let Hindus identify issues that they would find difficult, I would anticipate several likely areas of disagreement: Christian evangelism and aggressiveness toward other religions; the entanglement of Christianity with Western power; the seeming tendency of Christian culture to become secular culture; the seeming lack of Christian appreciation for spiritual practice; and the Christian refusal to be as generous toward the beliefs of others as toward odd Christian beliefs.

If there is an atmosphere of mutual respect and trust, theological differences may allow Catholics to talk to Hindus about worship. It is likely that many Catholics might, at least at the start, find temple worship incomprehensible, or quite opposed to many Christian liturgical habits: suspicions about myriad deities, idolatry, and incomprehension about teeming crowds may be expected. Even images, such as those I presented just a moment ago, may disturb the amateur observer who has other ideas about "how God ought to appear." So too, from periodic eruptions in this regard, many Christians seem deeply suspicious even of yoga, worrying whether it might lead Christians away from God. Hindus who practice yoga *and* devote themselves to a God or Goddess may find themselves having to explain how yoga is compatible with interpersonal, divine-human devotion.

Or we might enter upon tougher discussions of sensitive ethical issues, such as caste structures and ways of living, and engage in more heated arguments about human well-being, and the problem of equality and hierarchy, liberty and oppression, within traditional structures of Indian and Hindu life. Some Christians might wish to complain to their Hindu friends about the problem of passivity in the face of social ills (even if it is hard to imagine today's India as a lethargic place!). While women have made marked progress toward equality in India, there are still places and communities—Hindu, but not only Hindu—in which women are victimized, vulnerable to violence, and receiving the full brunt of poverty. In turn, Hindus might wish to challenge Catholics about the behavior of largely Christian nations, the unfair accumulation of wealth in the Christian West, or the ills evident in Europe and North America. Of course, both Hindus and Catholics may wish to join in lamenting the loss of spiritual values in both India and the West.

But such allergic matters need not be divisive, as if honest intellectual disagreements must lead to violence. Catholics and Protestant Christians still disagree on many issues of theology and practice, but today we do not expect to see the animosity and violence that wracked Christian Europe three or four centuries ago. Disagreements should be noted and not passed over in silence, yet considered with equanimity; argument rooted in mutual respect is the kind of argument that can be beneficial. Interreligious theological and ethical disputes will be no more quickly resolved than theological disputes within the Christian and Catholic communities, but we can help our communities greatly by learning to argue intelligently with each other.

But what matters more basically is that such disputes, however argued, occur within the frame of a richer mutual understanding rooted in the kind of practices I have indicated previously, so that it is persons who know one another, and not simply institutions enacting policy decisions, who are talking to one another on the most difficult issues.

VII. Which Catholics?

All the above, particularly as practically oriented, involve finally a sense of who is bested suited for the Catholic-Hindu engagement, with respect to which projects.

We are Catholics—in the West, in India, in other cultures. Obviously, Catholics in India have a particular stake in shaping the Catholic relation to the Hindu traditions. Not only are they a small minority in a Hindu population of nearly a billion, but many of these Catholics either have Hindu family members and relatives, or remember Hindu roots for their own Catholic identities. We who are Catholics of and in the West, however, have a distinct and irreplaceable role to play, discerning how Catholics and Hindus might shape a relationship appropriate to the American scene, in a good sense "Americanizing the Catholic-Hindu relationship."

We are of and in the Catholic Church—as representing our faith, and as simple faithful individuals. Official dialogues and official pronouncements necessarily have a central place in defining any Catholic encounter with another religious tradition, and so by way of example I cited the 2007 statement of the CDF above. This is not to claim that such documents arise from a Catholic-Hindu encounter, or are of any obvious direct value in shaping a Catholic encounter with the Hindu traditions. But they do set parameters of Catholic rootedness, an all-encompassing Christic view of the world, and yet still, Catholic openness to the mystery of God working in the Hindu traditions, specifically in rites and practices, images and beliefs that none of us will see wane or disappear merely because of what we believe about the destiny of the world in Christ.

We are practicing Catholics who encounter Hindu traditions as practiced in living Hindu communities. Actual personal encounters and practices must still ground any Catholic venture to encounter the Hindu traditions intellectually and institutionally. It is to the benefit of all that both Catholics and Hindus realize that without elements of practice and experience, even a well-informed perspective will fall short of "really" engaging Hinduism as an interwoven whole of religious traditions.

We are theologians. Theological inquiries of course require trained experts who know the Catholic tradition but also are educated in Hindu learning, acquired in any of the many possible ways, but primarily through texts. There are innumerable links to be made, with an eye to both similarity and difference, between Hindu philosophical and theological positions on any given issue, and Catholic counterparts. So too, there is room still for the theology of religions discipline, in which Catholic theologians reflect on the meaning and presuppositions of the encounter—though not as if to decide in advance whether it is possible, but rather so as to reflect on learning and encounters that have in fact taken place.

We are Catholics, not Hindus. It goes without saying that all of the above is preliminary and preparatory for an actual dialogue, and requires first Hindu reflections on the encounter with Catholics. Actual Hindus will bring particular perspectives and positions to the conversation, and will not merely stand in for "the typical Hindu." And, again, from a Hindu starting point this entire essay would look very different.

VIII. Encounter, (First of All) for Its Own Sake

In the preceding pages I have suggested, by way of implication, that the Catholic-Hindu dialogue I have in mind is demanding, long-term, defined and intensified by the situation in which we find ourselves—and worthwhile in itself. This last marker requires further comment. It is not, first of all, meant to preclude evident benefits that occur along the way, such as the ending of stereotypes, the cultivation of mutual respect leading to friendship, or the fostering of the ability to work together on projects of common concern. Yet by stressing the disciplined learning that must occur, I have looked toward deep changes in the Catholic who engages in the encounter. Similarly, I have saved a place for the clear-minded recognition of theological similarities and differences, and for arguments about such differences. I have also noted the way in which dialogue will inevitably continue to be linked to a consistent representation of Catholic identity, which includes testimony to the centrality of Christ, even under the rubric of "evangelization." In this context, dialogue might then seem inevitably subordinate to that evangelization; yet were conversion to be a goal to which dialogue were simply and entirely instrumental, the dialogue would clearly fail, and so too the evangelization. So some honest recognition of both theologically stated goals and on-the-street realities must be part of an overall assessment of the encounter's finality.

But I would still argue that the Catholic-Hindu encounter inestimably enriches its participants in a way that is a good in itself. It leads us to look more deeply into our own identities and commitments and into our own ways of manifesting and practicing our identities as Catholics. While the end goal will never be that all of us become Hindu-Catholics, it does seem likely that this particular encounter, in its comprehensiveness and necessarily imaginative enactment, adds new dimensions to our being Catholic; by encountering Hindu traditions, we gain more than in our human capacities we can give. As "A Doctrinal Note on Some Aspects of Evangelization" says, "Evangelization does not only entail the possibility of enrichment for those who are evangelized; it is also an enrichment for the one who does the evangelizing, as well as for the entire Church"[27]—as I had learned in my first experiences of Hinduism in Kathmandu, some thirty-five years ago.

Or, as Pope Benedict put it in Washington, D.C. on April 17, 2008:

> Dear friends, let our sincere dialogue and cooperation inspire all people
> to ponder the deeper questions of their origin and destiny. May the followers of all religions stand together in defending and promoting life
> and religious freedom everywhere. By giving ourselves generously to
> this sacred task—through dialogue and countless small acts of love,

understanding and compassion—we can be instruments of peace for the whole human family.[28]

Notes

1 Two qualifications are in order. First, I deliberately speak from a Catholic perspective, not wishing to generalize regarding the much wider range of Christian views. It is an important yet rather distinct project, not undertaken here, to look into the ways in which Hindus might best learn from Christians, in accord with Hindu sensitivities. Second, I largely try not to speak for Hindus, rather leaving to Hindu writers the reverse dynamic of "Hindu-Catholic" encounters. The responses to this lecture by Professor Chapple and Swami Sarvadevananda aptly begin the process of incorporating the needed other voices.

2 Some of the ideas developed here found earlier expression in the *Cambridge Dictionary of Christian Theology*, ed. David Fergusson, Karen Kilby, Ian McFarland, and Iain Torrance (Cambridge: Cambridge University Press, 2010).

3 For instance, Gavin Flood, *An Introduction to Hinduism* (Cambridge: Cambridge University Press, 1996); and Axel Michaels, *Hinduism: Past and Present* (Princeton: Princeton University Press, 2004). On the problem of the reference of "Hinduism," see Brian K. Pennington, *Was Hinduism Invented? Britons, Indians, and Colonial Construction of Religion* (New York: Oxford University Press, 2005); and *Hinduism Reconsidered*, ed. Günther-Dietz Sontheimer and Hermann Kulke (New Delhi: Manohar, 1989).

4 On this list of points regarding Hinduism, see also Francis X. Clooney, S.J., "Getting Particular: A Christian Studies Hinduism," in *Comparative Theology: Deep Learning across Religious Borders* (Malden, Mass.: Wiley-Blackwell, 2010), 69–86.

5 As for the Protestant missionary tradition in India, likewise rich and varied, one could begin with the pioneer Lutheran missionary Bartolomeo Ziegenbalg (1682–1719) and figures like Nehemiah Goreh (1825–1895). Given my focus on the situation in the theological frame of reference and here in the United States, I do not attempt here to discuss the contemporary work of the Indian Catholic Church in working out its relationships with the Hindu community.

6 See Corinne G. Dempsey, *Kerala Christian Sainthood: Collisions of Culture and Worldview in South India* (New York: Oxford University Press, 2001); Corinne G. Dempsey and Selva J. Raj, *Popular Christianity in India: Riting between the Lines* (Albany: State University of New York Press, 2002); Eliza Kent, *Converting Women: Gender and Protestant Christianity in Colonial South India* (New York: Oxford University Press, 2004).

7 We must also acknowledge the variety of Hindu responses to this encounter with Christianity and its theological possibilities. Traditional pandits argued with missionary scholars, defending Hindu beliefs against unanticipated new challenges. In the nineteenth century, figures such as Rammohun Roy (1772–1833), Keshab Chander Sen (1838–1884), and Swami Vivekananda (1863–1902) engaged Christian thought in theologically interesting ways, while the early twentieth century witnessed impressive comparative studies by the Saiva scholar Nallaswami Pillai (1864–1920) and his contemporary, the Vaisnava scholar Alkondavilli Govindacharya. In recent decades Hindu intellectuals have been more vigorously critical of (foreign) Christian presence in India, and of social and political dimensions of Christian mission. Mostly reactive to Christian initiatives, Hindus seem in general to have been only minimally interested in Christian theology; even the potentially useful word *theology* has not been not widely used. Given the growing Hindu population in the West, and the engagement of young Hindu scholars in the study of religion, it may be that the Christian-Hindu theological exchange will now flourish more vigorously outside of India. For detailed consideration of the Hindu response to Christian missionaries, see Bob Robinson, *Christians Meeting Hindus: An Analysis and Theological*

Critique of the Hindu-Christian Encounter in India (Oxford: Regnum, 2005), and his extensive bibliography.

8 But here too, I must leave it to Indians, particularly Hindus, to indicate how they now evaluate the history of Catholic-Hindu encounters.

9 This 2007 document does not mention Hinduism, or any specific religious tradition. But there are documents composed in the Indian and Asian contexts that are directly relevant, both the work of the South Asian and Asian bishops' conferences and of individual theologians. Nevertheless, the Vatican documents can be taken as setting up the framework for most Catholic perspectives on dialogue.

10 N. 7. The quoted passage is from Vatican II's *Dei Verbum* (1965), n. 8. Dei Verbum is another of the Vatican II documents, included in any volume of documents such as includes Lumen gentium; so too, Verbum Dei and Ad Gentes.

11 N. 8 of *Lumen Gentium*.

12 N. 8 of "Doctrinal Note," with an imbedded quotation, *Ad Gentes* (1965), n. 13.

13 N. 8. *Dei Verbum*, n. 8.

14 "Doctrinal Note", n. 7.

15 "Doctrinal Note" n. 7, citing Benedict XVI's Homily at the Mass inaugurating his pontificate (Rome, April 24, 2005).

16 After the lecture on which this essay is based, Pope Benedict XVI spoke to a group of interreligious leaders in Washington, D.C., on April 17, 2008. In his address, the pope stressed the importance of dialogue as a project that Catholics and people of other faiths should share on multiple levels. See the text of the address at http://www.vatican.va/holy_father/benedict_xvi/speeches/2008/april/documents/hf_ben-xvi_spe_20080417_other-religions_en.html.

17 Again, it is from both Hinduism and Catholicism that I have learned the importance of this turn to the practical, and required engaged and participatory learning.

18 Found, respectively, in *Seeing through Texts* (Albany: State University of New York Press, 1996); *Divine Mother, Blessed Mother* (Oxford: Oxford University Press, 2005); *Beyond Compare* (Washington, D.C.: Georgetown University Press, 2008); and a spring 2008 course on the *Yoga Sutras* read with the Spiritual Exercises.

19 For a good starting point for the Catholic reader, see Bede Griffiths, *River of Compassion: A Christian Commentary on the Bhagavad Gita* (New York: Continuum, 1995); and Daniel Sheridan, *Loving God: Krsna and Christ: A Christian Commentary on the Narada Sutras* (Leuven: Peeters, 2007).

20 *The Truth, the Way, the Life: Christian Commentary on the Three Holy Mantras of the Srivaisnava Hindus* (Leuven: Peeters, 2008).

21 *Carama Sloka*, part 1.

22 *Carama Sloka*, part 2. In my book, as in this chart, I divide the *Carama Sloka* (Bhagavad Gita 18.66) into parts, since it seems to be a divine invitation (b) but also a divine response (d, e).

23 The biblical quotations are (a) Romans 8.15; (c) Luke 23.26; (b, d, and e) Matthew 19.21.

24 For further discussion of learning one's own and another tradition together, see also my *Beyond Compare: St. Francis de Sales and Sri Vedanta Desika on Loving Surrender to God* (Washington, D.C.: Georgetown University Press, 2008).

25 See, for instance, Jacques Dupuis, *Christianity and the Religions: From Confrontation to Dialogue* (Maryknoll, N.Y.: Orbis, 2002), especially chapter 10, "Interreligious Prayer," 236–252.

26 In this section I largely suggest likely Christian problems regarding Hinduism—not because I find merit in all such problems, or because problems head only in this direction, but because in this instance it is best that I speak "for" Catholics, while waiting for Hindu critiques of Christian and Catholic views.

27 N. 8. *Dei Verbum*, n. 8.

28 Pope Benedict XVI (speech to interreligious leaders, Washington, D.C., April 17, 2008), http://www.vatican.va/holy_father/benedict_xvi/speeches/2008/april/documents/hf_ben-xvi_spe_20080417_other-religions_en.html.

A Response to Francis X. Clooney

Hinduism in Southern California

CHRISTOPHER KEY CHAPPLE

Francis Clooney cites important Second Vatican Council documents that paved the way for members of the Christian Catholic faith to explore the faith traditions of others. Because of this institutional willingness to engage beyond the traditional scriptures of the Christian faith and in the tradition of the "recovery" of classical Greek philosophy during the time of Thomas Aquinas as well as the amazing work of the early Jesuits, Catholic theologians have pioneered in the field of interreligious and intercultural communication. Frank Clooney has continued this tradition, placing people and texts in dialogue with one another.

To echo Clooney's opening remarks, Vatican II, in part with input from Pope Benedict XVI, declared that truth is found in various traditions and cultures. It must be recognized and respected. *Nostra Aetate* proclaims that

> religions to be found everywhere strive variously to answer the restless searchings of the human heart by proposing "ways" which consist of teachings, rules of life, and sacred ceremonies. The Catholic Church rejects nothing which is true and holy in these religions. (*Nostra Aetate,* 2)

The text goes on to say that the world's religions "often reflect a ray of that Truth which enlightens all [people]" and that for Hinduism this includes a "searching philosophical inquiry" and that "Buddhism in its multiple forms acknowledges the radical insufficiency of this shifting world." My response will focus on the "searching philosophical inquiry of Hinduism," (*Nostra Aetate,* 2) particularly as it has manifested in Southern California.

India stretches one thousand miles from west to east, and one thousand miles from north to south. The western deserts contain the remnants of a long-lost civilization in the Indus River and Saraswati River valleys that flourished five thousand years ago. These early peoples traded with Egypt and Mesopotamia, and left ruins of impressive cities with running water. From their artifacts, it appears that these people venerated animals, held women in high regard, and developed what look to be early practices akin to yoga. Most likely due to over-irrigation of the adjacent farmland, these cities were abandoned, and a forest-based culture emerged traceable to the historical period. About twenty-five hundred year ago, while similar developments were occurring in Greece and in China, philosophers transmitted teachings that have determined the shape of Indian culture as we know it today. Oral texts such as the Vedas and the Upanishads, as well as the teachings of the Buddha and the Jina, formed the foundation for a broad civilization that for today's purposes we can refer to as Indic. The borders of Indic civilization stretched beyond modern India, and grew to include Indo-China (now referred to as Southeast Asia), and the archi-pelago of Indonesia. Perhaps India's most successful export has been Buddhism, which at one time stretched from Persia across Central Asia through East Asia and all the way to Hawaii, the only state in the Union that has more Buddhists than Roman Catholics.

What characterizes Indic thought? Frank Clooney has provided us with ten points that serve to describe the overarching characteristics of Hinduism, and I would like to affirm his observations as follows. Virtually all the traditions that arise in India stand in some relationship to its earliest sacred literature, the Vedas, either in alignment or in opposition. If we examine the early Vedic hymns, dating from thirty-five hundred years ago, they offer an interesting view of the origin and continuation of the universe. First, the frequently cited Hymn of Creation states that we cannot ever really know the origin of things, that even the Gods and Goddesses arose after Creation itself, and that the emergence of the world stems from human desire. Every human action, according to the Vedas and the Upanishads, wells up from stirrings deep within the human body and mind. By knowing one's own interior landscape one can discover the patterns of how other people behave and how society most optimally can be structured. The Upanishads are known for a series of great theological pronouncements (*mahavakyas*), including *Tat Tvam Asi* (you are that); God is one without a second; and that the deepest layers of one's spirit or *atman* connect with and reflect the nature of God (Brahman). The Upanishads also emphasize the importance of food, declaring food to be God, and the importance of the senses and particularly the breath. This emphasis on getting in touch with one's breath carried over into the devel-opment of Yoga exercises or Pranayama that allow one to understand the power and flow of breathing, an important part of the spiritual practice of Yoga.

Hinduism speaks positively about the presence of spirit or soul and advocates meditation and ritual as means to establish a connection through one's mind and body with higher states of awareness. Buddhism, on the other hand, protests that there is no abiding spirit, that all constructed phenomena including religious ritual and teachings, cannot accomplish the ultimate task of human existence, namely to identify the root cause of human desire and suffering, and, through meditation, systematically purify one's karma and achieve a state of transcendence known as nirvana. Otherwise, argued the Buddha, one is condemned to an endless round of meaningless pursuits, birth after birth.

A third major strand of Indic thought can be found in Jainism, which takes yet another approach. Rather than denying the existence of soul as in Buddhism, Jainism sees soul in all things: in clods of earth, in the bacteria-laden breeze, in plants, and of course in animals and humans. The path of Jainism, which boasts the world's oldest continuous religious orders (both men and women), mandates a scrupulous practice of nonviolence and has inspired Mahatma Gandhi.

Religious traditions in India also include Islam, which manifests in a very beautiful, devotional form deeply influenced by the Sufism of Rumi. Sikhism was born in India, inspired in part by the mystical poetry of Kabir. Other faith communities of note within India include the Parsis, who practice Zoroastrianism, an ancient form of Judaism that might have originated at the time of the Babylonian exile, and various styles of Christianity, including that of the Mar Thomas Christians of South India who, according to indigenous accounts, were converted by the apostle Thomas.

In his public remarks, Fr. Clooney suggested that Hinduism is less well known in America than Buddhism. In the section that follows, I will point out various ways in which key teachings of Hinduism, particularly Vedanta and Yoga, not only were well known in America since the nineteenth century but also helped shape foundational aspects of modern American thought, including the Transcendentalism of Emerson and Thoreau, and the Pragmatism of William James.

American fascination with Indian thought and practice began in the nineteenth century, when Transcendentalists discovered the newly translated texts of the Vedas and Upanishads. Emerson wrote a poem in honor of Brahman, and Thoreau declared himself to be a Yogi during his sojourn at Walden Pond. Academic discussions and essays gave way to a genuine culture encounter upon the convening of the Parliament of the World's Religions in Chicago in 1893. The most pronounced Hindu voice was set forth by Swami Vivekananda, whose address to the convention proclaimed a commonality among all faiths, and brought the audience to its feet.

Swami Vivekananda, who had been part of a monastic revival in India, subsequently traveled throughout North America and Europe, lecturing on Vedanta. His order established schools and hospitals throughout India, inspired in part by the Swami's dedication to bringing the benefits of modern technology to an India that had been largely impoverished by British colonial rule. He spent a fair amount of time in Pasadena, where he wrote the classic book *Raja Yoga*. His followers eventually opened the Vedanta Center in Hollywood, the Ananda Ashram in La Canada, Vivekananda House in Pasadena, a convent in Montecito, and a monastery in Tabruco Canyon in Orange County. In many ways, it can be said that the age of interreligious dialogue was born in Southern California. The famous short story writer Christopher Isherwood (whose writings eventually became famous as the musical *Cabaret*) came to study and live at the Vedanta Society in the 1940s and helped the Swami Prabhavananda publish several books that helped popularize Hindu ideas and practices, including a lyrical translation of the Bhagavad Gita and a translation of Patanjali's *Yoga Sutras* under the title *How to Know God*.

The Theosophical Society also arrived in Southern California early in the twentieth century. The mystic savant Madame Blavatsky and her successor Annie Besant discovered great wisdom in the traditions of India; their followers helped spark a Buddhist revival in Sri Lanka and a rediscovery on classical Yoga in South India. In addition to their international headquarters in Adyar, near modern Chennai, their organization maintained branches throughout the world, including South Central Los Angeles and in Hollywood. Annie Besant had arranged for a young South Indian Brahmin, Krishnamurti, to be groomed to assume leadership of the Theosophical Society, a task that he eventually rejected. In the 1920s, the Theosophical Society purchased extensive landholdings in Ojai, eventually developing the Krotona School and the Happy Valley School, while Krishnamurti's followers on adjacent property built the Krishnamurti Foundation of America and the Oak Grove School, all of which flourish today. Krishnamurti's numerous books have had a profound impact on American cultural ideas, particularly in the fields of counseling and scientific speculation.

Another shining star in the California Hindu pantheon was Paramahamsa Yogananda, who established the Self Realization Fellowship Shrine in the Pacific Palisades area of Los Angeles more than fifty years ago. Like Swami Vivekananda, he was a native of Calcutta (now known as Kolkata). Paramahamsa Yogananda wrote the *Autobiography of Yogi* in 1946, which is still in print and widely distributed. It has introduced Indian thought to three generations of Americans, and includes stories about his meetings with Calvin Coolidge, Luther Burbank, and Mahatma Gandhi. Gandhi took initiation in Kriya Yoga from Yogananda and a portion of Gandhi's ashes are interred at the Lake Shrine.

In the 1960s, with the countercultural revolution and the Beatles' popularization of things Indian, two different types of Yoga took up permanent residence in Los Angeles: Bhakti or devotional and Hatha or physical Yoga. A. C. Bhaktivedanta Swami Prabhupada established the International Society for Krishna Conciousness on Watseka Avenue near Culver City. This organization emphasizes devotion to Sri Krishna as the supreme deity beyond all others, developing a theology of worship that requires elaborate rituals and frequent prayers. For years, it has maintained an excellent vegetarian restaurant and boutique.

Swami Vishnudevananda, author of the *Complete Illustrated Guide to Yoga*, established the Sivananda Yoga Vedanta Center in Larchmont in the 1960s, which moved to Abbot Kinney Boulevard in the 1980s and is now on Ocean Avenue in Marina del Rey. Many of my students have participated in introductory Yoga posture classes there and many of the hundreds of Yoga teachers in Los Angeles have completed their teacher training, either in the Bahamas or in Kerala, South India.

Since the late 1980s and into the 1990s, Hatha Yoga studios have proliferated, most notably Anna Forest Yoga Academy and Yoga Works in Santa Monica, among countless others. Many of these teachers have trained in the lineage of a South Indian master, Sri Krishnamacharya, who taught Yoga to B. K. S. Iyengar, Patabhi Jois, B. K. S. Desikachar, and Srivatsa Ramaswami, who has been teaching through Loyola Marymount University's Center for Religion and Spirituality for several years.

Along with the cultural revolution that made Yoga in various forms widely popular in the 1960s, the civil rights movement brought profound changes to America's demographics. Because of the Chinese Exclusion Act of 1882, virtually no persons of Asian origin were allowed to settle in the United States. These bans on large-scale immigration were lifted in 1965 under the administration of Lyndon B. Johnson, as an extension of a governmental intention to undo all forms of prejudice in America. As a result, increased numbers of students migrated to America from India, as well as medical interns and engineers trained in India who were recruited for their expertise. Once these professionals became established, they sponsored other family members to immigrate to America.

What began with a core group of a few thousand has since expanded to more than two million souls with origins in India, most of whom practice the Hindu faith. Persons of Indian origin and Indian descent compose the wealthiest single ethnic group in America. Starting in the late 1970s these communities began building Hindu temples in the traditional style, starting in Pittsburgh, and then expanding to Queens, New York, and Malibu, California. Now there are hundreds of Hindu temples throughout North America, which serve both as sites for religious worship and as vehicles for the maintenance of Hindu culture.

The Hindu faith has fully entered into a place of cultural and philosophical prominence. Hundreds of American professors have been trained not only in classical languages of India including Sanskrit and Tamil but many have also learned vernacular languages such as Hindi and Gujarati. Several professional organizations and journals have emerged that seek to ask the big questions, once reserved for Christian theologians: how do Hindus regard the use of reproductive technology? genetic manipulation? environmental degradation? contemporary cosmology? treatment of animals? These questions and many others are being actively engaged by scholars and prominent members of the Hindu community, indicating a renewal and a maturity of a tradition that was was often in the past described by the British as world-denying, backward, and superstitious. More than fifteen million Americans practice Yoga on a regular basis, and many words that originate in Indian thought have become part of standard English usage, including *karma* and *dharma*.

Frank Clooney calls for friendship and mutual learning between Catholics and Hindus. Today, many Hindu home altars will include an image of Jesus alongside statues and representations of Hindu gods, goddesses, and saints. As Clooney has suggested, many Christian theologians have been inspired by the vast scope of imagination that characterizes the Hindu world. Advocates for social justice worldwide have all received guidance from Mahatma Gandhi, the famous Hindu who corresponded with Tolstoy. Gandhi built communal ashrams along egalitarian models, rankling many of his Hindu devotees who were uncomfortable working alongside persons of different castes and religions. Yet Gandhi stood firm in his affirmation that God dwells within each person and created a model for social engagement that has since been followed by Christian advocates of liberation theology.

Many years ago, boundaries between people and cultures and faiths were demarcated by skin tone, national allegiances, and deeply held beliefs. Today, throughout the world, we live in a state of constant migration, of continual encounter with difference. Frank Clooney has embraced the openness of this new world and provided excellent models through which to celebrate the joy of learning about and willingness to be changed by the ways of others.

A Response to Francis X. Clooney

SWAMI SARVADEVANANDA

I feel extremely honored to have been asked to respond to the thought-provoking presentation of Professor Francis Clooney of Harvard titled "Some Catholic Reflections on the Catholic-Hindu Encounter." I greatly admire and appreciate his positive approach to bridging the apparent distinctions of these two ancient religions, Hinduism and Christianity. Because his essay is based on his thirty-five years of contemplating Hinduism's "potential and actual place" in his own life, it conveys profound insights and understanding. This response highlights and develops a number of his points.

The Vedas and the Upanishads comprise the basic texts that Hindus consider foundational to their faith. Recent controversies about their dates of origin matter little so long as it is understood that these scriptures originated from the ancient Rishis (sages) of India who passed on for the edification of all mankind their direct perceptions of the Divine. Professor Clooney's suggestion that such texts arise from a "polytheistic heritage" highlights a critical point. Historically, Hindu worship has been disparaged by Christians as "idolatry" prohibited by biblical injunctions.[1] To eliminate any doubt on this issue it must emphatically be stressed that Hindus do not worship stones and blocks of wood. A casual observance of a Hindu worship ceremony may create such an impression, but a deeper understanding will demonstrate that through the use of symbols the Hindu approaches, in time, the realization of the limitless undivided consciousness of the Absolute, called Brahman. This realization dawns gradually at the end of a progression starting with devotion to various aspects of the Divine exemplified in one or more forms. The various symbols appeal to the worshipper's individual tastes and are "custom fit" to suit his mind's unique temperament and tendencies. However, images of Shiva, Kali, Rama, Krishna, Lakshmi, and Saraswati are considered to be only different facets of the same Reality. Contemplating deeply on a particular image of a God, Goddess, or incarnation, the Hindu worships the aspects of the indivisible Absolute represented in that form. These images eventually evoke an appreciation for the infinite attributes of God. Ultimately, they lead to the realization that the Absolute is too vast, too unknowable to be reduced to a single idea—and that He is not bound by our little notions of time, space, and causation.

It is by such constant contemplation on the Divine in its myriad forms that, step-by-step, the worshipper begins to recognize God's all-pervasiveness, which in turn frees him still further to approach an even greater mystery—that the Absolute lies beyond even the ken of his mind with all of its fleeting attractions and aversions. Taken in this light, these images, though apparently limited, compose an ever-broadening pathway to the direct perception of the Absolute, which pulsates at the back of every name and form. In similar fashion the holy cross stands through history as a sacred reminder of Christ's unflinching surrender to the will of the Father—His unlimited compassion—His redeeming mercy. The sacramental wine and bread, the holy cross, the crown of thorns—each persist in modern consciousness as profound symbols of Christ's sacrifice. From the image of the star of Bethlehem to the stone rolled away from His tomb, Christianity is replete with symbols that are not themselves truth, but which represent it, to remind us of Christ's divinity. The use of symbols is, moreover, a practical approach, for the mind cannot conceive of the unlimited except by means of symbolism.

Diversity is a fact of temporal life. It is not only nature that teems with diversity, religions branch out and sects multiply. Though centered on Christ, Christianity has developed into more than two hundred sects. Countless sects have arisen in Hinduism as well, giving freedom to individuals to approach the Infinite as their hearts' dictate. This diversity stands to reason, for the Creator has placed within man this indomitable quest for truth in all of its multifaceted expressions. To ascribe to that Creator, then, a rigid inflexible approach for realizing Him would ignore the vast infinitude of God. God has created this world and He is not finished with His creation; meaning that God is also beyond the creation. Hindus accept that God is not only immanent, but at the same time, transcendent; that this universe, the cosmos and beyond, is saturated with God. This is the realization of the sages of the Upanishads. That is why the great American philosopher William James said, "The paragon of all monistic systems is the Vedanta Philosophy of Hindostan."[2] Hinduism is not polytheistic or monotheistic—but it is monistic.

A question may arise whether all Hindus are monistic. True, there are followers of all types of philosophies among the Hindus. But wherever the aspirant may start his journey, he will ultimately arrive at one conclusive experience where he will lose all consciousness of body, mind, intellect, and ego until individual identity dissolves into infinite light, consciousness, bliss. The great saint of nineteenth-century India, Sri Ramakrishna, going to Samadhi; the experiences of the Christian mystics losing outward awareness; Ramana Maharshi's state of beyond-body consciousness—all these prove the accessibility of that truth.

The little body-bound ego merges into the cosmic limitless ego. This is the long sought-after experience at the core of all religions. The complete set of the Hindu tradition, described by Professor Clooney, is complex and difficult to understand except by focusing on the goal of all the religions. As Swami Vivekananda describes it:

> Each soul is potentially divine. The goal is to manifest this Divinity within, by controlling nature, external and internal. Do this either by work, or worship, or psychic control, or philosophy—by one or more or all of these—and be free. This is the whole of religion. Doctrines, or dogmas, or rituals, or books, or temples, or forms, are but secondary details.[3]

Our focus should go to the core of religion, to love all, to see God everywhere, and cast off all limitations. Man will not understand these goals unless his heart becomes pure by ceaseless prayer and meditation on God. Theological encounters give scope for understanding one another's paths so that we may develop not merely respect, but love for one another. Ultimately, we should attain that state of clarity when we will accept the Other's path as equally valid. Professor Clooney narrates the historic relationship of the Hindu and Catholic traditions to the present. As Swami Vivekananda stated:

> Thus in India there never was any religious persecution by the Hindus, but only that wonderful reverence, which they have for all the religions of the world. They sheltered a portion of the Hebrews, when they were driven out of their own country: and the Malabar Jews remain as a result. They received at another time the remnant of the Persians, when they were almost annihilated; and they remain to this day, as a part of us and loved by us, as the modern Parsees of Bombay. There were Christians who claimed to have come with St. Thomas, the disciple of Jesus Christ; and they were allowed to settle in India and hold their own opinions; and a colony of them is even now in existence in India. And this spirit of toleration has not died out. It will not and cannot die there.[4]

Today there are growing criticisms and reactions among Hindus against the methods used in some conversions to Christianity in India. Free, sincere, and openhearted dialogue between Christian and Hindu leaders in India can solve the disagreements on these points. Hindus have always welcomed witnesses to the gospel in India; only forceful conversions have been eschewed. Spreading the gospel of Christ is welcome so long as it does not result in the breaking of family bonds or in the destruction of social peace; so long as it respects each individual's right to answer the call of his heart without political pressure, fear of force, or economic duress. Honest, respectful dialogue will allow us to discern instances where evangelism devolves into brutal coercion taking unfair advantage of poverty, illiteracy, or political weakness. The solution lies in coming together with a focus on similarities that will engender mutual respect, not merely regard this as a political issue.

A review of the historical context through which Hindus have passed will supply an important component to understanding the Hindu frame of reference. For centuries, strong resentments have arisen among Hindus against orthodox Brahmins who aggressively enforced a caste system with all of its obvious evils, taking advantage of the poverty of the masses, treating them as outcasts and "untouchables" while beating their own drums and lauding themselves as supreme. Such oppressive denigration led to a backlash of resentment and intolerance among Indians toward any message that told them that they were inherently unworthy.

It is also helpful to an understanding of the Hindu mind to know that the Indian temperament has long been steeped in the concept that diversity is the natural course for society. From Vedic times the Hindus adopted the concept that "Truth is one—the sages call it by various names" (*Ekam Sat Viprah Bahudha Vadanti*). Thus it was easy for Hindus to accept Christ and His followers, to absorb and assimilate Christianity. Although not considering themselves Christian, many Hindus worship Christ as one of their beloved chosen ideals, as another incarnation of God. Christ has become a part of the spiritual tradition of India. All over the centers of the Ramakrishna Order in India and the Vedanta Societies in the Western world, Christmas is observed with great devotion. Christ is worshipped like any Hindu God. Sri Ramakrishna himself practiced Christianity, which resulted in a vivid vision of Christ. His disciple, Swami Brahmananda, had a similar vision of Christ during the reading of "The Sermon on the Mount" on Christmas. Swami Vivekananda too had a wonderful experience pertaining to Christ on his ocean passage past the island of Crete.

Professor Clooney observes that "Hindus seem in general to have been only minimally interested in Christian theology." This is very true. To bring them into dialogue, one should note the following characteristics. The majority of Hindus place less emphasis on discussing theological concepts than they do on following spiritual practices in their daily lives. Although Hindus respect the idea, given by their sages and scriptures, that intellectual understanding is of value, they place an even greater importance on the realization of God through a well-suited path. Moreover, due to the proliferation of sects in Hinduism, most Hindus consider Christianity as just another sect. And while sects, in and of themselves, are not considered bad, sectarianism itself is seen as a limitation to avoid. The Hindu would, accordingly, find it quite a foreign concept to be told that his worship of a particular god will lead to his own destruction but that adherence to another god would alone vouchsafe a place for him in heaven.

Hinduism can at least be classified into three main perspectives:

1. *Partisans*: The concept similar to its Christian counterpart that Christ is the only way to God can also be found among the practitioners of dualistic religions in India. Hinduism is not without its fanatics. This can be seen within the outer extremes of the practice of *Ishta-Nistha* (or intense love for one's own beloved chosen deity). This single-pointed focus of the lovers of Krishna, Shiva, Rama, Mother, and Christ on their chosen ideal has its benefits—such intense devotion is very much needed for God realization and thus such devotees are rare and very special. While there is a great depth to their practice, many of this type tend to lack broad-mindedness, as evidenced by the fact that they often cannot tolerate those from the "other" persuasion. They are like a frog living in a small well that believes that his well alone comprises the entire cosmos. This inability to look beyond their own perspective breeds intolerance, arrogance, dissension, and ultimately, war with others who do not follow their path. There is a story in the Purana that the devotees of Shiva and Rama in their unmitigated intolerance for one another, went on fighting, not knowing that He who is Shiva is also Rama! The history of the world is replete with the horrors of wars that have sprung from the rage of such fanatical exclusionism.

2. *Eclectics*: Eclectics are of a better mind-set. These aspirants appreciate the noble teachers of all religions and collect those teachings they consider the best. Selecting and practicing what they prefer and rejecting that which they dislike, they are doubtless broad-minded in their approach but they also tend to run on superficial cosmopolitanism. They may plunge into any path with wide-eyed abandon, as one would succumb to the enticements of a changing fad, but often with the unfortunate result of belittling the teachings that they then discard in favor of a newer season's trend. Through a succession of such unstructured selections they may indeed forge a new path of their own, but such path can often be devoid of spiritual vigor, due to the absence of any underpinnings in a long-standing saintly tradition. Although having its apparent benefits, this proclivity may create a danger of its own, for at such time as an experience or vision may arise, there will be none other there to proclaim that it is valid, as opposed to a mere hallucination of mind.

3. *Harmonizers*: The third perspective engenders synthesis and harmony. These aspirants recognize that diversity is the law of nature and that diverse religious paths are bound to exist. They focus deeply in their own journey just as the partisan does—but simultaneously they view others with a broadness of understanding that is as deep as the ocean and as vast as the sky. They carry an abiding respect and love for all others who call on God in another form. It is their

great delight to see that someone has developed a deep love of God by a different path. They lovingly accept every seeker as a fellow traveler on the spiritual journey. Mere tolerance for others is not a high enough ideal, because there is in that tolerance a cloaked sense of superiority. Acceptance is the idea of the Harmonizer.

All of our apparent conflicts could be readily dissolved if Hindus and Catholics could only take this third approach. Given their assimilating tendencies, it may perhaps be easier for the Hindu to follow the path of harmony, while it is more challenging for the Christian. One reason for this is that the theology of the Bible has often been interpreted in its most limited and exclusionary sense. When viewed from a broader perspective, it can be seen that when Christ stressed acceptance of Him, He did not solely mean acceptance of His name and form, so much as His message of unconditional love and unity. We see this breadth of understanding in the unparalleled lives of Christian saints who followed pointedly the path of love for all, which Christ's life exemplified. If we read the Sermon on the Mount, *The Imitation of Christ*, *The Way of The Pilgrim*, and similar spiritual texts, we cannot help finding the way to build up our spiritual lives, to generate an intense love for all, and to move into a single-pointed absorption in God. These texts, from which anyone can draw spiritual sustenance, are extremely catholic and universal in their approach. The lives of the saints exemplified therein stand as reminders of the command for unity, of the duty to love one another even as God has loved us. Dialogue on these lines can diffuse much misunderstanding.

The Second Vatican Council, as found in the *Nostra Aetate*, and the 2007 statement from the Vatican's Congregation for the Doctrine of Faith, cited by Professor Clooney, laud the importance of recognizing diverse religious traditions and contain the grounds for reconciliation. Professor Clooney's exposition of the parallels in Hindu and Christian traditions, and indeed his very search for such similarities, offers encouraging signs of progress that recognizes unity within diversity. We see in these two great religions similarities in the use of incense, candles, icons, prayers, prayer beads, and vigil. We find unity too in that all-important moment when every Hindu and Christian aspirant alike, at last laying aside his struggle and striving, surrenders himself to God. Austerity, prayer, devotion, selfless service, the absence of ego, humility, love, compassion, crying for the vision of God—these are the shared goals of both traditions, exemplified in the lives of saints of both traditions. The enlightened paths of holy saints from both traditions inspire us to expand our vision and fix our hearts and minds on the same goal, the direct perception of God.

Hindus, like Christians, can deepen their spiritual lives by making comparisons and initiating dialogue. Consider the following parallels. Hindus are inspired to think of the transcendent love that the cowherd girls bore for Krishna. Christians contemplate the love St. Teresa of Avila bore for Christ. The deep suffering of the stigmata born by St. Francis after intense meditations on Christ, recalls the sixteenth-century Indian saint Sri Chaitanya, whose body burned in the agony of his separation from his beloved Krishna. St. Francis's reference to the "noble treasure of holy poverty"[5] describes the same vow of austerity and poverty assumed by the Hindu monk and devout householder. Intention of the heart, not so much as outward expression, is the key. St. Francis "converted a very great multitude of men and women from a state of sin to remorse and penance,"[6] reminding us that what is needed is a conversion, not to a dogma, but to a selfless heart; a transformation, not to the exclusionism of a sect, but to the openness and acceptance of a trusting child of God. The *Spiritual Canticle* of St. John of the Cross reveals his agonizing experience of the dark night of the soul, and in relief of the same, the living flame of love for his beloved Lord. It parallels the "Srimad Bhagavatam," wherein the cowherd girls' divine love for Krishna was expressed as unbearable anguish upon the least separation from Him, and unbounded joy at His return.

In the annals of history, we find several great people who came in India to harmonize conflicting beliefs. Emperor Ashok, Akbar, Guru Nanak, Sri Chaitanya, and other saints achieved great success in instilling harmony and left a deep impact on society. In the nineteenth century, one man's life stands as a shining example of this principle of harmony. Sri Ramakrishna, a simple, uneducated person, lived a life of intense spiritual practices and became the very embodiment of interfaith by experiencing the truth of each religion in which he immersed himself. He reconciled in a single life the apparent conflicts between dualism, qualified nondualism, and absolute dualism; God the personal (*savika-lpa*, or with form), God the impersonal (*nirvikalpa*, or without form); God the immanent, transcendent, and beyond. He also harmonized the different paths of spiritual discipline: knowledge, devotion, service, and yoga. People of various beliefs—whether Sikh, Christian, Muslim, Mother worshippers, or followers of Shiva, Krishna, or Rama—found in him a person who had reached the highest culmination of their path. This great ideal of harmony was brought to the West by Ramakrishna's exemplary disciple, Swami Vivekananda, who traveled the length and breadth of the United States spreading the ideal of harmony and unity.

These brilliant examples lead us to the ultimate experience, when we will know only oneness. This is the culmination of all dialogue—the experience of God. In that state, all doubts and intellectual confusions fall away. In such a man, the ego is destroyed, and bliss remains for him and through him, for the entire world. To have any value, our spirituality must be transformative, making us pure and humble, inspiring love for others without regard for differences in beliefs. As like calls unto like, the similarities of our beliefs will kindle an awareness of our interconnectedness. Diving deep into our own spiritual practice, our contemplation of God will expand the breadth of our vision. Unconditional love will arise in us from our proximity to Him. Focusing on external details and differences will be abandoned altogether. For as Sri Ramakrishna said, "You have come to the orchard to eat mangoes. Eat the mangoes. What is the good of calculating how many trees there are in the orchard, how many thousands of branches, and how many millions of leaves? One cannot realize Truth by futile arguments and reasoning."[7] Religion is the framework within which God's presence can flourish within us. But religion loses its inner significance when our attention becomes trapped into the little dogmas, doctrines, and sociopolitical issues that divide us.

Realized souls see God. They talk to Him as palpably as we talk to one another. St. Francis talked to God. A young friar fell unconscious when he "perceived a marvelous light completely surrounding St. Francis and in that light he saw Christ and the blessed Virgin Mary and St. John the Baptist and St. John the Evangelist and a great throng of angels, who were talking with St Francis."[8] Sri Ramakrishna lived in the world of visions, asking the Divine for guidance at every step. Therefore we see that these profound experiences are truly within our grasp; they are not relegated to the realms of fantastic historical accounts. As the lives of these saints instruct us, however, it will take a total transformation of our focus—an unconditional immersion in God. In that awareness, all limitations and divisions cease, comparisons and fear of others fall away. God alone remains.

Notes

1 See, for example, 1 Corinthians 9–10.
2 *World Thinkers on Ramakrishna-Vivekananda* edited by Swami Lokeswarananda (Calcutta: The Ramakrishna Mission Institute of Culture, 1992), 32.
3 *The Complete Works of Swami Vivekananda* (Kolkata: Advaita Ashrama, 2009): I:257.
4 Ibid., I:391.
5 *The Little Flowers of St. Francis*, trans. Raphael Brown (Garden City, N.Y.: Hanover House, 1958), 68.
6 Ibid., 107.
7 *The Gospel of Sri Ramakrishna* (New York: Ramakrishna Vivekananda Center, 2007), 496.
8 Ibid., 78–79.

Francis X. Clooney Continues the Dialogue

FRANCIS X. CLOONEY, S.J.

I am grateful to Professor Christopher Chapple and Swami Sarvadevananda for their generous responses to my lecture; they are particularly gracious, since I spoke rather informally at our meeting, sharing with them in advance only a very detailed outline of the comments I would make, along with a related article. Now that they have read my written text, and I have read their responses, I all the more appreciate the exchange, and am particularly glad to see one of my basic hopes confirmed: the Hindu-Christian encounter has to be worked out in actual, multilevel dialogue, by the kinds of practices I have suggested—and so, almost by definition, continues to evolve over time. My respondents give concrete specificity to my comments, with further insights into Hinduism in the context of the United States (Chapple) and as synthesized in accord with the Ramakrishna Vedanta Society's understanding of Hinduism (Sarvadevananda).

Professor Chapple helpfully reminds us of the vivid and growing presence of Hinduism in nineteenth- and twentieth-century America and how very many Americans have eagerly taken up yoga in particular. These facts cannot be denied, even if, as I would still claim, Hinduism has less of a hold on the American mind and imagination, and less a place in the media, than Buddhism and Islam. It is not incidental that there is a relatively smaller group of Americans of non-Indian origin willing to call themselves "Hindu," while "American Buddhists" are quite common. Admittedly, this may have to do not with a lack of Hindu presence in America, but with the complicated nature of Hinduism—which, as I acknowledge in my lecture, is hard to pin down for the sake of concise claims or media consumption. It may also have to do with the close intersection between "being-Indian" and "being-Hindu" in the minds of many people, including Hindus. Few of us imagine that to practice Zen or Vipassana we need to become Japanese or Burmese, whereas "Hinduism" seems for many to entail a familial and cultural commitment as well as a religious one, as if by religious conversion one, as it were, marries into a large Indian family. Accordingly, perhaps, many people who welcome swamis or practice yoga do not think of themselves as also choosing Hinduism.

Professor Chapple is correct in pointing to the growing presence of Hindus from all parts of India in American life, as full participants in conversations about the issues that face us today, ranging from reproductive technology to the environment to the quality of education. This dialogue—pervasive and ongoing—might still be cultivated in the ways I have suggested, but the starting point is that "we Americans" are Hindu as well as Catholic, and we will always be engaged in implicit, lived dialogues on many issues beyond the explicitly religious ones.

In his many fine insights Swami Sarvadevananda does what is fundamentally necessary for any future growth of Hindu-Christian understanding: he brings an actual Hindu voice, of a particular Hindu community, into the dialogue. Readers will note that not everything Swami says about the essence of Hinduism and the vision of God affirmed by theistic and monistic seers fits easily with my characterization of Hinduism. This is perfectly fine, since a Vedanta Society swami and a Catholic priest are fortunate when we have complementary viewpoints; we need not expect identical opinions. We do well to hear and learn from different perspectives, both voices from within our traditions and voices, from outside, showing us how we look to others, and our exchange can enrich both our appreciations of the Hindu-Christian relationship.

Swami Sarvadevananda also gives honest and helpful insights into the history of Hinduism as reflected upon by modern Hindus, for instance regarding abuses related to caste, and we all need to take such insights seriously, just as we likewise celebrate the importance of diversity in the tradition. In dialogue, it is often easier for us to be tough on our own tradition while more gentle and respectful with the other, and so even in this oblique way we face truths about ourselves by speaking with people of another faith tradition. Swami's classification of Hindus as partisans, eclectics, and harmonizers—distinctions of course applicable to other traditions as well—is helpful. It reminds us that if Catholics and other Christians find it hard to come up with a single Christian view of religions, there is no reason to expect that Hindus would have a single, simple attitude toward us. For my part, I would be sympathetic with the partisans as well as the harmonizers, given how powerfully partisans can communicate to us the truth of their own traditions. In some dialogues, it is most interesting to speak with partisans.

Our Hindu-Catholic relationship is not driven by the same history or urgency as the Jewish-Catholic and Muslim-Catholic dialogues, and there is work to be done if it is not to be taken for granted and left in abeyance. I hope my comments, enriched and complexified by those of Professor Chapple and Swami Sarvadevananda, provide a realistic sketch of what we need to think about and do, so that our relationship can thrive and, in word and spirit, go well beyond the generalities of "Christian" and "Hindu" that too often dominate discussions of dialogue.

SUGGESTIONS FOR FURTHER READING

1. Francis X. Clooney, S.J., *Comparative Theology: Deep Learning across Religious Borders* (Malden, Mass.: Wiley-Blackwell, 2010). A study of learning across religious borders, with particular attention given to the Hindu and Catholic traditions.

2. Francis X. Clooney, S.J., *Hindu Wisdom for All God's Children* (Maryknoll, N.Y.: Orbis, 1998; Eugene, Ore.: Wipf and Stock, 2005). A theologically attuned introduction to seven major themes in Hinduism, with attention given to how Christians can learn from them.

3. Anantanand Rambachan, *The Advaita Worldview: God, World, and Humanity* (Albany: State University of New York Press, 2006). A leading contemporary Hindu theologian's reflections, grounded in Hindu nondualism, yet open to a renewed thinking about God.

4. Bob Robinson, *Christians Meeting Hindus: An Analysis and Theological Critique of the Hindu-Christian Encounter in India* (Oxford: Regnum, 2005). A survey and analysis of how Hindus and Christians have interacted over the centuries and particularly in recent decades.

5. Michelle Voss Roberts, *Dualities: A Theology of Difference* (Louisville: Westminster/John Knox, 2010). A fresh new inquiry into duality and nonduality, seen in light of medieval Christian and Hindu women's mystical writings.

5

Off the Map

The Catholic Church and Its Dialogue with Buddhists

JAMES L. FREDERICKS

In the fall of 1549, Francis Xavier, SJ, began a series of conversations with the Venerable Ninshitsu, a Zen monk of the Sōtō sect and abbot of Fukushōji Temple in Kagoshima, Japan. Ninshitsu welcomed the Catholic saint warmly. In November of that year, Xavier wrote to Ignatius Loyola reporting that "this Ninshitsu is an amazingly good friend of mine."[1] No doubt, part of the reason behind this warm reception is the fact that the Zen monk presumed that his strange new friend, so different in other respects, was a Buddhist like himself. Xavier had arrived at Fukushōji tonsured and in flowing robes, as any respectable monk would. Furthermore, he spoke reverently of *Dainichi* and *Hotoke-sama* (Xavier's translator, a Japanese convert to Christianity named Anjirō, rendered the Portuguese *Dios* using the name of the cosmic Buddha that is the source of the universe and *Señor Jesus* simply as "Lord Buddha"). Most of all, Xavier had come to Japan from fabled *Tenjiku*, the Japanese word for India, the land where the *dharma* had first been preached. This came as a great surprise to Xavier, because, two years earlier, while Xavier was still in India, Anjirō had told him about *Tenjiku*, which lay "beyond Tartary" according to Anjirō, never realizing that he was in *Tenjiku* at the time. Xavier had resolved that, after converting Japan and Cathay, he would move on to convert the land where the religion of the monks had originated. Xavier's Buddhist friend, Ninshitsu, however, had his geography straight, referring to Xavier as a *Tenjiku-jin*, or a "man of *Tenjiku*" and presuming that Xavier was bringing a new *sutra* for study (Anjirō was translating *scriptura* as *O-kyō*, the Japanese term for *sutra*).

The Roman Catholic dialogue with Buddhists has come a long way since the initial conversations of St. Francis Xavier and the Ven. Ninshitsu. In 1996, for example, Buddhist and Catholic monks met at the Trappist Abbey in Gethsemani, Kentucky—Thomas Merton's monastery—at the request of the Dalai Lama, who, as a young monk, had met Merton there. The meeting brought together Theravada, Mahayana, and Varjayana monks with Benedictines, Trappists, and Catholic laypeople for discussions in-depth on topics such as ultimate reality and spiritual practice, prayer and meditation, community life and spiritual direction, social responsibility and the virtuous life.[2]

In this essay, I will argue that the Roman Catholic dialogue with Buddhists, perhaps more than any other of the church's dialogues, drives us off our theological road map of religions. This "road map," articulated most authoritatively by Pope John Paul II, provides a comprehensive Christian theological interpretation of the meaning and status of other religions, vis-à-vis the Roman Catholic Church. Our dialogue with Buddhism runs us off this map. By no means do I think this situation is lamentable. In fact, I welcome it. Buddhism's refusal to appear in its assigned place on the map demonstrates that the time has come for us to shift our energies from the need for a comprehensive Christian theological interpretation of Buddhism to the project of entering into dialogue in-depth with Buddhists where they are: off the map. The Catholic Church needs to shift from theological thinking *about* Buddhism to thinking theologically *with* Buddhists. Specifically, I want to make three points.

First, I want to give a sketch of Pope John Paul II's theology of religions. The last pope, in a series of encyclicals over his long papacy, developed a comprehensive Christian theological interpretation of the meaning and status of other religions in relation to the Catholic Church. I will claim that the pope's theology of religions adequately responds to the demands that Christian faith places on us in our attempts to understand the meaning of religious diversity. By "adequate," I mean that this theology precludes any exclusivist view of the principle *extra ecclesiam nulla salus* (outside the church, no salvation). The pope's view of other religions also rules out the relativism of what is often called the "pluralist" philosophy of religions. In doing so, John Paul II has succeeded in responding to the twofold demand that Christian faith imposes on any theological interpretation of the diversity of faiths: (1) the centrality of Christ (which implies the integral role of the church) in the economy of salvation, and (2) the universality of the offer of grace in the Incarnation of the Word and the continuing work of the Holy Spirit. The pope meets these criteria by means of a "fulfillment theology"[3] that recognizes that the religious aspirations of all human beings find their ultimate fulfillment in the one mediation of grace, which is Christ, witnessed to by the church.

Second, I will argue that, although John Paul II's fulfillment theology is adequate to the demands of Christian orthodoxy, this theology is not helpful in regard to the church's responsibility to engage other religious communities in interreligious dialogue. Moreover, I believe that the inadequacy of the pope's fulfillment theology is perhaps nowhere more visible than in our dialogue with Buddhists. Catholics with expertise in the dialogues with Jews, Hindus, Muslims, Jains, Daoists, and others no doubt will have their own observations to offer regarding the adequacy of the pope's theology of religions as a basis for their dialogues. For that matter, their dialogue partners may have comments to offer as well. My point is simply that significant problems arise when the church's official theology of religions is employed as a framework for dialogue with the Buddhist community. I base this statement on my years of dialogue with Theravada, Mahayana, and Vajrayana Buddhists in the United States, Japan, China, and Taiwan.

My third point has to do with properly appreciating the pope's achievement. His Christian theological interpretation of the meaning and soteriological status of other religions may be inadequate to the needs of the church in its dialogue with Buddhists, but I will not propose that it be put aside. Instead, I will recommend that we recognize that a sea change has occurred in the Catholic Church. A fifty-year period of theological development has come to a successful completion in the theology of John Paul II. In this half-century, Catholics have moved from an aggressively apologetic posture in regard to other religious traditions, to an attitude of openness and even esteem for the other religious paths. I recognize that this transformation has been uneven and inconsistent at times, but even still, there has been a genuine change in Catholics from the back pew in the local parish to the Apostolic Palace in the Vatican that is not to be dismissed. Although I do not think the pope's theology should be abandoned, I do think we must recognize that his theological achievement brings a period of intellectual development to an end. Catholics now have a comprehensive Christian theology for interpreting the meaning of other religions. And this comprehensive theory is not adequate to the needs of the church in regard to interreligious dialogue, at least dialogue with Buddhists. Thus, I recommend that we shift away from this concern for *theoria* (a theology of religions that answers to the demands of Christian faith) to the actual *praxis* of dialogue with those who follow other religious paths.

John Paul II and the Council

In his encyclical *Redemptoris Missio* (1990), John Paul II cites the Gospel of John to the effect that "the Spirit blows where he wills" (John 3:8). "I have repeatedly called this fact to mind," the pope writes, "and it has guided me in my meetings with a wide variety of peoples."[4] The pope's readers may confidently assume that "wide variety of peoples" refers to those who follow other religious paths, for John Paul goes on to offer a comment on his famous (and to some, infamous) meeting in Assisi in 1986, where he gathered together with leaders of various religious communities for prayer.

> Excluding any mistaken interpretation, the interreligious meeting held in Assisi was meant to confirm my conviction that every authentic prayer is prompted by the Holy Spirit, who is mysteriously present in every human heart.[5]

The Assisi meeting, therefore, was a reflection of the pope's pneumatology. The Holy Spirit, who "blows where he wills," can be discerned within the hearts of believers who follow different religious paths. John Paul's interest in establishing a comprehensive theology of religions in pneumatology remained with him throughout his long pontificate.

This concern can be traced as a thread winding through several of his encyclicals. For example, in *Redemptor Hominis* (1979), his first encyclical, the pope sees in the belief of non-Christian believers an "effect of the Spirit of truth operating outside the visible confines of the Mystical Body," which is so impressive that Christians should be "ashamed at being often themselves so disposed to doubt concerning the truths revealed by God and proclaimed by the Church."[6] In *Dominus et Vivificantem*, speaking of the Spirit's role in binding us to the saving mystery of Christ's death and resurrection, the pope cites *Gaudium et spes* 22 which states that "we ought to believe that the Holy Spirit, in a manner known only to God, offers to every man the possibility of being associated with this Pascal Mystery." (DV 53).

The background to the pope's pneumatology can be found in *Gaudium et spes*, the "Pastoral Constitution on the Church" of the Second Vatican Council. According to this document, "the Christian man" has been "conformed to the likeness of [the] Son" by the Holy Spirit. Furthermore, this Spirit "renews" the whole man.[7] After noting this, the Pastoral Constitution goes on to make an observation that will be decisive for John Paul:

> All this holds true not only for Christians, but for all men of good will in whose hearts grace works in an unseen way. For, since Christ died for all men, and since the ultimate vocation of man is in fact one, and divine, we ought to believe that the Holy Spirit in a manner known only to God offers to every man the possibility of being associated with this paschal mystery.[8]

The pope's frequent citation of this passage from *Gaudium et spes* is an indication of the emphasis he places on the universal activity of the Holy Spirit in the lives of all human beings. Human beings, in their vast diversity, are called to one and the same supernatural destiny. Therefore, the Spirit's offer of incorporation into the Paschal Mystery must be in some sense available to all. Let me note, however, that *Gaudium et spes* has little to say regarding the nature of this universal offer of salvation, except to say that grace is active invisibly in the hearts of all individuals of goodwill, presumably including individuals of goodwill who are not baptized Christians.

Gaudium et spes, par. 22 makes clear that the offer of salvation is universal. All human beings, regardless of their religious practice, can be saved through the activity of the Holy Spirit. What does this mean, however, in regard to the soteriological status of the other religious paths? Are Buddhists and Muslims, Hindus and Jains, Baha'is and Zoroastrians saved in spite of their religious beliefs and practices? Or can we say that the Holy Spirit touches a Buddhist by means of her practice of the *dharma*? *Gaudium et spes*, and the council as a whole for that matter, is unambiguous about the offer of saving grace to non-Christian believers. The soteriological efficacy of the other religious traditions, however, is a question left unresolved by the council. The point to be taken here is not that the council refused to address the issue, but rather that the various statements made by the council are inconclusive or ambiguous, allowing for a conflict of interpretations.[9]

For example, in *Ad gentes*, 3, the council teaches that "the universal design of God for the salvation of the human race is carried out not only, as it were, secretly in the soul of a man." This language seems to be at variance with *Gaudium et spes*, par. 22, which teaches that grace is active invisibly. In *Ad gentes*, Christian believers should expect to find the saving work of the Spirit mediated by social institutions, which presumably would include religious institutions. Religions, however, are not mentioned. In fact, religions might be intended for inclusion among the "attempts" that need to be "enlightened and healed," as noted further on in section three of *Ad gentes*. In contrast, *Lumen Gentium*, 17, teaches that grace is available not only in the hearts of individuals, but also in their rites and customs. As with *Ad gentes*, 3, the text does not refer to religions explicitly, even though excluding religious traditions from the category "rites and customs" would seem to require a very contrived reading of the document.

The roots of the council's ambiguity can be traced back to preconciliar theological discussions in Europe concerning other religious traditions.[10] The work of Henri deLubac, Hans Urs von Balthasar, and Jean Daniélou, S.J., was widely influential at the council on a variety of topics, including its multiple statements on the status of those who follow other religious paths. Generally, these theologians took a cautious approach to the question. According to Daniélou, other religions are "touching and often very beautiful attempts" on the part of human beings to know God.[11] Christianity, however, must be distinguished from other religions. In Christianity, the universal human quest for God is fulfilled with a supernatural grace that is not available in other religions. To be sure, the other religious paths offer to their adherents a real knowledge of God, universally available through human reason. Moreover, this preliminary knowledge has a supernatural finality. The religious belief of these other religions, however, must be placed in stark contrast with the "supernatural faith" enjoyed by Christians, which comes only from God's active intervention into the human quest for the divine in the unfolding of a history of salvation that begins with Abraham and culminates in Christ. Based on this scholastic distinction between the natural light of reason and supernatural grace, Daniélou concludes that all the religions of the world, with the singular exception of Christianity, are human creations of the natural order.

Also visible in the council documents is the work of theologians such as Gustave Thils, H. R. Schlette, and Karl Rahner, S.J. Rahner's basic position is that the other religious paths cannot be taken by Christians to be merely natural expressions of the human quest for God. Hinduism and Islam, Buddhism and Daoism, to say nothing of Judaism, are supernatural fulfillments of that quest. Therefore, the other religions are intended by God for the salvation of human beings. As with Daniélou's theology of religions, Rahner's views hinge on a theology of grace. According to Rahner, the human person is not related to God in a purely private and interior way. Grace, because it is always becoming incarnate, cannot be separated from the social and cultural lives of human beings. This requires Christians to recognize that grace is mediated to human beings by their own religious beliefs and practices. Furthermore, the grace that is mediated must be recognized as supernatural: God willfully entering into the history of specific human beings with the intention of incorporating them into the divine plan of salvation. Rahner's theology of grace leads to two conclusions. First, Rahner concludes that the other religions cannot be seen as merely natural expressions of human wisdom. Buddhism, for example, cannot be merely a *preparatio evangelii* (a preparation for the gospel) and nothing more. The religions must be recognized as the result of supernatural acts of God that make saving grace available to human beings. Second, those who follow other religious paths must be related to the church—not formally incorporated into the Paschal Mystery by baptism, but in some mysterious way.[12] This is because there is but one great mediation of grace: Jesus Christ present in his Mystical Body, the church.

The ambiguity of the council regarding the soteriological value of the other religious paths plays out in terms of this contrast between Daniélou's more restrictive and Rahner's more expansive understanding of the working of grace. For example, in *Ad gentes*, 3, the council speaks of the attempts, even religious attempts, of the human race to "seek after God" and finding God "perchance."

Furthermore, these attempts need to be "enlightened and healed." Even still, the other religious paths are not evil or worthless for they "may sometimes serve as leading strings toward God, or as a preparation for the Gospel" and thus find their fulfillment in Christian faith. The text represents Daniélou's theology of religions. But this very same section also leaves open the door to a Rahnerian approach when it says "this universal design of God for the salvation of the human race is carried out not only, as it were, secretly in the soul of a man." An openness to Rahner's theology of religions can also be seen in *Gaudium et spes*, 22, where it states that "we ought to believe that the Holy Spirit in a manner known only to God offers to every man the possibility of being associated with this paschal mystery." Statements such as these must not be overinterpreted. They move in a Rahnerian direction to the extent that they recognize grace to be operative and efficacious in the lives of people who are not Christians. They do not go as far as Rahner does in explicitly recognizing the other religious paths as mediations of Christ's salvation.

These considerations about the Second Vatican Council provide a context for interpreting the contribution of John Paul II to the discussion. The pope, in his ordinary magisterium, moves decidedly beyond the council by taking a Rahnerian approach to the theology of religions. Of course, I am not claiming that John Paul is indebted to Rahner himself. Instead, I am claiming that the pope resolves the ambiguity of the council by turning to a pneumatology in which the working of the Holy Spirit is recognizable within the concrete, social, and cultural contexts of the human person—much as Karl Rahner argued. For the pope, the Holy Spirit is at work in every genuine human act of transcendence. And, in keeping with his phenomenological approach to the human person, these acts of transcendence cannot be separated from our material, social, and cultural life. Therefore, the saving grace of the Holy Spirit empowers the human person's self-realization through self-transcendence by means of our "rites and customs" as taught in *Ad gentes*, 3. This must mean that a Buddhist is touched by God's grace by means of Buddhist religious practice, not despite it.

Some twenty years after Vatican II, Rahner commented on the council's caution and ambiguity regarding the soteriological value of religions other than Christianity. An essential problem for the church's theologians was left open by the council, he observed.[13] Now, forty years after the promulgation of *Nostra Aetate* and with the completion of John Paul II's pontificate, we can recognize that the pope has taken the council's restraint as the starting point for his teaching, not the end point. The pope looked on the council's ambiguity as an opportunity to respond to the church's need for a comprehensive theology of religions fully responsive to the demands of Christian faith. In section 28 of *Redemptoris Missio* (1990), for example, the pope teaches that the Spirit's "presence and activity are universal" and that the working of the Spirit is to be found "in human initiatives—including religious ones—and in mankind's efforts to attain truth, goodness and God himself." The pope's willingness to mention religious initiatives explicitly must be placed against the hesitancy of the council in this regard. And that the pope sees this explicit reference to religions as an interpretation of the council is evident in his copious citations of *Ad gentes* and *Gaudium et spes*.[14]

The Spirit's saving work in the other religious traditions, however, does not make the church superfluous. Neither can the Spirit's activity be understood as an economy of salvation competing with that of Christ. In par. 10 of *Redemptoris Missio*, for example, John Paul teaches that, for those who have not entered the church by means of baptism,

> salvation in Christ is accessible by virtue of a grace which, while having a mysterious relationship to the Church, does not make them formally part of the Church but enlightens them in a way which is accommodated to their spiritual and material situation.[15]

He then goes on to cite par. 22 of *Gaudium et spes* once again, where the council affirms Catholic belief that all human beings are called to one and the same divine destiny and that, therefore, Christians must recognize the fact that the Holy Spirit offers to all human beings the possibility of being associated with the Paschal Mystery "in a manner known only to God." In my view, par. 10 of *Redemptoris Missio* is best read in light of par. 5 of that same encyclical, where the pope stresses Christ's one, universal mediation but also recognizes the possibility of "participated forms of mediation of different kinds and degrees"[16] in which other religious communities share, in various ways but always by means of the Holy Spirit, in the one saving mediation of grace that is Christ. These forms of mediation cannot be understood as "parallel or complementary" to Christ's universal mediation. Thus John Paul II is both grounded in the council and moving beyond it by means of a theology of the universal activity of the Holy Spirit. The Second Vatican Council was unambiguous in affirming that other religious believers can be saved. The pope goes a step further in teaching that the other religions are mediations of the grace of Christ, the unique mediator, through the universal work of the Holy Spirit. Buddhists, according to this theology of religions, are saved, not despite their practice of the *dharma*, but by means of it. This is because the Buddhist community is linked in some way to Christ and the church. The *dharma* is not salvific, at least in the Christian understanding of salvation, in its own right.

Let me summarize these considerations in three points. First, John Paul II's theology of religions responds to the demands of Christian faith. It recognizes the uniqueness of Christ as the one mediation of grace and simultaneously affirms the universality of the offer of grace rooted in the activity of the Holy Spirit within every authentic act of transcendence. Second, the pope's pneumatology recognizes that other religious believers are saved by means of their religious practices, not in spite of them. This affirmation, however, must not be interpreted as meaning that religions are paths to salvation independent of the Christ-event and the church as its continuation within history. Instead, the pope recognizes the other religions as "participated forms of mediation" of the grace of Christ and that, therefore, religious believers are related in some mysterious way to the church. In this respect, the pope's theology of religions serves as a corrective to exclusivist interpretations of *extra ecclesiam nulla salus* as well as to relativist approaches to religious diversity in which Christianity is construed as one path among others.[17] Third, this theology of religions is a theology of fulfillment. Although the universal human religious quest is marked by the grace of the Holy Spirit, this quest finds its ultimate fulfillment in an explicit Christian faith in Christ and membership in the church. Thus, even while affirming the soteriological value of other religious traditions, John Paul II sees the relationship between the many religious paths and Christianity as one of aspiration and fulfillment.

The Dialogue with Buddhists

How are we to evaluate this theological road map of religious diversity? John Paul II's fulfillment theology brings to a conclusion fifty years of reflection on the meaning and soteriological value of other religious traditions. Catholic thinking about other religions has moved from the triumphalism of *extra ecclesia*, at least in its exclusivist interpretation, to the relative openness of "participated forms of mediation." In this, the pope's achievement is to have provided the church with a theology of religions that is responsive to the multiple demands of Christian faith. Fidelity to the demands of tradition, however, is not the sole criterion for evaluating a theology of religions. Like theology in general, the pope's pneumatological approach to religious diversity must be judged not only in terms of its fidelity to tradition but also by its ability to serve the pastoral needs of the church. In this latter regard, I do not believe that John Paul II's response to the religious diversity of the world can be counted a success. At least, this is the case in regard to the church's dialogue with Buddhism. In this regard, I want to address a very practical problem that confronts Catholics when the official fulfillment theology is used as a theological foundation for interreligious dialogue: what I call "the domestication of difference."

The tendency to marginalize and control difference and privilege similarity must be recognized as an unwelcome epiphenomenon of the Catholic Church's fulfillment theology of religions. This confronts us with a theological *aporia*: a fulfillment theology is demanded by the richness of Christian faith, and yet this very theology also amounts to a rhetorical strategy that results in keeping not only the threat but also the transformative power, of the Other under control. This problem can be seen in Roman Catholicism's preconciliar exclusivist theology. The destabilizing power of the other religions (in both their similarity and difference) was kept safely at bay under a rubric of "error," or "natural religion," and so forth. The church's current fulfillment theology has not freed itself from this tendency to defend against the power of the Other. The destabilizing and potentially transformative power of the other religions is safely handled by reducing them to the status of a "preparation for the gospel" (*preparatio evangelii*) or "seed of the Word" (*Logos spermatikos*) or a "participated form of mediation" of the same saving grace of Christ witnessed to by Roman Catholics.[18] Perhaps no one should be surprised that the need to defend oneself from the destabilizing power of the Other should take the form of reducing that Other to a paler and unthreatening version of oneself. Be that as it may, I want to argue that the church's fulfillment theology leads to a domestication of difference in which the religious Other is rendered a relatively obscure reflection of the same truths witnessed to more explicitly in Christianity. This phenomenon is especially evident in our dialogue with Buddhism. Once difference is safely domesticated, Buddhism no longer poses a challenge to Christianity. The strangeness of Buddhism will never require me as a Christian to think in new ways about my faith. Therefore, when employed as a basis or framework for interreligious dialogue, the church's theology of religions has the perhaps unintended but decidedly unhelpful effect of cutting us off from the transforming power of the encounter with other religious believers. Let me offer several examples taken from my own experience of dialogue with Buddhists.

The Zen philosopher Shin'ichi Hisamatsu was the teacher of one of my own Buddhist teachers, Masao Abe. Hisamatsu used to speak of Zen as the "negation of holiness."[19] In Hisamatsu's view, the "holiness" that Zen negates is not an ethical quality (the moral purity of the saints, for example). Hisamatsu meant the holiness of God as the supreme Thou, which is not contained within the world, but rather transcends the world as its Creator. The holiness that Zen negates is the otherness of the God of Abraham, Isaac, and Jacob, the supreme subjectivity that Karl Barth often called *Ganz Anderer* (the Wholly Other). The aim of Zen practice, according to Hisamatsu, is not to connect with this transcendent Creator by means of faith. In fact, Zen does not seek to transcend this world at all. According to Hisamatsu, Zen teaches that the holiness and otherness of Christianity's Hebraic God must be negated in the process of "awakening" to reality in its pure immanence. Only after the negation of the holiness of God does the "true suchness of all" (what Japanese Buddhists call *shin-nyo*) arise. Hisamatsu's Zen constitutes a dramatic alternative to the Hebraic legacy in Christian theism. In place of the transcendent majesty and supreme subjectivity of Barth's "Wholly Other," Zen directs us to awaken to the pure immanence of the world in its "suchness," or what my teacher Masao Abe calls "wonderous being."[20]

If we take Buddhists like Hisamatsu and Abe at their word, Christians must come to the conclusion that Zen and Christianity have very different ways of construing ultimate reality and the goal of religious practice. In fact, in "true suchness" and the "holiness" of the Maker of heaven and earth, Buddhists and Christians would seem to be talking about dramatically different realities. This difference should be of great theological interest to Christians. Zen challenges the Hebraic legacy in the Christian doctrine of God by providing a genuinely religious alternative to it. This challenge carries with it opportunities for Christian reflection on the doctrine of creation and environmental ethics, to say nothing of the theology of revelation. Recognizing this difference would not only be helpful to Christians in recognizing something important about Buddhism as a religion but it might also allow Christians to begin to ask difficult questions about the doctrine of God that cannot arise from within a purely Christian standpoint. Let me also add that if Zen's "suchness" negates the transcendence of the Christian God, then the Christian God negates Zen's "suchness" as well, providing an opportunity for further dialogue with Buddhists in greater depth. For now, I only want to establish that difference ought to be of genuine theological interest in our dialogues with Buddhists. Difference marks the beginning of dialogue, not its end. However, when Catholics take the official fulfillment theology of religions as a guiding principle for dialogue, this uncomfortable theological disparity separating Buddhism and Christianity is pushed to one side in order to give attention to points of Buddhist doctrine and practice that seem familiar and comfortable to Christian believers. The focus of dialogue is safely restricted to meditation practices, for instance, and their relationship to established Christian spiritual principles, such as the notion of spiritual abandonment or "abiding within God." A fulfillment theology that directs us to look for the Holy Spirit at work in the lives of our dialogue partners aids and abets this domestication of difference. Let me state once again that my view is not that the fulfillment theology is wrong. In fact, I believe that it is demanded by Christian faith. Rather, my point is that this theology of religions is not suitable as a basis for dialogue, at least not suitable for dialogue with Buddhists.

My second example has to do with my dialogues with Buddhists in Japan and China on the role of anger in our spiritual practices. In Buddhist tradition, anger is counted, along with ignorance and craving, as one of the "three poisons."

The Buddhist placement of anger among the three poisons seem to be roughly equivalent to what the Christian spiritual tradition intends by including anger on the list of the "seven deadly sins." The Christian notion of righteous anger, however, is a major stumbling block for Buddhists. Once, in Los Angeles, I was involved in a discussion with Theravada monks who were complaining about rude behavior and aggressive proselytizing by (some) Evangelical Christians. I recommended that we begin to document these incidents and eventually take this information to Evangelical pastors to enlist their leadership in addressing this problem. A monk from Sri Lanka objected. The proper practice of the *dharma*, he noted, does not allow monks to remember insults. Anger and pride are signs of the illusion of selfhood and must be renounced. I answered that, in this case, the anger was justified by the injustice being suffered by the monks. My Buddhist friend replied that, like attachment to anger, the attachment to justice must also be renounced.

In my view, the deep suspicion that Buddhists harbor in regard to what Christians consider the virtue of "righteous anger" is theologically significant. Buddhists and Christians have different ways of imagining human flourishing and the virtues that promote this flourishing. For my Theravada Buddhist friend, no anger can be "righteous," or as he would put it, "skillful." Anger remains a poison to be renounced. The notion that some anger is "justified" by hope in the coming kingdom of God is simply unintelligible to most of the Buddhists I know. Basing our dialogue on the theology of fulfillment, however, tends to shift attention toward a discussion of virtues that Buddhists and Christians have in common—for example, humility, self-renunciation, compassion—as confirmation of the work of the Holy Spirit in the religious lives of Buddhists. The notion of renouncing attachment to justice, even as attachment to righteous anger is renounced, does not fit snuggly into Catholic presuppositions regarding the working of the Holy Spirit.

A third example has to do with Buddhists and their views of human rights. The Roman Catholic Church has embraced the notion of human rights only since 1963 with the promulgation of the encyclical *Pacem in Terris*. Today, there is a debate among Buddhists regarding the appropriateness of the rhetoric of human rights for the practice of the *dharma*.[21] Buddhists like the Dalai Lama and Ananda Guruge, for example, believe human rights to be consonant with the most basic teachings of Buddhism. On the other hand, Buddhists like Craig Ihara argue that human rights are foreign to Buddhism and incompatible with Buddhist doctrine. Moreover, introducing such a notion "would significantly transform the nature of Buddhism ethics."[22] This is because the assertion of human rights promotes an adversarial mentality and is incompatible with the practice of compassion. Human rights also promote a "negative notion of freedom" that presumes the existence of a substantial self. Therefore, "it probably would be a mistake to introduce the notion of rights into Buddhist ethics."[23] The highly respected Thai monk, Phra Dhammapidok, is also leery of human rights as a strategy for realizing Buddhist ethical ideals. Human rights are impermanent human inventions that lead to social division and strife. Dhammapidok believes that the ethos of rights does not measure up to the demands of Buddhism's ethics of compassion and fears that the embrace of human rights by Buddhists will distort the *dharma*. Of course, Buddhists who are skeptical about human rights are not suggesting that waterboarding, slavery, and the denial of *habeas corpus*, for example, are to be condoned. Instead, they look on the ethos of human rights as a strategy for achieving certain political ends (however laudable) in a way that is not compatible with the practice of Buddhism.

The hesitancy of these Buddhists regarding the rhetoric of human rights should be of immense theological interest to Christians. Christian morality, like its Buddhist counterpart, is a virtue ethics rooted in the selfless practice of love (*agape*) and compassion (*karuna*). To what extent does Buddhist skepticism about the appropriateness of human rights also apply to Christianity? If the proper Christian response to injustice is the patient practice of love, then what role should the assertion of rights play in Christian social ethics? I predict that a dialogue with Buddhists about human rights will lead quickly to a discussion about the nature of the individual. Some Buddhists are skeptical about human rights because they see rights as promoting the illusion of a substantial self. Catholics have embraced a doctrine of rights based on a theology of the human person as the image of God (*imago Dei*). The contrast between the hesitancy of some Buddhists and the enthusiasm of many Roman Catholics regarding the rhetoric of human rights, however, is an inconvenient truth from the perspective of the fulfillment theology of religions. Once again, the church's theology of religions shifts attention away from certain aspects of Buddhist teaching in order to highlight other aspects that are more amenable to a preconceived Roman Catholic view of our dialogue partners.

My fourth example has to do with Buddhist and Christian meditation practices. A teacher of Zen and an old friend advises his students to practice a mental exercise as they enter the *dōjō* for meditation. He tells them to remember the last line of the inscription above the gate of hell in Dante's *Inferno*, "Abandon all hope you who enter here." The point of this exercise is hardly to suggest that the practice of *zazen* (seated meditation) is like a stroll through Dante's hell (although your knees may think so after an hour on the cushion). The inscription reminds all who enter that the proper practice of *zazen* requires the renouncing of what Christians know as eschatological hope. In Zen, one does not "wait in joyful hope" for the coming of a savior. *Zazen* requires the radical abandonment of all attachments, including attachment to hope in a future enlightenment, let alone salvation in the eschatological coming of a savior. Since the pioneering efforts of Catholic monks like Thomas Merton, Roman Catholics in many parts of the world have taken up the serious practice of Buddhist meditation, to the extent that some Catholic monks have even received ordination as Zen teachers.

The Roman Catholic practice of *zazen* opens up a host of interesting questions, both for our dialogue with Buddhists and for the dialogue within Christianity between spirituality and systematic theology. What is the relationship between the Christian eschatological hope and the Buddhist doctrine of "emptiness" (which requires the abandonment of all hope)? What is the relationship between Buddhist meditation and Christian contemplation? In the practice of *zazen*, does a Roman Catholic find union with God? Is *zazen* a way for cultivating what Christian spiritual tradition calls the "practice of the presence of God"? If not, then what is happening when a Roman Catholic practices *zazen*? And how is this related to Christian spirituality? These are not rhetorical questions. I think these questions are very much worth pursuing and I have no doubt that Christians will be enriched by their Buddhist teachers in asking these questions. I also recognize that this is a very sensitive issue for many Roman Catholics who practice Buddhist meditation, and for some Buddhists as well. Let me state clearly that my purpose in raising these questions is not to discourage Roman Catholic experimentation with Buddhist meditation. Rather, my hope is to promote a much deeper level of dialogue. Moreover, my purpose is to show that the church's fulfillment theology is not helpful in promoting this dialogue. Roman Catholics who are engaged in the practice of Buddhist meditation sometimes insist to me that *zazen* promotes Christian contemplation. Lurking behind this interpretation of *zazen* is the church's theology of religions, which emphasizes the work of the Holy Spirit in the religious practices of other religions. Once again, Buddhism is reduced to a version of what Roman Catholics already know, in this case contemplation understood as communion with God in the Holy Spirit. Buddhism is reduced to more of the same. Difference is domesticated.

The point of all of these examples is to show that Buddhism and Christianity are not only similar, they are also different in theologically significant ways. Basing our dialogue with Buddhism on a fulfillment theology, however, tends to privilege the points of similarity and marginalize the differences as being of lesser significance. More than forty years ago, the Second Vatican Council, in its "Declaration on the Relation of the Church to Non-Christian Religions" (*Nostra Aetate*), famously taught that

> the Catholic Church rejects nothing that is true and holy in these religions. She regards with sincere reverence those ways of conduct and of life, those precepts and teachings which, though differing in many

aspects from the ones she holds and sets forth, nonetheless often reflect a ray of that Truth which enlightens all men.[24]

This expression of what might be called the Catholic Church's "theological map of religions" highlights the problem I am exploring in this essay. If all that is "true and holy" in Buddhism is what Christianity already knows to be true and holy, then the matters in which Buddhism differs from Christianity should be of only marginal theological significance to Christians. In the case of our dialogue with Buddhism, at least, this must be counted a momentous loss to the theological value of interreligious dialogue.

Some Practical Suggestions

Catholics, in dialogue with Buddhists, need to deal with a significant challenge. Even as we acknowledge our fulfillment theology as a genuine achievement over these last fifty years, we must ask, at what point does our theology of religions so interfere with our ability to listen to our dialogue partners that we fail to hear what they are saying? To what extent does our theology of religions, however adequate it may be to the demands of Christian faith, impede our practice of interreligious dialogue? We must recognize that this theology is based solely on intra-Christian theological requirements. It responds to problems endemic to Christianity, namely, how it is that the vast majority of human beings who are alive today and have lived in the past are not damned by being unincorporated into Christ and the church. Buddhists, I hasten to add, are not asking this question. Moreover, if we enter into dialogue with Buddhists with the answer to this question paramount in our minds, Catholics should not be surprised if they fail to hear what Buddhists are saying, at least on some topics of real theological significance. The fulfillment theology of the Catholic Church is adequate to the demands of Christian faith, but not helpful in supporting the church in its need to engage other religious believers in dialogue. In light of this problem, I wish to conclude by offering a few practical suggestions.

First, despite the inadequacy of our fulfillment theology as a basis or framework for interreligious dialogue, I do not recommend abandoning it. The pneumatology of John Paul II should be recognized and welcomed as a major achievement of the postconciliar church. John Paul's fulfillment theology is adequate to the demands of Christian faith in that it embraces not only the uniqueness of Christ and inseparability of the church from Christ but also recognizes the universal saving activity of the Holy Spirit. The alternatives to this fulfillment theology are inadequate in one way or another. The "exclusivist theology" of Karl Barth, for example, fails to appreciate the universal activity of the Spirit.

Thus Barth fails to see that "every authentic prayer is prompted by the Holy Spirit, who is mysteriously present in every human heart" as the pope attests in *Redemptoris Missio*, 29. The so-called "pluralist hypothesis" of John Hick, to give another example, fails to account for the centrality of the Christ-event in the economy of salvation.

My second practical proposal has to do with our need to keep the church's fulfillment theology in historical perspective. The pneumatology of John Paul II has brought a fifty-year development of Roman Catholic thinking to a close. We have gone from an exclusivist view of *extra ecclesia nulla salus* to an appreciation of other religious communities as "participated forms of mediation" of the one, saving grace of Christ. The church has also gone from the defensive, indeed, beleaguered mentality of the Counter-Reformation to the spirit of *aggiornamento* that led to the promulgation of *Nostra Aetate* and the establishment of what is today called the Pontifical Council for Interreligious Dialogue. John Paul's pneumatological theology of religions has succeeded in getting the Catholic Church's own theological house in order regarding religious diversity in a postcolonial world.

John Paul's pontificate, however, marks not only the end of an era but also the beginning of a new era for the Catholic Church. The pope brought an era to a close by developing a fulfillment theology, beyond the initial steps of the Second Vatican Council, in his encyclicals. Attention must be paid as well, not only to the pope's writings but also his activities. John Paul II was the first pope to enter a synagogue and a mosque. On his extensive travels, he unfailingly met with Jews, Muslims, Hindus, Jains, Zoroastrians, Buddhists, and others. In this new era, less energy need be invested in the theological question of the meaning and status of other religious traditions so that more energy can be devoted to actual dialogue with these traditions. The church needs to shift its attention from *theoria* (the theology of religions) to *praxis* (the dialogue with those who follow other faiths).

This leads to my third practical suggestion. Catholics need to recognize interreligious dialogue as a new form of ministry in the church. Perhaps it is more revealing to say that dialogue with other religious communities is a ministry of the church. By "ministry," I mean, of course, the church's service to the world. In the twenty-first century, dialogue with other religions will be an increasingly important way in which the church responds to the needs of a world in which religious identity is reasserting itself for good or for ill. But by "ministry," I also mean a way in which the church realizes itself concretely in history.[25] By entering into dialogue, the church comes to be what the Holy Spirit is empowering the church to become: a sign of unity and hope for the world. In effect, I am suggesting that we respond to the council's call for dialogue (*Nostra Aetate*, 2) remembering that in Christ the church is "like a sacrament or as a sign and instrument" of "the unity of the whole human race" (*Lumen Gentium*, 1). Contrary to socio-logical theories that predicted the inevitable demise of religion in the advent of modernity, globalization is bringing about a resurgence of religious practice. In some parts of the world, religious identity is taking the place of failed national identities. The twenty-first century has already been scarred by violence and intolerance in the name of various religions. The Catholic Church needs to respond to this problem. Dialogue with other religious communities needs to become a central pastoral activity for the church. By means of its multiple dialogues, the church becomes what the Spirit is calling it to be: a "sign and instrument" of solidarity among religious communities.

Given this situation, Catholics need to realize that the pastoral purpose of interreligious dialogue is certainly not evangelization, if this be understood as converting the dialogue partner to Christianity. Neither is the pastoral purpose of this church ministry merely to confirm our theological presuppositions about other religious believers, however irenic these views may be. Herein we find the difficulty I have tried to outline in using the church's fulfillment theology as a basis for our dialogue with Buddhists. The purpose of interreligious dialogue is pastoral: to establish bonds of solidarity with other religious communities. In this way, the church becomes what the church has been raised up by the Spirit to be: a kind of sacrament of the unity of people in a world whose religious diver-sity is more vast and more wondrous than those trying to find their way with a road map can imagine.

Notes

1 Joseph Costelloe, *The Letters and Instructions of Francis Xavier* (St. Louis: Institute of Jesuit Sources, 1992), 300.

2 For an account of this landmark event, see *The Gethsamani Encounter*, ed. Donald W. Mitchell and James Wiseman, O.S.B. eds., (New York: Continuum, 1998).

3 The category "fulfillment theology" is taken from the work of Paul Knitter. See his *Introducing Theologies of Religions* (Maryknoll, N.Y.: Orbis, 2002), 63ff.

4 *Redemptoris missio*, par. 29.

5 Ibid. The pope took a similar position in his radio address from Manila in 1981. For a tran-script of this address, see *Interreligious Dialogue: The Official Teaching of the Catholic Church (1963–1995)*, ed. Francesco Gioia (Boston: Pauline, 1994), 371–372.

6 *Redemptor hominis*, par. 6.

7 *Gaudium et spes*, par. 22.

8 Ibid.

9 For an authoritative analysis of the council's multiple statements on the status of other reli-gious traditions, see Jacques Dupuis, *Jesus Christ at the Encounter of World Religions* (Maryknoll, N.Y.: Orbis, 1981).

10 For a discussion of theological developments prior to the council, see Jacques Dupuis, *Toward a Christian Theology of Religious Pluralism* (Maryknoll, N.Y.: Orbis, 1997), 130–157.

11 Jean Daniélou, *The Salvation of the Nations*, (South Bend, Ind.: University of Notre Dame Press, 1962), 8. For Daniélou's theology of religions, also see *Mythes païens, mystère Chrétien*

(Paris: Fayard, 1966); "Christianity and the Non-Christian Religions," in *Word in History*, ed. P. Burke (New York: Sheed & Ward, 1966), 86–101; and *The Lord of History: Reflections on the Inner Meaning of History* (London: Longmans, 1958), 107–121. For von Balthasar's view, see "Catholicism and the Religions," *Communio* 5 (U.S. edition) (1978). 6–14.

12 Among Rahner's more influential essays on this topic, see "Christianity and the Non-Christian Religions," *Theological Investigations* 5 (London: Darton, Longman and Todd, 1966), 115–134; "Observations on the Problem of the 'Anonymous Christian,'" *Theological Investigations* 14 (London: Darton, Longman and Todd, 1976), 280–298.

13 Karl Rahner, "On the Importance of Non-Christian Religions for Salvation," *Theological Investigations* 18 (New York: Crossroad, 1983), 288–295.

14 In *Redemptoris Missio*, the pope cites *Ad gentes*, par. 3, 11, 15; and *Gaudium et spes*, par. 10–11, 22, 26, 38, 41, 92–93.

15 *Redemptoris Missio*, par. 10.

16 The Latin text reads, "mediationes participatae diversi generis et ordinis."

17 For official statements in regard to the principle *extra ecclesiam*, see the declaration of the Congregation for the Doctrine of the Faith, *Dominus Iesus* 20, especially note 82. For an analysis of the historical development of church teaching on this issue, see Francis Sullivan, *Salvation Outside the Church?* (Mahwah N.J.: Paulist, 1992). On the question of religious relativism, see *Dominus Iesus* 4. Also see the 1996 document of the International Theological Commission, "Christianity and the World Religions," *Origins* 27, no. 10 (August 14, 1997): 149–166, especially nos. 4–22, and the talk given by Cardinal Joseph Ratzinger titled "Relativism: The Central Problem for the Faith Today," *Origins* 26, no. 20 (October 31, 1996): 309–317.

18 See James L. Fredericks, *Buddhists and Christians: Through Comparative Theology to Solidarity* (Maryknoll N.Y.: Orbis, 2004), 17–19.

19 Shin'ichi Hisamatsu, "Zen as the Negation of Holiness," in *The Buddha Eye: An Anthology of the Kyoto School* (New York: Crossroad, 1982), 169–178.

20 Masao Abe, *Zen and Western Thought* (Honolulu: University of Hawaii Press, 1985), 130.

21 See *Buddhism and Human Rights*, ed. Damien Keown, Charles Prebish, and Wayne Husted (Surrey, England: Curzon, 1998).

22 Craig Ihara, "Why There Are No Rights in Buddhism," in ibid., 44.

23 Ibid., 51.

24 *Nostra Aetate*, par. 2.

25 For the notion of the church's self-realization (*Selbstvollzug*) within history, see Karl Rahner, *Selbstvollzug Der Kirche* (Berlin: Herder, 1998); and *The Church and the Sacraments* (Berlin: Herder, 1963).

A Response to James L. Fredericks

ANSELM KYONGSUK MIN

I want to congratulate James Fredericks on an exciting presentation. I find his historical account of the evolution of the Catholic theology of religions from the Second Vatican Council to John Paul II quite masterful; his delineation of issues on the four important topics of ultimate reality, anger, human rights, and meditation practices quite provocative; and his three practical recommendations quite relevant. His whole presentation was straightforward, powerful, and compelling.

Ultimately, I think we are in profound agreement on the substantive issues, but perhaps we differ on the way of getting there. There are four issues in particular between us, which I would like to briefly explore. They are the value of the fulfillment theology of religions, the purpose of dialogue, the theological basis of the witness that Fredericks calls on the church to bear to the solidarity of humanity, and the proper approach to how a religion can transcend and open itself to the religious Other. I do not address the issues raised by his comparative discussions of the four topics because this will require a discussion all by itself.

For Fredericks, the fulfillment theology of religions recognizes the work of the Holy Spirit in the religions of the world as such, yet subordinates their salvific value to their participation in the mediating work of Christ, who remains central. As the culmination of a whole era of theological struggles to come to terms with the diversity of religions in the world, this theology is better than any of the two alternatives, exclusivism, which denies the universal activity of the Holy Spirit, and pluralism, which denies the centrality of Christ. And yet Fredericks insists that this theology is inadequate and unsuitable as a theology of religions because it does not allow us to listen to our dialogue partners and learn from them, especially the destabilizing and potentially transformative potential of other religions. It stresses the similarities between Catholicism and other religions, tries to reduce others to a version of Catholicism, and does not allow Catholics to hear truly the Other when that person is so different so as to radically challenge them, as in the case of Buddhism.

Now, one would expect that if someone should find a theology inadequate, he or she would also propose a modification, or abandonment, or some alternative.

Instead, Fredericks insists that we should not abandon it. Is it because it still contains the essential truths of Catholicism not worth sacrificing for the sake of learning from Buddhism? Is it because the alternatives are worse? Doesn't he insist, though, that it is inadequate and unsuitable? If so, what does he propose to do about it? Instead of discussing what to do with the fulfillment theology, other than just leaving it aside for a while, Fredericks proposes to shift from thinking theologically *about* other religions to thinking theologically *with* them, from a theoretical reconstruction of a theology of religions to the praxis of dialogue with them. I suspect he is advocating some sort of a temporary suspension or moratorium on theological evaluations of the Other. I do not know exactly why he wants this shift, but is it possible that he is hoping that as a result of dialogue with others we will eventually learn something in light of which we can perhaps modify the fulfillment theology of religions? I wish he were a little clearer on this point.

This raises at least four related questions, on the value of the fulfillment theology of religions, the nature and purpose of interreligious dialogue, the task of the church in relation to other religions, and how and the extent to which a religion can rightly be expected to open and transcend itself to the Other. He judges the fulfillment theology of religions inadequate and unsuitable for dialogue, especially for learning from and being transformed as a result. Not only is Fredericks setting up suitability for dialogue as the measure or criterion for the value of Catholic theology but he is also suggesting that the purpose of dialogue is to be transformed by the Other, not to convert or evangelize. What, then, does he propose for the mission of the church? As a sign and instrument of the unity of the human race, the mission of the church is, I argue, to become a sacrament of the solidarity of all humanity.

First, then, on the value of the fulfillment theology of religions. For all his positive statements about it, Fredericks clearly sees it as more negative than positive because it "domesticates difference." On the other hand, I value it more positively than he does because I do not use the same criterion of suitability for dialogue as the measure of the adequacy of a doctrine. I use, rather, the criterion of adequacy to existential and historical problems of human life itself, and I will argue later that other religions too should be evaluated by this criterion.

From the perspective of existential and historical adequacy, the fulfillment theology of religions contains many elements. It contains the anthropological reflections on the unity of all humanity and indeed of all creation; their interdependence in sin and grace; the absolute, transcendent seriousness of sin or what we do to another in this world by way of hate and alienation; and the human impossibility of saving ourselves from the consequences of sin. It also contains the theological responses: the incarnation of the Son culminating in the crucifixion and resurrection of Jesus, the invitation to all humanity and all creation to share in the atonement and resurrection of Jesus, Jesus' hypostatic union that enables him to represent and participate in our sufferings and hopes, the work of the Holy Spirit who reconciles all humanity and all creation as brothers and sisters in the body of Christ the Son so that all may become sons and daughters of the Father, and the love of the Father who sends the Son and the Holy Spirit precisely on these missions.

Although this theology is thoroughly based on the Christian perspective, its content is thoroughly universalist, not sectarian. It orients Christians to think in terms of all humanity, all creation, their interdependent destiny in sin and grace, their solidarity in the body of Christ, the reconciling and solidarity-creating role of the Holy Spirit, and the love of the triune God who at the same time infinitely transcends the creature and condemns all reduction to creaturely parochialism, sectarianism, and ideology. This theology contains the Christian responses to the basic existential questions arising from our creatureliness; our mutual dependence; our responsibility for sinful alienation from one another; our ontological, moral, and spiritual anxieties; our search for definitive fulfillment. In the explicit recognition of the activity of the Holy Spirit in all humanity and all creation, and the universal significance of Christ's crucifixion and resurrection, this theology also addresses the compelling historical problem of our time, the reality and consciousness of human division along the lines of class, race, gender, and religion. It encourages Catholics to think in terms of solidarity with them, to provide preferential love for the oppressed Others among them, and to regard Others positively, indeed learn from them when they are ideologically different, and look for the presence of God's saving grace in them, for precisely the "ways unknown to us" in which the Holy Spirit operates. It encourages Catholics to do all these with good theological conscience, with the feeling that they are fulfilling, not betraying, their deepest mission and identity.

Fredericks may ask, rightly, whether this way of thinking and acting does not still remain anchored in the Christian perspective and whether it is not in danger of domesticating difference. And the answer, of course, is yes to both concerns. However, this is not peculiar to the Christian attempt but to all group attempts to understand the Other. Can the Buddhist attempt to understand the Christian doctrine of the incarnation, perhaps at the antipodes of the Buddhist doctrine of no self, without in some way being anchored in Buddhism itself, or do we want the Buddhist to cease being a Buddhist in order to understand Christianity without domesticating the Christian difference? And if the Buddhist does so as a Buddhist, can he escape the danger of domesticating difference?

I wonder whether it is theoretically legitimate and practically feasible to require that a religion put aside or abandon, for fear of domesticating religious differences, a central doctrine of its own that it regards so important as to identify itself with it. Without going into an elaborate discussion of this, let me just say that no religion should and can effect an even temporary suspension of a central identifying doctrine because it has to sustain itself as an institution with its liturgical, administrative, educational, and spiritual structures, all of which are permeated by that doctrine. An individual theologian may be able to suspend belief in a particular doctrine for the sake of dialogue, but not the institutional religion as such. Still, in pushing the limits of dialogue allowed by that doctrine, the religion can grow by learning from others and integrating that into one's identity, which as a result also expands. (This, in fact, has been the history of Christian theology as well as the history of Buddhism.) As each religion expands its sense of identity, it can to that extent come closer to religious Others. This, I think, in all its implications, is all that we can expect. In the matter of dialogue, as in all other things, we should not nurture a hope that is not based on reality, as we cannot afford to remain blind to the demands of the *kairos*, which is to listen to the Other, but without requiring that we suspend belief in something central and cease to be ourselves.

This raises a fundamental question of the nature and purpose of dialogue itself, the second point of this essay. Is dialogue so important that it should become the measure of the adequacy of doctrines? Fredericks says that the purpose of dialogue is not to convert or evangelize. I think he is quite correct in saying this, but one would think that the purpose of dialogue is not only to learn from the Other but also to share what we honestly think is the good news with those who do not know it. We want the Buddhists to share with us the best insights they have, their dharma, but why not also share with them the best insights we have?

Now I think we should be careful here. When I say that we have not only to learn from Others but also share what we have with them, it may sound like the question is simply us versus them, *our* truths versus *their* truths. There is some plausibility about this way of posing the issue. We have been—and I must say, all religions have been—using truths as ideological weapons in a struggle for power in the world. Therefore, we cannot deny the ideological, abusive potential of the habit of regarding truths as *our* truths or *their* truths.

This way of posing the problem, however, I think, is fundamentally mistaken. When Buddhism claims the Four Holy Truths, it does not claim them as *its* truths in the sense that they are its own possession that it can then manipulate in any way it wants as a means to promoting its own power. Buddhism claims them because they are true, not because they are *its* truth, and therefore not only for Buddhists but also for all humanity. It will be ludicrous to say that the doctrine of no self applies only to the Buddhists, but not to Christians. In fact, it is not Buddhists who claim the Four Holy Truths; it is the Four Holy Truths that claim the Buddhists and make them what they are. In the same way, when Christianity claims Christ as the unique mediator of the salvation of all humanity and indeed of all creation, it does so because it is true, and therefore for all humanity, not because it is *its* truth, which makes Christians feel superior, or because it is true only for Christians. This is why Christians have been willing to die to bear witness to the truth about Christ; it is hardly something that they possess and that they can then bandy around to threaten other people. It is the truth that claims Christians, not Christians who claim the truth. I think this experience of truth as something that claims us and challenges us to change our ways, rather than as something we can claim and subordinate to our own ends, is phenomenologically true of all genuine experience of truths. The language of possession and superiority is simply a category mistake in the sphere of truth.

If truth is something that claims and addresses us precisely in its universality, then, dialogue cannot be a one-way street of learning from the Other, however important this might be. If it is a genuine dialogue, not a monologue, it should also involve sharing what we consider as truths with our dialogue partners, not because they are *our* truths, which makes no sense, but precisely because they are truths *for all*. Christians cannot claim that Christ is only for them any more than Buddhists can claim that the Buddha is only for the Buddhists. Both claims, if they are genuine truth claims, are universal and must be universal. However different the content of these truths, they must be shared and then engaged in all seriousness.

Converting or evangelizing in the sense of conquering others with *our* truths is sheer arrogance that should be stopped; it is also based on a silly assumption that such truths can be the possession of a particular group. However, sharing with others truths that claim us and to which we subject ourselves because that is the way we see and cannot see otherwise is precisely the point of all religious dialogue. Only then will it be a true encounter of truth with truth, and only then will the dialogue be about something truly substantive, something truly central to human life as such. Without that sharing dialogue becomes monologue. Isn't this precisely what "thinking *with* the Buddhists," not "*about* the Buddhists," that Fredericks suggests, should involve?

If this is the case, then, it will not do to merely set aside the fulfillment theology of religions for the time being for the sake of the praxis of dialogue. If there is something true that claims the faith of Christians in the claims about the universality of the Holy Spirit and the centrality of Christ, then these two things must also be shared and become part of the dialogue with the Buddhists, not simply set aside. Christians will not and should not simply set aside something so central to them as the centrality of Christ for the sake of dialogue, any more than Buddhists will and should set aside something so central to them as the insubstantiality of the self or any one of the Four Holy Truths. This will make dialogue very difficult indeed, but also genuine. This difficulty is only appropriate to the gravity of the matter at issue. Negotiations on central issues of life are never meant to be easy.

This raises a serious issue with regard to the importance of dialogue itself. Is dialogue important for its own sake, or is it important only because it leads us better to the truth of life that we seek together? If the latter, then, inadequacy or unsuitability for dialogue cannot be a major criterion for the inadequacy of a doctrine, however important the dialogue might be. What is more important is its adequacy to human life itself, to which the truths of other religions must also be subjected. The central question is not whether the fulfillment theology makes it difficult for Christians to hear the Buddhist partner in the dialogue, or, to put the question on Buddhist terms, whether the doctrine of no self prevents Buddhists from really listening to Christians about their theology of the incarnation and social justice, but whether both Buddhism and Christianity are adequate to the existential challenges of human life itself, whether this has to do with the great suffering and oppression in many parts of the world, the massive trivializing, pluralizing, and relativizing tendencies of the Internet, the horrendous consequences of global imperialism, or the massive destruction of the environment. I think we should change the focus of dialogue from the encounter of one religious doctrine with another religious doctrine to the examination of the adequacy of both doctrines, both religions, to the challenges of life itself, some of which I enumerated in mentioning the component truths of the fulfillment theology of religions earlier. In this case, it will be a genuine turn from theory to praxis. (I am not unaware, of course, of how difficult it is to make this change, because we do tend to interpret the challenges of life itself in the horizon of our doctrines.)

Frederick's understanding of the purpose of dialogue leads us to the third point of this essay: the task of the church. He says that the mission of the church is not to evangelize, which is fair enough if we take "evangelization" in the pejorative sense of converting others to our perspective, but to become a sacrament of solidarity of all humanity. My question, then, is, on what theological basis could the church be a sacrament of the solidarity of all humanity? If we put aside the fulfillment theology of religions, where do we find a theological basis of that solidarity? After all, the church can be a sign of solidarity of all humanity only because the church is the body of Christ and as such called upon to signify and actualize precisely the unity in Christ for which all human beings are intended by the triune God and for which the Holy Spirit operates to empower. If this fulfillment theology of religions, which so richly documents this idea of human solidarity, is to be set aside for the sake of the praxis of dialogue, from what other source can we provide the theological basis for the mission of the church as a sacrament of human solidarity? Appeal to the mere fact of human interdependence? Simply accept the Buddhist doctrine of codependent origination of all things? Should the church forget about its Christian identity because that still conceals unworthy preoccupation with identity and selfhood? Should the church then simply become Buddhist? Would this be a coherent position to claim, either intellectually or pastorally?

Finally, for all I have been saying, I also recognize the need for dialogue as a compelling contemporary imperative and the seriousness of the challenge posed by genuine and serious dialogue to review and reexamine our own cherished beliefs. Catholics should know this very well because the debates of Vatican II and since have been precisely debates about how to respond to these challenges. However, this requires a very sophisticated approach. It will not do to simply ask Catholics to give up some of their doctrines as some pluralists do because they seem to be in conflict with some of the seemingly self-evident truths of the secular world or with the truths of other religions. No religion will ever just give up some of their own truths for this reason, nor should it, in my view, especially if the doctrines at issue are so central to it as to define its very identity. I think this is the case with the universalist claims of Christology in Christianity and with the Four Holy Truths in Buddhism.

What do we do then? I think we can do two things here: first, we can practice the hermeneutics of distance and the hermeneutics of depth. We need always to become more aware of the inevitable distance between the objective reality of the truth claimed and the adequacy of our subjective grasp of that reality. In matters of ultimate concern dealing with human destiny, such a distance always exists, as, for example, between the objective, transcendent reality of the triune God in God's incomprehensible essence and our collective subjective grasp of that reality in our Trinitarian dogmas and theologies. Our human tendency across all the religions is to simply identify the two and then seek to impose our subjective grasp of the truth with the absoluteness due the object itself. But the consequence of such absolutization has been disastrous enough. This means that with regard to the centrality of Christ, we need to be much more reserved, without ceasing to be committed, about the adequacy of our own understanding of that centrality. This reservation may in fact be what is called for in what I think is Frederick's proposal, if I understand him correctly, to postpone the work on the theology of religions because we do not know enough about other religions and concentrate instead on learning about other religions and from other religions.

The second thing we can do as Catholics is to do what we do well. We never say that our dogmas and doctrines, our human grasp of revealed truths, are wrong, but we often practice the hermeneutics of depth with regard to dogmatic statements, inquiring about how a doctrine originated—how it was formulated, with what conceptualities, responding to what deep concerns of the time, and with what assumptions. Especially by delving into the concerns and assumptions and showing the inadequacy of these concerns and assumptions we come up with a way of reformulating the doctrine. This has been the story of our new understanding of many ethical issues, especially sexual ethics, just war theory, and the traditional doctrine that there is no salvation outside the church. In any case, without denying the validity of the current formulations of dogma, we can always go deeper into its existential and historical meaning, and through this depth hermeneutics we may be able to understand dogma in such a way that we find *within* the dogma itself, in its own depth, a principle of self-transcendence, a principle whereby we can transcend its current formulation without denying its validity, although we do relativize that validity. This will be exactly the process of the development of dogma, which is also the process of the enrichment of dogma. Karl Rahner has been masterful in doing this in his "ontological" reinterpretation of the "ontic" statements of doctrine. I think we should do more of that. We cannot bluntly ask religions, our own or those of others, to change or give up their age-old doctrines, especially their central defining doctrines, but we can ask them to go into the depth of such doctrines to see in them a principle of self-criticism, self-transcendence, and self-enrichment. In that depth, which is ultimately the depth of life itself to which we all belong together, we can perhaps come closer to one another and even find one another.[1]

Note

1 I have elaborated on many of the issues of religious pluralism and interreligious dialogue in my two books, *The Solidarity of Others in a Divided World: A Postmodern Theology after Postmodernism* (New York: T&T Clark, 2004), 134–197; and *Paths to the Triune God: An Encounter between Aquinas and Recent Theologies* (Notre Dame, Ind.: University of Notre Dame Press, 2005), 51–130.

A Response to James L. Fredericks

Sharing the Karma

HUAIYU CHEN

James Fredericks suggests shifting the Catholic Church's focus from theological thinking about Buddhism to thinking theologically with Buddhists. This is a welcome suggestion in contemporary dialogue between Catholicism and Buddhism. As is well known, Buddhism is not just a philosophical tradition or a moral teaching. It includes three indispensable jewels: Buddha, Dharma (i.e., the Buddha's teaching), and Sangha (i.e., the monastic order). In this sense, Fredericks can be understood as suggesting that we think with the Sangha or monastic order, not just with the Buddha and Dharma. Thinking with the Dharma has something to do with Buddhist philosophy and theology. In the past decades there have been many dialogues between Catholic bishops and some Buddhist religious leaders, where these Buddhist religious leaders have been seen as representing the Buddhist community, but not in the way that bishops can represent the Catholic Church. Buddhist leaders should not be viewed as the representatives of the Buddha, or the Dharma, or the Sangha. They represent only the particular Buddhist organizations or sectarian affiliations. Having dialogue with Buddhists make more sense in terms of going beyond the conventional conversation model with Buddhist leaders. That is why thinking with the Buddhists is important. In the following discussion, I will at first summarize key points made by Fredericks viewpoints and then offer some reflections on the difficulty of the dialogue historically and on the necessity and possibility of the dialogue in a contemporary context.

From a Buddhist perspective on the dialogue, I would like to highlight several points as a response to Professor Fredericks. First of all, Fredericks's suggestions certainly will bring the dialogue between Catholics and Buddhist to a new phase, a dialogue in terms of praxis. Second, historically speaking, the Buddhists seemed to be inferior to the Catholics in terms of the modern intellectual world. This fact causes some problems. Third, the diversity of Buddhist communities also poses some challenges in its dialogue with Catholicism. For Buddhism, no single Buddhist theology is endorsed by all Buddhist communities. No single Buddhist leader can be recognized in the contemporary world with the same universal authority as the pope in the Catholic Church.

A Historical Retrospect: Difficulties and Necessities

For me, the apparent historical inferiority of Buddhism to Catholicism seems to have a negative impact on the dialogue between Buddhism and Catholicism. From the very beginning in the early modern period, Catholicism actively dominated the dialogue with religions of the East. For instance, Catholic travelers encountered Buddhists as early as the thirteenth century when they visited the Mongol court. A Flemish Franciscan missionary, William of Rubruck, traveled clear across Eurasia to visit Kharakorum.[1] It seems that the Buddhists welcomed the connection and dialogue initiated by the Catholics. In the medieval and early modern period, the Catholic Church was dominant, influential, and central to the world. The Buddhist community, to the extent that it viewed itself in contrast to the homogenous Catholic Church, viewed itself as peripheral, less influential, and marginal—at least in the grand scope of world history. Moreover, the then-existing history of Buddhism, in the sense of modern historiography, was written by Western Christian scholars.[2] For more than a millennium, the Catholic Church has been one of the largest and most influential religious organizations in the world. Yet for a long time, the rest of the world beyond Asia viewed Buddhism as a mystical Oriental belief system. In some Asian countries, such as China and Japan, Buddhists had close connection and frequent dialogue with Confucians and Shintoists. In China, however, it never influenced the state and society as did Confucianism. Although the Jesuits began their dialogue with Buddhists as early as 1549, Europe only became familiar with Buddhism in the nineteenth century. Before that time, Buddhism should perhaps be viewed as an Asian religion rather than a world religion. However, nowadays, Buddhist organizations from various traditions have sunk their roots firmly in Europe and North America. The world we are living in is multireligious, multilingual, and multicultural, so dialogue is absolutely necessary.

In the twentieth century, the Catholic Church was an aggressive religious power in the East, while the Buddhist community found itself on the defensive. Since the era of colonialism, beyond its mainstream position in North America and Europe, the Catholic Church was also influential among African, Asian, and Latin American people. Confronted with Catholic Christianity, Buddhism was challenged even in its homeland of South Asia, Southeast Asia, and East Asia. Only after World War II, and especially in the past twenty years, Buddhism has become a real world religion, stretching across the boundaries of ethnicities, countries, cultures, and languages, spreading to Europe and North America. Given the historical experience of many Asian countries during the colonial era, Buddhism has been connected with nationalism, both politically and culturally.[3] It has been utilized as an ideological tool against European hegemony. For instance, in early twentieth-century China, many Buddhists attempted to use Buddhism as an element in the reconstruction of a coherent national spirit in response to the challenge from Western religions, including Catholicism.

Many negative elements have affected the dialogue between Catholicism and Buddhism. First of all, as the historical experiences mentioned above, the Buddhists seem not to be well prepared intellectually to engage in the dialogue in terms of theology. Most Buddhists have very little knowledge about Catholicism; in fact, only a few Buddhists would be interested in understanding Catholicism. If we look at the intellectual world, we may find many Catholics who have published works on Buddhism and have taught Buddhism at the college level. There are numerous Catholic Buddhologists,[4] yet there are very few, if any, Buddhist scholars of Catholicism. It would be difficult to find many Buddhists who would be able to teach Christianity at the college level. Although modern intellectual traditions have received a great deal of their intellectual sources from Islamic and Byzantine thought, they have been created in Western Europe.[5] Without a background in Catholicism, it is unlikely that a theological dialogue will be possible. This lack of Catholic background in the Buddhist intellectual world creates one-way dialogue, which means that the Buddhists have to listen to Catholic Christian understandings. This situation repeats what in fact happened in the colonial period. From a Buddhist perspective, acquiring a better understanding of Catholicism is a demanding task. Since dialogue requires participants who have a mutual understanding of Catholicism and Buddhism, Buddhist scholars need to be more active in American intellectual life. Buddhist scholars, therefore, need a better understanding of other religions, and in particular, Catholicism.

The diversity of Buddhist traditions poses another challenge that needs to be taken into account. Unlike Catholic Christians, who in general are unified in their understanding of God, Christ, and the church in Rome, Buddhists have neither a unified church nor a unified theology when it comes to understanding the Buddha and Dharma. For instance, many Mahayana traditions advocate following the Dharma rather than following the Buddha. Daoxuan (596–677), a medieval Chinese master, taught that since the Buddha did not set down all the regulations for monastic life, Chinese masters are free to make some new rules for monastic life in the Chinese Buddhist monastic community, based on their understanding of so-called true Dharma.[6] As Professor Fredericks has acknowledged, there is no single voice when it comes to human rights within Buddhism. In fact, many basic teachings within Buddhism are contested, including the

Buddha and the Dharma. What is a true Dharma? There is no single answer. Moreover, many different Buddhist traditions also have different answers and reactions to the political situations Buddhists confront, such as those in Tibet, Burma, Taiwan, and Japan.

In the meantime, the dialogue between Buddhism and Catholicism also faces an institutional problem. Up to the present time, the Buddhist Sangha was never unified in order to be a single church. There are many Sanghas (or many monastic orders) and many Buddhist communities (such as Theravada Buddhist communities and Mahayana Buddhist communities). In many Asian countries, such as Thailand, Sri Lanka, China, and Japan, there are numerous Buddhist communities. No single Buddhist leader can represent Buddhism as a whole. A Buddhist leader usually represents his lineage of a particular Buddhist order. For instance, His Holiness the fourteenth Dalai Lama is often viewed as the single representative of Tibetan Buddhism. Actually, he is the head of the Gelug sect. There are many other sects in Tibet and even within the Gelug sect; some Tibetan Buddhists are under the leadership of the Panchen Lama. Perhaps it is better to say that the fourteenth Dalai Lama can be viewed as the political-religious leader of Tibet, because the title "Dalai Lama" was granted to the political and religious leader of Tibet by the court of the central government in the fourteenth century.[7] Unlike the pope in the Catholic Church, there is no Buddhist "pope" in Buddhist world.

A Contemporary Context: Concerns and Opportunities

Compared to traditional societies, the contemporary world is much smaller. The communities with different cultures, religions, institutions, and languages become bound together. It is impossible to live in a remote region where a single religious tradition can exclusively be separated from the material and spiritual influence outside. Therefore, the dialogue between different religious groups becomes more necessary than ever before. Nevertheless, as Professor Fredericks has suggested, Christians and Buddhists share some common virtues, such as humility, self-renunciation, compassion, and love. These virtues do bring Christians and Buddhists to the same table when human beings face difficulties, such as political, economic, and environmental crises. By shifting the focus from a dialogue of theology to dialogue of practice, I am able to highlight several social issues Catholic Christians and Buddhists could focus on together. These issues include war and violence, sustainable development, gender and health, and environment.

For instance, one of the major issues today is the problem of global warming, which has a profound impact on all our lives from east to west and north to south. The problem of HIV/AIDS is another global issue. In many remote villages, Catholics and Buddhists have shared their understanding of and made contributions to addressing local social crises. Why not look at these efforts as a dialogue in practice?

In terms of Buddhist doctrine, people have two kinds of karma: collective or shared karma (*gongye*) and individual or nonshared karma (*bieye* or *bugongye*).[8] Shared karma refers to the karma that has been shared by a group of people who have been growing up in the same geographical region, the same political condition, and the same cultural milieu. This shared karma exists because a group of people are together responsible for the effect. For the many issues I have mentioned above, shared karma can help us understand why both Buddhists and Catholics together suffer from violence and environmental degradation.

Shared karma can also help us understand violence and war against a specific group. A group of people have a shared karma for what they have done together. Therefore, they share the same effect from the same cause. One example is the attack by Islamic extremists on the World Trade Center on September 11, 2001. The World Trade Center's Twin Towers collapsed. Thousands of people died; they were from different countries and cultures and worked in or were touring the World Trade Center. Numerous families suffered the loss of their relatives and friends, and thousands more lost their jobs after the attack.[9] As a civilian target, the World Trade Center was not supposed to be on the list of targets for those who despise the United States. Yet it was attacked. From a Buddhist point of view, this violence can be understood as a kind of shared karma.[10] It seems that the victims have a shared karma by what they had done. Those victims contributed to free-market capitalism, elected and, through paying taxes, supported their government in the war against Islam. These people had a shared karma against the Muslims who suffered American imperialist expansion, politically, economically, and culturally. The understanding of shared karma seems to explain why the attack took place on the civilians who worked in the World Trade Center. It explains why the terrorists despised everyone who worked in the World Trade Center buildings, because the victims were seen as sharing the same responsibility with the American government.

Individual-karma theory also works in this case. Why was the World Trade Center attacked and not other civilian targets? The reason is the World Trade Center employees' individual karma. Individual karma refers to the unique karma attached to a particular being. The World Trade Center uniquely stands as the symbol of prosperous capitalism, as a center for international economic power. For many Islamic extremists, the international trade practices of the West are unfair to Muslims. Many Muslims suffer under poor economic conditions because of the American imperialist economic order. By destroying the World Trade Center's Twin Towers, the terrorists sought to shake the nerves of the capitalists all over the world. Moreover, for those extremists, the World Trade Center happened to be the highest building in New York City, the capital of the world economy. It was an easily identifiable target from the air. From a military technical viewpoint, using a commercial airplane to attack the highest building in New York City is much easier. In view of this analysis, the employees who worked in these buildings suffered their individual karma that is not shared with those employees who worked in other skyscrapers in New York City.

There is no way of knowing how many Buddhists or Catholics perished in the attack onf the WTC. Nevertheless, Catholics and Buddhists can do something together in order to prevent a similar attack on any other civilian targets in the United States. As a consequence of the common prosperity of this world, they have shared karma and shared responsibilities. As Fredericks suggests, a dialogue, to be worthwhile, should serve the needs of the world. We need to reduce violence and attacks on civilians. He also notes that Catholicism and Buddhism share the same virtue of compassion. Even though the concepts of human rights in Catholicism and Buddhism are different, each individual's life is a common concern. Buddhists do not agree with the Christian idea of an afterlife. The end of life in this world is, for the Buddhist, a starting point of the next life. Purifying bad karma prepares for the journey to the next life.

Besides violence, gender and health are other issues that deserve to be addressed by Catholics and Buddhists together. From a historical viewpoint, both Catholicism and Buddhism have had a negative attitude toward women. Women rarely entered the high-ranking class in both Catholic and Buddhist communities. In the Lotus Sutra, women were told that they could achieve Buddhahood only after transforming their bodies into those of males. Nowadays, numerous Catholic women work in Africa to save people's lives. In Taiwan, Buddhist nuns and other Buddhist females play a crucial role in numerous charitable organizations, especially Foguangshan and Ciji organizations.

Finally, there is a shared karma, it seems, for all people on the planet, and that is the reality of global warming. Global warming is due to the bad karma shared by all people who have contributed to consuming oil and exhausting other natural resources. How could Buddhist and Catholic compassion contribute to the resolution of this problem? As Fredericks remarks, both Buddhism and Catholicism advocate the virtue of humility. To my understanding, Catholics believe that God is the creator of all things, and that human sin destroys things. Buddhism's idea of impermanence teaches that all things are rising and falling, and that human beings themselves are rising and falling. Because both human beings and nature are created by God, they are not different, and are not different in the process of rising and falling. If humility can take deeper root in the human heart, a mutual understanding of this world can be achieved between Buddhists and Catholics.

Notes

1 Paul Pelliot, "Les Mongols et la papauté," in *Documents nouveaux édités, traduits et commentés by M. Paul Pelliot*, with the collaboration of Borghezio, Masse, and Tisserant, *Revue de l'Orient chrétien*, 3e sér. 3 (23), 1922/23, 3–30; 4 (24), 1924, 225–335; 8 (28), 1931, 3–84 and William of Rubruck, *The Mission of Friar William of Rubruck: His Journey to the Court of the Great Khan Mongke, 1253–1255*, trans. Peter Jackson and David Morgan (London: Hakluyt Society, 1990).

2 This scholarship can be called missionary Buddhology. How the missionaries in the modern era talk about Buddhism should be pursued further. A few works have touched on the issue about how Western scholarship reconstructed the image of Buddhism or decided what were or were not fruitful avenues of research. See, for instance, Charles Hallisey, "Roads Taken and Not Taken in the Study of Theravada Buddhism," in *Curators of the Buddha: The Study of Buddhism under Colonialism*, ed. Donald S. Lopez (Chicago: University of Chicago Press, 1995), 31–61.

3 For the case in Japan, see Robert H. Sharf, "The Zen of Japanese Nationalism," *History of Religions* 33, no. 1 (1993): 1–43.

4 Although there is no accurate list of these Catholic Buddhism scholars, I assume that most Catholic higher education institutions would have hired Catholic scholars to teach Asian religions, including Buddhism. These scholars are either trained in Buddhism as an area of specialization or in Asian religions in general. In either sense, they are qualified to teach Buddhism at the college level. Yet Buddhist scholars in the United States or Europe usually are not trained to teach Catholic Christianity.

5 Marcia L. Colish, *The Medieval Foundation of the Western Intellectual Tradition, 400–1400* (New Haven, Conn.: Yale University Press, 1997).

6 Daoxuan, "Liangchu qingzhong yi," in *Taishō shinshū daizokyō*, ed. Takakusu Junjirō and Watanabe Kaigyoku (Tokyo: Taishō shinshū daizokyō kankokai, 1924–1934), 45:849–850.

7 Hugh E. Richardson, *Tibet and Its History*, 2nd ed., rev. and updated (Boston: Shambhala, 1984), 59–60.

8 [Maitreya], *Yogācāra-bhūmi-śāstra*, trans. Xuanzang, *Taishō shinshu daizōkyō* 30 (no. 1517): 664b.

9 National Commission on Terrorist Attacks, *The 9/11 Commission Report: Final Report of the National Commission on Terrorist Attacks upon the United States* (New York: Norton, 2004).

10 For a good Buddhist remark on the karma in this event, see Ven. Yifa, *Safeguarding the Heart: A Buddhist Response to Suffering and September 11* (New York: Lantern, 2002), 26–34.

James L. Fredericks Continues the Dialogue

JAMES L. FREDERICKS

Let me express my gratitude to Professors Huaiyu Chen and Anselm Min for their careful reading of my essay and their very different responses to it. Taken together, the two professors raise a multitude of provocative issues. I wish to make only a few observations by way of response.

Professor Chen observes that, in comparison to their Christian counterparts, Buddhist leaders are relatively ill prepared for interreligious dialogue and lack a suitable intellectual preparation for it. Sadly, I have to agree with him. Let me offer an observation as to why this is the case and some hopes for the future.

In many parts of Asia today, Buddhism still functions sociologically as a folk religion, in which the dharma is closely identified with culture. This "enchantment," however, is coming to an end as traditionally Buddhist societies modernize and the relationship between these modernized Asian societies and traditional Buddhism becomes problematic. Buddhist leaders need to articulate an understanding of the dharma that meets the needs of people in societies where Buddhist faith can no longer be taken for granted. This process is already visible in societies like those of Taiwan, Japan, and Korea. I am also aware that the disjunction of culture and dharma can be overcome by distorting Buddhism into an ideology in the service of nationalism. This happened in Japan in the 1930s and 1940s as Professor Chen has indicated. Examples of Buddhist nationalism can also be observed at times in Sri Lanka and Thailand. On the other hand, the demise of folk-Buddhism is also leading to the rise of a transnational, transcultural Buddhist community as Professor Chen has also indicated. These Buddhists are articulating an understanding of the dharma that responds to the complex needs of their rapidly changing societies. They are often more disposed to interreligious dialogue than their forebears. Take for example the new prominence of "Engaged Buddhism" and its complex relationship with Christian social activism. Also, there are several prominent examples of reformed Buddhists movements in Taiwan. Let me draw attention to the work of Dharma Master Hsin Tao of Ling Jiou Shan. Since 9/11, Master Hsin Tao has dedicated his efforts to dialogue with Muslims. Dharma Master Hsing Yun of Fo Guang Shan and Dharma Master Cheng Yen (a Taiwanese Buddhist nun and the founder of the Tzu Chi Foundation), promote a "humanistic Buddhism" that is open to dialogue with Christians.

In addition, I count Professor Chen himself as an example of a Buddhist ready for interreligious dialogue. His readiness is visible in his willingness to work out Buddhist responses to significant social and political problems in conversation with Christian teachings. For example, Professor Chen approaches the challenge of global warming in terms of the Buddhist notion of "shared *karma*." He begins by noting that the threat posed by climate change connects human beings on this planet in an unparalleled way. Today, we must recognize that we are linked by a collective or "shared karma," in contrast to our individual karmic debts, the more traditional way of Buddhist thinking. He then asks how this Buddhist way of conceiving karma might relate to the Christian doctrine of creation and how the virtue of humility might provide a basis for cooperation among Christians and Buddhists in addressing the issue.

Applying the notion of shared karma to the terrorist attack on the World Trade Center, however, is considerably more difficult for Christians to accept. People from vastly different backgrounds became victims of terrorism on 9/11, Professor Chen notes, and these victims shared in the same effect from the same cause. The victims were participants, in one way or the other, in a global economic system that provoked a violent act by a group of terrorists. In accordance with the law of karma, the cause (participation in global economic activity) has produced an effect (the attack). In Professor Chen's view, the atrocity of 9/11 was the karmic fruition of the collective acts of the victims as participants in an "imperialist economic order."

This interpretation of the terrorist attack will be abruptly dismissed by many Christians. With their eschatological sense of time's fulfillment, Christians want to interpret the terrorist attack in terms of justice for the victims and judgment against the terrorists. For not a few Christians, the atrocity called out to heaven for an apocalyptic crusade and a "war on terror." Instead of dismissing Professor Chen's approach to the terrorist attack, Christians would do well to inquire more deeply into the Buddhist doctrine of karma. All sentient beings are imprisoned in the realm of suffering (*samsara*) by their karma. The proper (Buddhist) response to this universal fact is compassion, not judgment. Karma inevitably leads to suffering (what Buddhists call *dukkha*). Furthermore, I presume that Professor Chen would agree that the Buddhist practice of compassion should be extended to all sentient beings, bound as they are by the law of karma—compassion toward those who suffered from karma's effects (the victims), but also those whose karmic acts will inevitably bear more sorrowful fruit in the future (the terrorists). In their dialogue with Buddhists,

Christians should ask how the doctrine of karma allows us to see how both the terrorists and the victims are bound together in a "shared karma" in which all sentient beings are interconnected in the realm of suffering by their compulsive need to act (karma). Exploring this issue by means of our dialogue with Buddhists may turn out to be helpful for thinking more deeply about themes in Catholic social teaching, such as "interdependence" and "the virtue of solidarity." Shared karma may bring deeper insight to Christian Liberation Theology understand of oppressor and oppressed as part of one social system.

Professor Anselm Min is critical of my proposal to place the project of a theology of religions aside in favor of the praxis of interreligious dialogue. Although he is not the first to take umbrage at what is the most controversial proposal in my work, I wish to thank him for being the most articulate and thorough in his critique. He objects to my claim that a theology of religions should be judged by its ability to support the church's responsibility to engage in interreligious dialogue. Instead, he argues that a theology of religions should be judged by its adequacy to existential and historical problems of life. Professor Min has a point. All Christian doctrines, seemingly, should be judged by this criterion, the theology of religions being no exception. However, I believe that the notion of a theology of religions needs to be singled out for special attention at this time in the recent history of the Catholic church. More than other Christian doctrines, the theology of religions has an impact on the church's ministry of dialogue.

This impact on dialogue is a mixed blessing at best. No doubt, the Catholic Church's fulfillment theology has motivated some Christians to seek out those who follow other religious paths and engage in dialogue. When I began my conversations with Buddhists more than twenty-five years ago, a version of this fulfillment theology was my guide. In time, however, I had to admit that this theology was not helpful to me in my attempt to understand Buddhists on their own terms. The negative impact of fulfillment theology on interreligious dialogue is even more serious, however.

Too often, I find Catholics focusing on this fulfillment theology in lieu of engaging in interreligious dialogue. This tendency is hard to document, but a real problem all the same. Talking about the importance and necessity of interreligious dialogue is much easier and less time-consuming than actually sitting down with Buddhists, listening to them as they present their views, learning their languages, studying their scriptures, and even sharing in their practices. Elaborate debates about how Buddhists are saved by Christ are an effective way for Christians to continue to talk to themselves and not to Buddhists. Even as I recognize with Anselm Min that every theology of religions needs to be judged by its adequacy to existential and historical problems of life, I am also asking him to recognize with me that theologies of religion, more than other Christian doctrines, succeed in distracting us from the difficult work of engaging in dialogue.

To be very precise, I am not proposing that the fulfillment theology be abandoned or even modified. I am certainly not suggesting (as Professor Min claims I do, rhetorically) that Catholics abandon their belief in the universality of the work of the Holy Spirit and become Buddhists in order to dialogue with them. Rather, I am asking Catholics to shift their energies from the question of a theology of religions to interreligious dialogue. My motivation is practical, not theoretical. Catholics should recognize the achievement of the church over the last fifty years in articulating a comprehensive theology of religious diversity, but also recognize that the fulfillment theology of religions is not helpful in the church's efforts at dialogue (at least with Buddhists). Catholics have succeeded in articulating a theology of religions adequate to the demands of Christian tradition. Now they need to devote their energies to interdialogue.

Furthermore, I must disagree somewhat with Professor Min when he claims that the fulfillment theology of religions is universalist and not sectarian. This theology is both universalist and sectarian, in my view.[1] Fulfillment theology is universalist, therefore, in that it encompasses all the religions and allows us to recognize in the religious lives of others the same grace witnessed to by Christian faith. This is good theology, adequate to the universality of the Christian religious vision.

I want to nuance Professor Min's position by noting that fulfillment theology is sectarian as well. Catholic fulfillment theology is what François Lyotard calls a "grand narrative."[2] The post-modern condition, according to Lyotard, is that all grand narratives have lost their innocence in the world today. In my view, Christian faith is the existential and historical truth (Min's words) that has universal value for every human being. My Buddhist friends, however, say the same thing about the *dharma*. In dialogue, these two grand narratives come face to face with one another. Inter-religious dialogue means not denying the otherness of the Other. This is what it means when I say that all grand narratives have lost their innocence. Let me be clear: I am not proposing religious relativism when I speak of the loss of innocence. I am saying that the universality of Christian faith has become "sectarian" in a world where all grand narratives have lost their innocence. Of all the possibilities for a theology of religions, fulfillment theology is the most adequate to the universal vision of Christian faith. Like all "grand narratives," the church's fulfillment theology makes universal claims that reflect the priorities of its specific sectarian perspective. The same is true of my Buddhist friends. A practical problem arises, however, when this "sectarian universalism" is used as a basis for dialogue with Buddhists. Our fulfillment theology does not allow us to recognize the "otherness" of Buddhism. Therefore, I am in complete agreement with Anselm Min that the Catholic Church's encompassing understanding of all religions should not be abandoned. (I fear that I have not been clear enough on this matter) Instead, Catholics should recognize that

(1) their church's fulfillment theology is a great achievement, (2) this project is complete, at least for the time being, and (3) now, Catholics need to devote their attention to the more pressing matter of building solidarity with other religious believers by means of interreligious dialogue. Buddhism runs Catholics off their theological map. This is not a bad way to be faithful to Christ.

Notes

1 François Lyotard, *The Post-modern Condition: A report on Knowledge* (Minniapolis: University of Minnesota Press, 1984), 37.
2 Ibid.

SUGGESTIONS FOR FURTHER READING

1. Donald W. Mitchell and James Wiseman, O.S.B., eds., *The Gethsamani Encounter* (New York: Continuum, 1998). A collection of papers given at the historic dialogue meeting called by the Dalai Lama at the Trappist monastery in Gethsamani, Kentucky. Topics include prayer and meditation, monastic life, the Christian understanding of God and the Buddhist understanding of emptiness.

2. Paul Knitter, *Introducing Theologies of Religions* (Maryknoll, N.Y.: Orbis, 2002). The best summary of the debate regarding the Christian theology of religions by a scholar who has worked in this field for many years.

3. Jacques Dupuis, *Toward a Christian Theology of Religious Pluralism* (Maryknoll, N.Y.: Orbis, 1997). A major publication that pushes the boundaries of how Catholics might best understand their relationship to other religions, especially Hinduism.

4. James L. Fredericks, *Buddhists and Christians: Through Comparative Theology to Solidarity* (Maryknoll, N.Y.: Orbis, 2004). An example of doing Christian theology comparatively in dialogue with Buddhism. This volume includes an analysis of the fulfilment theology of religions, an introduction to Buddhist doctrine, and a comparison of Thomas Aquinas and the Buddhist philosopher Nagarjuna.

5. Masai Abe, *Zen and Western Thought* (Honolulu: University of Hawaii Press, 1985). A collection of essays by one of the great pioneers of Buddhist-Christian dialogue. The essays address the Christian notion of God and the Buddhist notion of emptiness.

6. Paul Mommaers and Jan van Braght, *Mysticism: Buddhist and Christian, Encounters with Jan van Ruusbroec* (N.Y.: Crossroad, 1995). One of the very

best examples comparing Buddhist teachings with Christian mysticism by two extremely knowledgeable scholars.

6. Francis X. Clooney, *Comparative Theology: Deep Learning Across Religious Borders* (Oxford: Blackwell Publishing, 2010). A general introduction to the practice of doing theology comparatively by one of the most influential thinkers in this field.

6

Catholicism and Confucianism

An Intercultural and Interreligious Dialogue:
Historical Perspectives and Contemporary Challenges

PETER C. PHAN

This essay explores the encounter between two systems of thought and ways of life whose fortunes in East Asia have been intertwined for more than four centuries and whose future prospects seem to be indissolubly wedded to each other. This task is made vastly complicated by the fact that there is a deep uncertainty about the identity of one of these two partners-in-dialogue. While there is a broad agreement as to what is meant by "Catholicism," there are sharp differences of opinion regarding "Confucianism." It has been seriously and extensively debated, for example, whether Confucianism is a religion at all or whether it is merely a philosophical anthropology or an ethical system or a sociopolitical theory, and even whether "Confucianism" itself is, historically speaking, a Western invention.

The subtitle of my essay, "An Intercultural and Interreligious Dialogue," indicates my own position in these debates. I believe that Confucianism is to be regarded as a philosophical anthropology, an ethical system, a sociopolitical theory, and a religious way of life, all at once. These distinct categories, while useful in academic discourse, are not adequate representations of what is commonly referred to as Asian religions in general and Confucianism in particular. To encompass all these aspects of Confucianism, I will use culture and religion as the two broad perspectives for my exposition of the encounter between Confucianism and Catholic Christianity.

I begin with a bird's-eye view of the basic teachings of Confucius and the main developments of Confucianism. Next I give an account of the encounter between Confucianism and Roman Catholicism in East Asia, mainly in China, from the sixteenth century to the present. I end with reflections on some of the most important issues confronting an intercultural and interreligious dialogue between Confucianism and Roman Catholicism.

It is to be noted that my essay has a narrowly circumscribed focus, that is, the dialogue between Confucianism and Roman Catholicism. More precisely, it will consider only some and not all the issues that are crucial for that dialogue. It does not deal with the encounter between Confucianism and Christianity in general nor with the relationship between the Roman Catholic Church and other Christian churches in China, on the one hand, and the Chinese political system and the Chinese government, on the other. It is, of course, impossible to wall off my reflections on the encounter between Roman Catholicism and Confucianism from these other larger issues and I will occasionally refer to them. I hope that my reflections will make a contribution, however small, to the understanding of the future of Christianity, and in particular of the Roman Catholic Church, in East Asia.

Kongzi, the *Ru* Tradition, and Confucianism

Kongzi, Kong Fuzi, Confucius

"Confucius" is the Latinization by sixteenth-century Jesuit missionaries in China—most probably Matteo Ricci—of the honorable title Kong Fuzi (literally, Master Kong). This Chinese expression itself was popularized if not invented by the Jesuits to designate a man proclaimed as China's greatest teacher of wisdom whose given name is Kong Qiu and courtesy name is Kong Zhongni and who was known to the Chinese as Kongzi—but not as Kong Fuzi, though the honorific *Fuzi* (master) was used by his disciples to address him or refer to him.[1] Born into a family of minor aristocracy in the small feudal state of Lu, near modern Qufu (Shandong Province) Confucius (551–479 B.C.E.) lived in an age of great social and political upheaval known as the Spring and Autumn Period (772–481 B.C.E.) of the Eastern Zhou Dynasty (771–256 B.C.E.). Of Confucius's life little is known with certainty, except that like others of his time, Confucius regarded public service as the proper goal of a gentleman (*junzi*). It is reported that at about the age of thirty-five, he visited the neighboring state of Qi but received no offer of employment from Duke Jing of Qi. He then returned to Lu and at the age of fifty took up a minor office of police commissioner. Disappointed with his failure to influence the duke of Lu, Confucius left Lu again and traveled for some thirteen years with a small band of disciples to visit various states. In around 484 Confucius returned to Lu, where he was made a low-ranking counselor. He died some five years later in 479 at the age of seventy-three.

In the *Lunyu* (literally, "ordered sayings"), popularly known in English as the *Analects*, a collection of 497 verses purportedly containing Confucius's conversations with his disciples and compiled by the latter about a hundred years after his death, Confucius was alleged to have summarized his life as follows:

> At fifteen, I set my mind upon learning; at thirty, I took my place in society; at forty, I became free of doubts; at fifty, I understood Heaven's Mandate; at sixty, my ear was attuned; and at seventy, I could follow my heart's desires without overstepping the bounds of propriety.[2]

This barest autobiographical outline, though reflecting a historical core, is symbolic of the various stages of intellectual and spiritual progress of the "Confucian Way." This way comprises three pairs of stages. The first pair (learning and taking one's place in society) focuses on study and ritual practice. The second pair (freedom from doubt and understanding Heaven's Mandate) emphasizes the necessity of fully internalizing the new way of life and compliance with the will of heaven. The third pair (being attuned and following one's heart's desires without overstepping the bounds of propriety) describes the state of complete harmonization between one's internal dispositions and the dictates of the moral order. These six stages contain all the essential elements of the so-called Confucian Way—personal self-cultivation through education for its own sake, sociopolitical engagement, and moral and spiritual transformation through compliance with a transcendent order of values. It is a way that can be practiced by anyone and does not necessarily correspond with any period of one's age.

Just as "Confucius" is the Latinization of the honorable title of Kong Fuzi, invented by the sixteenth-century Jesuits for Kongzi, so the term "Confucianism" is also a Jesuit invention for the system of thought purported to be originally taught by the Chinese Master. As Paul Rule has noted, until Nicholas Trigault published Matteo Ricci's journals in 1615, no European had ever discussed Confucius and the thought system associated with him, Confucianism. However, "Confucianism," if understood to mean some philosophical system or religious organization founded *ex nihilo* by Confucius, in the way Buddhism is founded by Siddhārtha Gotama and Christianity by Jesus of Nazareth, then it is a misnomer. In fact, Confucius explicitly disclaimed any intention to establish new teachings or practices.[3] Rather, living in a state of political instability and moral decay of the Spring and Autumn Period of the Eastern Zhou Dynasty, Confucius believed that the only way to reestablish harmony and prosperity in society is to return to the "Way of the Ancients," especially as embodied by the legendary sage kings (the Jade, Shun, Yao, Yellow, and Yu emperors) and later by the founders of the Zhou Dynasty (King Wen, King Wu, and the duke of Zhou).

The *Ru* Tradition

Prior to Confucius there had been an intellectual tradition to which he made appeal as a normative fount of wisdom and as a way of life, and which is often referred to as *ru*.[4] That Confucius referred to this tradition, urging his disciple Zixia to be "a gentleman *ru*" (*junzi ru*) rather than "a petty *ru*" (*xiaoren ru*) is reported in the *Analects* (6.13). However, what is meant by *ru*, both etymologically and historically, is extremely obscure and has by no means been settled despite extensive scholarly studies. Etymologically, *ru* is said to be derived from the character *xu*, which itself is composed of two parts, meaning "cloud" and "above sky," as well as associated with other homophonous characters meaning "wet," "soft," and "weak." These etymologies suggest that *ru* were people versed not in the military arts but in ritual, music, and dance.[5] Historically, according to Zhang Binglin (1869–1936), *ru* refers to three different kinds of people in the government office of the Zhou Dynasty: first, to intellectuals or gentlemen equipped with skills and expertise in one or more areas of social life (*shu shi*); second, to professionals versed in the six arts of ritual, music, archery, charioteering, history, and mathematics; and third, to people who assisted the ruler to follow the way of yin-yang and to educate the people on this way.[6]

By the time of the Warring States Period (479–221 B.C.E.) Confucius, as Han Feizi, a well-known critic of Confucius's ideas and practices, points out, was recognized as the most preeminent master in the *ru* tradition. From here it was but a small step to identify *ru* with the teaching of Confucius, and the members of the *ru* tradition with his disciples. A complex of expressions associated with *ru* such as *rujia* (*ru* family), *rujiao* (*ru* teaching), *ruxue* (*ru* learning), and *ruzhe* (the *ru*) are used to designate what is now referred to as Confucianism and the adherents of the Confucian Way. Not that Confucianism is identical with *ru*. As has been mentioned, Confucius claimed to be only a transmitter and not an inventor of tradition. Nevertheless, there is no gainsaying the fact that in transmitting the Way of the Ancients, Confucius had transformed it or at least is regarded to have done so by later writers, so that *ru* no longer refers merely to masters of dance, music, and ritual but to a specific tradition of thought and learning associated with Confucius and a community of scholars committed to studying and transmitting it.

Long before Confucius, there had existed, therefore, a tradition of learning that he claimed to have transmitted. This intellectual tradition was initiated by the Zhou Dynasty, especially the duke of Zhou, who wanted to institute an official system of education (*guan xue*) to train specialists for civil service. This educational system was weakened during the Spring and Autumn Period by the rise of semi-independent states and was replaced by private learning and education (*si xue*). Confucius was one of the earliest teachers to initiate this educational system and was said to have had three thousand students, of whom seventy-two were intimate disciples. Eventually this community of Confucius's disciples was known as the *rujia*, that is, a family or fellowship of the followers of the Confucian Way, devoted to the study and restoration of the Way of the ancient sage kings.

The Way of the sage kings is believed to be embodied in certain ancient writings or records. It was Confucius's lifelong ambition to collect, edit, preserve, and transmit them to later generations.[7] The earliest mention of the so-called Confucian classics is found in the *Book of Zhuangzi*, a Daoist work compiled during the Warring States Period. This work lists "Six Classics" (*liujing*): The *Classic of Poetry* or *Odes* (*shijing*), the *Classic of Documents* or *History* (*shujing* or *shangshu*), the *Records of Ritual* (composed of three texts: *Ceremonials* [*Yili*], *Rites Records* [*Liji*], and *Zhou Rites* [*Zhouli*]), the *Classic of Changes* (*yijing*), the *Spring and Autumn Annals* (*chunqiu*), and the *Classic of Music* (*yuejing*).[8] The last book is no longer extant (or has never existed); probably it was burned by order of the first emperor of the Qin Dynasty in 213 B.C.E., so that today reference is made to the "Five Classics" (*Wujing*).[9] These Five Classics, which deal with politics, legend, history, poetry, ritual, philosophy, and religion, were regarded as the foundational sources of Confucianism and were made the subject for civil service examinations.

In addition to the Five Classics, during the Song Dynasty, Zhu Xi (1130–1200) singled out the *Analects*, two chapters of the *Record of Ritual*, namely, the *Great Learning* (*Daxue*) and the *Doctrine of the Mean* (*Zhongyong*), and the *Book of Mengzi* (Mencius) to form the "Four Masters" (*Sizi*), later designated as the "Four Books" (*Sishu*), which were also made the subject of civil service examinations by the Yuan Dynasty (1260–1370) in 1313.

Confucianism

Partly because Confucianism was made by Emperor Wu (r. 141–87 B.C.E.) of the Han Dynasty (206 B.C.E.–220 C.E.) into the state orthodoxy in 136 B.C.E., with the worship of Confucius as the state cult, and Confucius himself awarded the title "Great Perfect, Most Holy Culture-Spreading First Teacher," and partly thanks to the Jesuit portraiture of the *xianru* (first *ru*) or *guru* (ancient *ru*), which they identified with the original teaching of Confucius, as the only orthodox teaching in China, Confucianism is often equated, in both Western and Eastern imagination, with "Chineseness" or Chinese culture. However, such identification is historically inaccurate since Confucius was only one of the great thinkers of his time and Confucianism was part of the "Hundred Families/Schools" (*baijia*) that flourished between 551–233 B.C.E. Sima Tan (ca. 170–110 B.C.E.), a court historian of the Western Han Dynasty, mentions six schools of philosophy vying for popular acceptance and imperial patronage during his time: beside Confucianism, Daoism (Laozi and Zhuangzi), Mohism (Mozi), the School of Law or Legalism (Han Feizi and Lizi), the School of Names (Hui Shi), and the School of Yin and Yang and the Five Phases (Agents or Elements). All these schools of thought, with sharply different views on fundamental philosophical issues and at times engaging in acrimonious polemics against one another, have contributed to the formation of what constitutes Chinese culture or "Chineseness."

Words ending in -ism tend to essentialize the realities they refer to, masking their historical permutations and multiplicity of forms. Like other cultural, philosophical, and religious traditions, Confucianism is by no means homogeneous but has undergone continual developments since its beginning in the sixth century B.C.E. to our time and contains within itself self-contradictory positions. Of course, Confucian basic teachings are rooted in the Five Classics and the Four Books, but already in the years immediately following the Master's death, there were among his self-proclaimed disciples, for example, Mengzi and Xunzi, profoundly different opinions regarding basic issues such as human nature and the process of self-cultivation.[10]

Even during the Western Han Dynasty (206 B.C.E.–8 C.E.), when, thanks to the efforts of Jia Yi (200–168 B.C.E.) and Dong Zhongshu (179–106 B.C.E.), Confucianism became the state-sponsored orthodoxy, there was a debate between the "Old Text" and "New Text" schools, so-called because the texts of the former are written in the pre-Han (archaic) script, whereas those of the latter in the script current during the Han Dynasty. The Old Text School arose as a reaction against the New Text School. The New Text School was championed by Dong Zhongshu and therefore accepted as orthodox, whereas the Old Text School was advocated by Liu Xin (? B.C.E.–23 C.E.) who was later accused of forging its texts. The New Text School tends to present Confucius not only as a sage but also as the "Uncrowned King," a divine being, and the "savior" of the world, whereas the Old Text School regards him simply as a transmitter of ancient wisdom. In addition, Han Confucianism became eclectic since it had to incorporate elements of Daoism and the School of Law and even apocryphal writings (chenwei) in order to be acceptable to all the citizens.

Differences in various Confucian traditions are more pronounced in the turbulent period following the collapse of the Eastern Han Dynasty (25–220 C.E.) known as the Six Dynasties period (222–589 C.E.) when the other two traditions, that is, Buddhism and Daoism, reemerged to form with Confucianism the "Three Teachings/Religions" (sanjiao). In their struggle against their competitors, Confucian scholars, notably Wang Bi (226–249 C.E.), developed a new form of hybrid Confucianism known as "The Study of Mystery" or "Mysterious Learning" (xuanxue), also referred to as Neo-Daoism. This form of learning, while remaining deeply rooted in the Confucian classics, interprets them, especially the *Classic of Change*, in Daoist language and categories. Mysterious Learning is the first serious and influential attempt to synthesize Confucianism and Daoism in order to resolve the debate about the relationship between moral codes/social institutions (*mingjiao*), which Confucianism favors, and the inborn tendencies of human nature (*ziran*), which Daoism promotes. The result is a new form of Confucianism enriched by the mystical elements of Daoism.

Another Confucian tradition emerged during the Song Dynasty (960–1279 C.E.), referred to in the West as Neo-Confucianism, which moves away from exegetical studies of the Confucian classics typical of the Han Learning to speculations on psychological and metaphysical issues of body-mind (*shenxin*) and nature-destiny (*xingming*). Major contributors to this new strand of Confucianism are the Five Masters of the Song Learning (*Song xue*): Zhou Dunyi (1017–1073), Shao Yong (1011–1077), Zhang Zai (1020–1077), and the two Cheng brothers, Cheng Hao (1032–1085) and Cheng Yi (1033–1107). However, the greatest master of the new school is Zhu Xi (1130–1200). As mentioned above, it was Zhu Xi who anthologized the "Four Books," which eventually became equal to the "Five Classics." In reinterpreting the Confucian tradition as a way of self-transformation, Chu Xi follows the Cheng brothers' view of the dual concepts of "principle" (*li*) and "matter" (*qi*) as constitutive of the cosmos. Hence, the "Neo-Confucian" tradition is often called the "Study of Principle" (*li xue*) or the Rationalist School or the Cheng-Zhu School. For Zhu Xi, to achieve self-transformation one must understand the *li* through the study of the classics (by "investigating things" [*gewu*]) and the practice of rituals. Zhu Xi's "School of Principle," which fuses scholarship with practice, and his commentaries on the classics became the required subject matter and norm for the civil service examinations from the Yuan Dynasty until the end of the Qing Dynasty.

However, Zhu Xi's interpretation of Confucianism did not go unchallenged. His contemporary Lu Jiuyuan (1139–1193) argues that the Supreme Ultimate that underlies and permeates all things is not *li* but *xin* (heart/mind). All human beings are endowed by heaven with the heart/mind, and therefore all have the innate ability to know intuitively what is good, to learn how to be good, and to do what is virtuous. This "Study of the Inner Mind" or "Learning of the Heart/Mind" (*xin xue*) School was developed and systematized under the Ming Dynasty (1368–1644) by Wang Yangming (1472–1529). Wang eschews complex textual exegesis to accumulate knowledge of external things as a way of self-transformation. Instead, he advocates knowing the "original substance" (*benti*) within and acting on one's innate affections as the means to achieve sagehood.[11]

Under the Manchu/Qing Dynasty (1644–1911), as part of anti-Qing sentiment, a movement called "Han Studies" (*Hanxue*) emerged. "Han Studies" proposes evidence-based research (*kaozheng*) and a return to the ancient classics beyond the distortions of Buddhist-inspired "Song Studies" (*Songxue*) embodied in the "School of Principle" and the "Study of the Inner Mind." Underlying "Han Studies" is the conviction that behind all the divergent and politically inspired "Confucianisms" there is a common and pure source residing in the authentic teaching of Kong Zi in which knowledge and action are united. Consequently, there was in this period a renewed interest in Confucius as a prophetic figure and religious founder.

Finally, as the Qing Dynasty was facing collapse and as the empire was repeatedly humiliated with unequal treaties by the Western powers, with their superior economic, technological, and military machinery, burning questions were raised by political and economic reformers regarding the social relevance of Confucianism for the new China—China with "science and democracy"— confronted with the urgent need of modernization. While the Qing Dynasty assiduously promoted the Cheng-Zhu School to bolster its own regime, Confucian scholars such as Kang Youwei (1858–1927) revived the debate between the Old Text School and the New Text School. Kang favored the latter with its apotheosis of Confucius and proposed to make Confucianism the state religion (*guojiao*) as a means to strengthen China, making *kongjiao* (Confucian teaching/religion or, better, "Confucianity") the Chinese equivalent of Christianity of the West. These scholars' political reform, which included constitutional monarchy, lasted only a hundred days in 1898, thwarted as it was by the Empress Dowager Cixi (1835–1908). After the fall of the Qing Dynasty (1911), there arose a powerful anti-Confucianism movement, crystal-ized in the May Fourth Movement (1919), led by radical liberals such as Chen Duxiu (1879–1942), Yi Baisha (1886–1921), Li Dazhao (1889–1927), and Hu Shi (1891–1962), laying all the ills of China at the feet of Confucius and Confucianism.

As a reaction against this extreme anti-Confucianism, a new movement led by Confucian scholars known as "Modern New Confucian Learning" (*xiandai xin ruxue*) came into existence. This movement may be divided into three periods. The first, before the founding of the People's Republic of China (1949), was led by two groups of prominent scholars: those favoring the Cheng-Zhu School ("New Learning of Principle" [*xin songsue* or *xin lixue*]) and those following the Lu-Wang School ("New Learning of the Heart/Mind" [*xin xinxue*]). Among the first group, the most distinguished scholar is Fung Yu-lan (1895–1990), and among the second, Xiong Shili (1885–1968). The second period, which took place mainly outside of mainland China—particularly in Hong Kong, Taiwan, and the United States—was led by scholars such as Tang Yunyi, Mou Zongsan, Xu Fuguan, and Fang Dongmei (Thomé H. Fang). In 1858 they published "A Declaration of Chinese Culture to the Scholars of the World" in which they maintain that Confucianism is not against democracy, science, and technology and that a modernized China cannot do without Confucian humanistic values. The third stage of Modern New Confucian Learning is being carried out by these scholars' students and disciples such as Cheng Chung-ying, Tu Wei-ming, Liu Shuxian, and Yu Yingshi, who present Confucianism as a holistic tradition and culture, including metaphysics, ethics, politics, religion, and spirituality, with positive implications for modernization as demonstrated in such countries as Japan, South Korea, Taiwan, Hong Kong, and Singapore.[12]

Meanwhile, in mainland China, the Chinese Communist Party, founded in 1921, criticized Confucianism as feudalistic and backward. Maoist ideology replaced Confucian ideology. Later, Confucianism suffered a terrible blow during the Cultural Revolution (1966–1976) with its iconoclastic policies against the "Four Olds": old customs, old habits, old culture, and old thinking— emblems for what was considered Confucianism. After the deaths of Zhou Enlai and Mao Zedong (both in 1976) and the arrest of the Gang of Four, research and publications on Confucianism became acceptable again. The government restored the Kong family mansion, cemetery, and Confucian temple in Qufu and opened it to the public. In the 1980s several international conferences on Confucius were held in Qufu. The China Confucius Foundation was established in 1984, and the Shandong Publishing Commission Office has published the *Guide to Confucian Culture*, a set of books on Confucius and Confucianism.

The main purpose of this exceedingly sketchy overview of Confucianism and its various schools and developments throughout its more than two-and-a-half-millennia history is to alert readers to the extreme complexity of a dialogue between Roman Catholicism and Confucianism. The preliminary question to such dialogue remains: with which Confucianism must the Catholic Church enter into dialogue? While a dialogue between Roman Catholicism and Confucianism can certainly dwell at the general level of the core philosophical, ethical, and religious concepts of both traditions, it is still necessary to be clear about how these concepts are understood, especially in different strands of Confucianism. Furthermore, from a practical point of view, such a dialogue cannot be carried out at the institutional or official levels since Confucianism, in contrast to Buddhism, Daoism, and other East Asian religions, does not have an authoritative teaching office (analogous to the Roman Catholic magisterium), a priesthood, and a governing authority. In fact, in China, Confucianism is not a religion recognized by the government.[13] The question is not only with *which* Confucianism but also with *whom* among Confucians should the dialogue be carried out. Before broaching these themes, a survey of the encounter between Roman Catholicism and Confucianism will provide some useful insights into how a dialogue between the two traditions should proceed in the future.

Confucianism and Roman Catholicism: A Historical Encounter

"The Luminous Religion from Daqin": Christianity's First Encounter with Chinese Religion

In 635 East Syrian Christianity in Persia, misleadingly referred to as the Nestorian Church, came to Xi'an, the ancient imperial capital in northwest China's Shaanxi Province, and was warmly welcome by the Tang emperor Taizong (r. 627–649).[14] On the stele erected in Xi'an in 781 and discovered in 1623/25, Christianity is called *Jingjiao* (the Luminous Religion or Religion of Light) of *Daqin* (Syria). The carved text of 1,756 Chinese characters, composed by the priest Jingjing (his Syriac name is Adam), is a unique record of the encounter between the Christian faith and Chinese religions in the eighth century.

The stele contains a lengthy exposition of the Christian faith in prose and a shorter summary in verse. The first exposition, the more important of the two, refers to the Trinity, the creation of the world, the original fall of humanity, Satan's rule, the incarnation, salvation, the Bible, baptism, evangelization, ministry, Christian morality, fasting, the liturgy of the hours, and the Eucharist. In expounding the essentials of the Christian faith Jingjing makes ample use of Buddhist, Daoist, and Confucian expressions. He describes God as "unchanging in perfect repose," a formula used by the *Daodejing* to describe the *Dao* (Way). God is said to have produced "the four cardinal points" (a basic concept of Chinese geomancy) and "the two principles of nature," that is, the yin and yang of Daoist and Confucian cosmology. He speaks of some people mistakenly identifying "nonexistence" (the Daoist "nameless nothingness") with "existence." He refers to Christianity as the ever-true and unchanging "Dao" itself. Jesus is said to have established his "new teaching of nonassertion," the key Daoist notion of *wu wei* (nonaction).

Jingjing also adopts Confucian expressions. The Messiah is said to teach "how to rule both families and kingdoms"—a Confucian phrase in the book of *Great Learning*. Buddhist concepts and images are also pressed into service. Jesus is said to have "hung up the bright sun" (i.e., crucifixion), taken an oar in "the vessel of mercy" (the boddhisattva or the Kuan-yin), and "ascended to the Palace of Light." In addition to this stele, there are numerous other Chinese written sources on Christianity of the T'ang period, often referred to as the "Dunhuang Documents," found in the library of the Dunhuang grottoes, which also contain a serious effort at interpreting the Christian faith in terms of Chinese religions.

The Catholic Church's First Entry into China

Unfortunately, when East Syrian Christianity disappeared with the fall of the Tang Dynasty in 907, its members scattered among the nomadic tribes in the north and northwest of China. Christianity did not come back to China until the time of the Mongolian/Yuan Dynasty (1279–1368), this time under the aegis of the Catholic Church. The mission to Rome in 1287 by Rabban Sauma (ca. 1225–1294), an Ulghur born in Beijing and a monk of the East Syrian Church, in the name of the Mongolian il-khan Arghun, revealed to the Roman Church the existence of Christians in Mongolia and China. The first Catholic missionary to enter China proper, sent by Pope Nicholas IV, was the Franciscan friar Giovanni da Montecorvino, who reached Khanbalik (Beijing) in 1294, shortly after the death of Kublai Khan. The missionary built a church there and reported in 1305 that there were six thousand converts. In 1307, Pope Clement V appointed him archbishop of Khanbalik and primate of Cathay (North China) and the entire Far East. When Giovanni da Montecorvino died in 1328, it was estimated that there were more than ten thousand Catholics. In 1338, at the request of the last Mongol emperor, Toghan Timur, Pope Benedict XII sent a group of missionaries, among whom was Giovanni da Marignolli. When the Yuan Dynasty collapsed in 1368, the Catholic Church, which then numbered thirty thousand and had enjoyed imperial support, disappeared with it. Compared with East Syrian Christianity, Roman Catholicism under the Yuan Dynasty cannot be said to have made a serious effort at communicating the Christian faith in terms, both cultural and religious, understandable to the Chinese. To the Chinese, the Catholic Church could not but appear as a foreign religion, politically protected by an occupying foreign power and financially supported by a foreign religious institution.

Catholic Presence under the Ming Dynasty: A Sustained Dialogue with Confucianism

Almost 185 years later, the Catholic Church attempted once more to enter China, which under the Ming Dynasty (1368–1644) had become isolationist, nationalist, and rigidly Confucian. Francis Xavier (1506–1552) left Japan for a mission in China in 1551 but died the following year on the small island of Sancian, within sight of the China coast, near Guangzhou.

Under the *padroado* (patronage) of Portugal, Francis Xavier's missionary dream was fulfilled by a small band of Jesuits, particularly Alessandro Valignano (1538–1606), Matteo Ricci (1552–1610), and Michele Ruggieri (1543–1607). From Macau, a small Portuguese colonial enclave (with a diocese established in 1576), Ricci and Ruggieri entered mainland China in 1583.

Following Valignano's accommodationist method, the two missionaries—
Ricci in particular—learned the language, studied the Chinese classics, dis-
carded the Buddhist monk's attire, presented themselves as members of the *ru*,
dressed in Confucian scholars' garb, and tried to convert the Chinese through
science (especially mathematics, astronomy, and map making). Ricci's goals
were to reach Beijing and to convert the emperor, and through him, the Chinese
people. Though he failed in his latter goal, he was allowed in 1600 by Emperor
Wanli to reside in Beijing. In the last ten years of his life, Ricci, known in Chinese
as Li Matou, was much more successful in his mission than in his previous
seventeen years. Among his converts were the so-called "Three Pillars of the
Chinese Church": Paul Hsu (Xu Guangshi), Leon Li (Li Zhizao), and Michael
Yang (Yang Tingyun), though the last was not taught by Ricci.

Other Jesuits who worked in Beijing until the fall of the Ming Dynasty
(1644) and beyond include Nicholas Longobardi (1559–1654), Adam Schall
(1592–1666), and Ferdinand Verbiest (1623–1688), the latter two directing the
prestigious Bureau of Astronomy. At the end of the Ming Dynasty there were
150,000 Chinese Catholics.

Roman Catholicism and Confucianism in Conflict under the Manchu (Qing) Dynasty

At the beginning of the Qing Dynasty, the prospects of Catholic missions were
promising. Thanks to his accurate prediction of the solar eclipse on September 1,
1644, Schall was appointed by the second Manchu emperor Shunzi director not
only of the Bureau of the Calendar but also of the Institute of Mathematics.
The emperor also gave the Jesuits a piece of land, a church, a residence in the
capital, and an annual subsidy. Verbiest, who succeeded Schall and served for
twenty years, was much decorated by the third Manchu emperor, Kangxi
(r. 1662–1723).

Unfortunately, internal struggles among missionaries soon threatened to
unravel Catholic missions in China. Until 1631, the Jesuits had enjoyed a mono-
poly in the China mission. After the 1630s, however, other religious orders
arrived, in particular, Dominicans (1631), Franciscans (1633), Augustinians
(1680), and members of *Missions Étrangères de Paris* (1683). These newcomers
brought with them not only conflicts between the two rival patronage systems—
the Spanish and the Portuguese—but also the nascent colonizing ambitions
of France and rivalries among religious orders. More tragically, they adopted
different attitudes toward Chinese cultural and religious practices, in particular
the sacrifice offered to Confucius and the veneration of ancestors. In Ricci's
footsteps, most Jesuits (with the notable exception of Niccolò Longobardi,
Ricci's successor) who worked mainly with the elite, tolerated these customs as

nonsuperstitious acts of political and civil nature, whereas the newly arrived missionaries, who labored among the uneducated masses, condemned them as idolatry.

These contrasting positions brought about what is known as the Chinese Rites Controversy, which began in 1633 and did not end until 1939. Popes Clement XI (in 1715) and Benedict XIV (in 1742) proscribed the Chinese rites. These condemnations proved disastrous for Catholic missions in China. In retaliation, the emperor Kangxi banished missionaries from China in 1722 unless they followed Ricci's policy, and his decision was confirmed by his successor Yongzheng. In the next 160 years sporadic persecutions broke out, Christians were ordered to apostatize, churches were seized, and native priests were forced to secularize. Nevertheless, the Chinese Catholic Church survived. In 1800, there were reportedly two hundred thousand Catholics in all of China.

Catholic Missions in the Nineteenth Century

At the beginning of the nineteenth century, Catholic missions in China were complicated by the arrival of Protestants, mostly British, who devoted much of their energies to education and medical welfare. With the new missionaries, other colonial powers appeared on the scene. The Opium War of 1839–1842 and 1856–1860, which humiliated China, concluded with favorable treaties for Great Britain, France, Russia, and the United States. These unequal treaties, besides forcing China to concede economic advantages to Western powers, stipulated the legal right for missionaries to preach and to erect churches in Chinese territories. Even the Chinese Christians were protected by the treaties as a special class, immune from Chinese laws. Catholic missions, in particular, were protected by France. Catholics were often segregated in isolated communities that were often regarded as foreign colonies, completely dependent on missionaries. In 1841, a Catholic mission prefecture was established in Hong Kong when the island was ceded as a British colony in that same year. From 1860 on, Catholic and Protestant missionaries flocked in great numbers to China, which soon became the world's largest mission field.

Eclipse of the Catholic Church under the Communist Regime in the Twentieth Century

By the middle of the nineteenth century, Christianity had been compromised by the Taiping Rebellion (1851–1864), led by Christian-inspired Hong Xiuquan, against the Qing Dynasty. At the beginning of the twentieth century, antiforeign sentiments were rumbling and exploded in the 1900 Boxer Uprising (1898–1900). Identified in the Chinese eyes with Western imperialism,

Christianity suffered heavily. With the overthrow of the Qing Dynasty (1911), in which Christians played a role, and with the establishment of the Republic of China (1912), led by the Christian Zhongshan (Sun Yat-sen), Christianity enjoyed what may be called its golden age (1900–1920). The number of Chinese Christians was estimated at 366,000 in 1920. Now the foreign religion was welcomed as an antidote to Chinese traditionalism. Its victory was, however, short-lived. In 1920, it was denounced by a group of college students as an anachronistic obstacle to China's modernization, and Christian missions were condemned as tools of Western imperialism. Again, anti-Christian movements broke out in 1924 and lasted until 1927, this time supported by political parties, both Nationalist and Communist. Thousands of missionaries had to leave, mission schools and hospitals had to be closed, and physical properties were damaged. In 1926 six Chinese priests were ordained bishops.

With the victory of the Communists over Jiang Jiashi's (Chiang Kai-shek) *Kuomingtang* in 1949, Christian, and in particular Roman Catholic, missions ended. The Three-Self Patriotic Movement Committee was founded in 1954, and all churches were required to join. In 1957, the Chinese Catholic Patriotic Association was established. As a result, there are two Catholic groups in China: the government-approved Patriotic Catholic Association and the so-called "Underground Church," loyal to Rome. In 1958, the first consecration of Catholic bishops without the approval of Rome took place. Since the 1980s there have been encouraging signs that the Vatican and Beijing have been working toward a rapprochement. Seminaries were allowed to open in Shanghai and Beijing in 1982 and 1983, respectively. In 2000, Pope John Paul II canonized 120 martyrs of China. Recently, two bishops were ordained with papal approval, following the appointment of a Vatican-approved bishop for Beijing.

However, relations between the Vatican and the Chinese government remain volatile and unpredictable, since the latter is still holding firm to the power to name bishops, and it has recently appointed several bishops without Vatican approval. Statistics of Chinese Christians are notoriously unreliable. Recent surveys put the number of Christians in mainland China at forty million, including twelve million Catholics, the rest being Protestants, especially Pentecostals.

Catholic *and/or* Confucian?

From this survey of the presence of the Catholic Church in China it is clear that the encounter between Christianity and Confucianism, which was initiated by the East Syrian Church in the seventh through ninth centuries, was taken up and expanded since the seventeenth century, principally by Jesuit missionaries with their accommodationist policies. The history of such accommodation—or to use the contemporary neologism of "inculturation"—is replete with triumphs and defeats, lights and shadows, humble acceptance and acrimonious rejection.[15] Though I have focused on China above, the same history of the encounter between Catholicism and Confucianism played out in countries within the Sinic sphere of influence, namely, Japan, South Korea, Taiwan, and Vietnam, not to mention overseas Chinese communities.

A thumbnail sketch of this complex history of the Catholic-Confucian encounter may be drawn on two canvasses: first, Catholic *and* Confucian, and, second, Catholic *or* Confucian. Of course, reality is much more complicated than these two stark options suggest. No Catholic would be totally for or totally against being a Confucian and vice versa. Both Catholicism and Confucianism contain beliefs and values that either side can appropriate, just as they also profess what one side considers as errors and unacceptable practices. The two alternatives however can serve as a useful heuristic device with which to view past approaches to the question of a possible dialogue between Catholicism and Confucianism.

On one side, then, there is the approach as practiced by the Jesuits, especially by Matteo Ricci and his followers. Alessandro Valignano (1539–1606), who, with the title of visitor general, was in charge of the Jesuit missions in East Asia, wanted Jesuit missionaries in China and Japan to "accommodate" Christianity to the local cultures, and as part of this policy he mandated a proficient knowledge of the native languages and personal adaptation to the local mores and customs. When Matteo Ricci arrived in Macao in 1582, he joined Michele Ruggieri in the study of the Chinese language and of the Five Classics and the Four Books and in the translation of these works into Latin. A year later, both Ricci and Ruggieri were allowed to enter China and to reside at Zhaoqing in the Guangdong Province. From there Ricci gradually moved north, through Shaozhou, Nanchang, Nanjing, and finally Beijing and established Jesuit houses in these four cities. It was during this northward journey that Ricci made a fateful decision to discard the Buddhist monk's outward appearances and dress in the *ru* garb, presenting himself and other Jesuits as the *ru*, *xiru* (Western scholars) or *daoren* (men of the Way).

Of course, it was not simply a matter of sartorial style. Rather, it was a missionary strategy, one that has had vast and lasting implications for the Catholic-Confucian dialogue. Since Buddhism has many parallels with Catholicism, especially in monastic practices, Ricci, with the encouragement of Wang Pan, the magistrate at Zhaoqing, adopted at first the Buddhist monk's indigent clothing to make himself a Chinese to the Chinese. Subsequently, however, he realized that Buddhist monks were held in low regard by the Chinese populace and that in order to gain a hearing from the Chinese, he had to present himself as a bona fide member of the *ru* and establish missionary contacts with these Confucian scholars who were part of the Ming imperial bureaucracy, with the hope that through them he could convert the emperor. It is in this intellectual environment that Ricci composed his most celebrated work, *Tianzhu shiyi* (the True Meaning of the Lord of Heaven), completed in 1596 and published in 1603. This work is presented as a dialogue between the "Chinese Scholar" and the "Western Scholar"—in fact, a dialogue between Confucianism and Catholicism on the basis of human reason alone.

Ricci is convinced that Confucianism as represented in the Five Classics— what he terms the "original" or "first" *ru*—is profoundly consonant with the Christian faith, with its belief in the one God designated as *Shangdi* (Lord on High) or *Tian* (heaven), in contrast to Song Confucianism (now called "Neo-Confucianism"), which became, through the hands of Zhu Xi, atheistic with its speculations on *li* and *qi* and distorted by Buddhist ideas. Consequently, Ricci vigorously attacks Buddhism and Daoism as superstitious sects and extols the original *ru* as the only embodiment of authentic Chinese culture and religion. Ricci was practicing the method of *bu ru yi fo* (supplement *ru*, excise Buddhism), to use the expression of one of his most celebrated converts, the scholar-doctor Paul Xu Guangxi.[16] In this context, Confucius is elevated to the status of a Christian/Jesuit saint (Ricci's honorific title for him is *santo*), and the *ru*, whom Ricci calls *la legge de' letterati* (order of the literati), becomes the equivalent of the Society of Jesus. Such "manufacturing" of Confucius and the *ru* reaches its peak in the influential and massive work edited by Philippe Couplet and his fellow Jesuits, *Confucius Sinarum Philosophus sive Scientia Sinensis* (1687).

At the other end of the spectrum of missionary method stands the attitude of most Mendicant Friars, Dominicans and Franciscans, who came to evangelize Southeast China (especially the Fujin Province) in the 1630s, and the members of *Missions Étrangères de Paris*, sent in the 1650s by the Holy Congregation for the Propagation of Faith, independent from the Portuguese *padroado*. These new arrivals worked mainly with the lower and poorer classes (whom, of course, the Jesuits did not neglect to evangelize, contrary to popular opinion). They were not versed in the Confucian classics nor were they interested in establishing a common cultural and religious ground between the Christian faith and the Chinese culture. Consequently, they were much more inclined to highlight the opposition between the "pagan" way of life of the Chinese and the new Christian life that conversion imposes.

The differences between the Jesuits and the other missionaries with regard to Confucianism came to a head in the so-called Chinese Rites Controversy, which lasted three hundred years and brought into collision two fundamentally diverse attitudes to Confucian practices. The issues at hand were the cult of Confucius and the veneration of ancestors, both sacred obligations, the former for the *ru*, the latter for all Chinese. Most Jesuits tend to regard the rituals connected with these two cults as acts of filial piety and of "civil and political" significance, not religious worship, and hence permissible. The Mendicant Friars and the members of *Missions Étrangères de Paris* (most notoriously Bishop Charles Maigrot) saw them as superstition and proposed they be banned. On the basis of conflicting reports from the missionaries, Rome issued confusing policies, at times prohibiting and at other times tolerating them. In 1742, a total and absolute prohibition of these practices was issued by Pope Benedict XIV in his decree *Ex quo singulari*. It was not until 1939 that Rome lifted the ban on the traditional rites in honor of Confucius and the ancestors on the grounds that they are only of "civil and political" import. In sum, then, a Chinese can be both Catholic *and* Confucian. One need not abandon one's Confucian heritage to be a Christian. The all-deciding question is of course, what is meant by "Confucian heritage"?

A Roman Catholic-Confucian Dialogue: Challenges and Prospects

As I hope to have made it clear, there are many schools and strands of Confucianism and there have been conflicting ways among Catholics in dealing with Confucianism. This double diversity must be kept in mind as we explore the encounter between Catholicism and Confucianism. In the remaining part of my essay I would like to highlight the new context in which Confucianism exists today, the challenges presented by this context to the encounter between Confucianism and Catholicism, and, finally, the prospects of a successful dialogue between these two religious traditions in East Asia.

A New Sociopolitical Context

There is no need to belabor the point that from the sixteenth to the twentieth centuries the context in which Catholicism encountered Confucianism in East Asia has changed drastically. In China, Japan, South Korea, and Vietnam, Confucianism has lost its preeminent position as an official religious and cultural tradition. Confucianism as a state-sponsored orthodoxy and the cult of Confucius—*kongjiao*—as a national religion (*guojiao*) have been dethroned. In their place, other ideologies are reigning supreme, Communism in China and Vietnam, and capitalism in most of other East Asian countries. Thirty years ago, Julia Ching, writing on the encounter between Confucianism and Christianity, already noted this radical change in context that required new modes and venues of such encounter:

> At that time (before the collapse of the Qing dynasty), there was yet an identifiable Confucian world, where certain well-known moral values

attributed to Confucian teachings were enshrined in the social order, and respected by legal institutions, in the countries of the Far East. Today, the situation has changes drastically.[17]

The drastic change Ching refers to is the dictatorial domination of Marxist socialism. Today, even that situation has also changed drastically. As far as economics is concerned, Communism, while still a one-party political system in China, North Korea, and Vietnam, is giving in to the forces of the free-market economy. Capitalism, at least under the Communist Party's control, is being experimented with and seems to be on the ascendance in China and Vietnam. With it, and with globalization, consumerism and materialism are rampant in all East Asian countries, especially among the youth.

In the meantime, questions are being raised about the cultural, moral, and religious values that should guide the lives of people and the nations where Confucianism was at one time the normative ideal. Of course, the fact that Confucianism is no longer the state-supported orthodoxy does not mean that its ideas and values have not been operative in the lives of individuals since the collapse of the Qing Dynasty in China and the advent of modernity in East Asia. Nor does it mean that there has been a total moral and religious vacuum in East Asian countries. There are other religions such as Buddhism, Daoism, Islam, and even Christianity, not to mention other popular religions, that continue to flourish, sometimes underground.

It has been mentioned that Confucianism has been enjoying a renaissance, albeit modest, in mainland China, and that it is vigorously practiced in other countries such as Taiwan, Hong Kong, Singapore, the Republic of Korea, and overseas East Asian communities. It has even been suggested that Confucianism, with its emphasis on community, hard work, egalitarianism, education, and harmony is the engine driving the economic miracle in the so-called Four Asian Tigers. Be that as it may, it is clear that the radically changed sociopolitical context of East Asian countries presents new challenges for the encounter between Catholicism and Confucianism.

New Challenges for Catholic-Confucian Encounter

At first glance, Catholicism and Confucianism seem to be on two different planes, having little to do with each other. The former is based on divine revelation, centered on God, and directed toward eternal salvation in union with the Triune God, whereas the latter makes no claim to divine origination, is centered on humanity, and aims at this-worldly perfection of sagehood. Given these fundamental differences, it was not surprising that many Christians, especially Protestant missionaries to China in the nineteenth century, have tended to regard a common understanding between the two traditions impossible or, if they attempt a dialogue at all, would end up by arguing for the superiority of Christianity, on the grounds that Christianity has access to truths that are in principle unknowable to human reason, whether corrupted or not.

It is to the credit of Matteo Ricci that in his *Tianzhu Shiyi* he bases the dialogue between the "Western Scholar" and the "Chinese Scholar" on what human reason—what he calls the *lumen naturale*—can discover as true and can be known with certainty by both Christians and Confucians. Hence, he rightly does not discuss the death and resurrection of Jesus in this book. Nevertheless, even Ricci feels the need to dedicate a major portion of his book to the questions of the existence of the one God, divine creation, the immortality of the soul, and other philosophical questions.

Today, in the current context of Marxist socialism and capitalism, the primary and urgent issue seems to be the meaning of being human, and it is here—philosophical anthropology—that Catholicism and Confucianism can undertake a first and most fruitful dialogue before broaching the question of God. On the one hand, anthropology has been the preferred starting point of modern and contemporary theology, even among Catholics. On the other hand, Confucianism is essentially about becoming and being a perfect human being (*junzi*). Here is not the place to expound the essentials of Confucian anthropology. As Julia Ching explains, there are ample opportunities for mutual enrichment between Confucianism and Catholicism in doctrines such as the essential openness of the human to the Transcendent, the basic moral character of human nature, the ideal of sagehood (*sheng*), self-cultivation in virtue unto death if necessary, conscience and natural law based on human nature, the heart/mind (*xin*) as the locus of the encounter between heaven and humans, the universal virtue of *ren*, the five human relationships, and the sense of community.[18]

This deepening of a common, albeit not identical, understanding of what it means to be human in the Catholic and Confucian traditions, enriching and correcting each other, is all the more urgent in societies such as those found in some East Asian countries where the question of God is not and cannot be explicitly raised, or where religious pluralism is such that a common understanding of the divine is not possible.

From the Catholic perspective, another area where a dialogue between Catholicism and Confucianism will be fruitful is ritual, liturgy, and worship. Admittedly, the cult of Confucius and the veneration of ancestors are no longer controversial, at least on the theological level. There are, however, aspects of Catholic worship and liturgy that will benefit greatly from an incorporation of the Confucian understanding of ritual (*li*). Whereas Catholic liturgy emphasizes strongly the transcendent dimension of worship as an act of cult directed toward God by the community, it often leaves undeveloped the personal, social, and political implications of worship. It is in this latter aspect that Catholic ritual can be enriched by the Confucian understanding and practice of ritual (*li*). Confucian *li* is variously translated as ritual, rites, ceremonies, moral codes, or the rules of propriety. As James Legge explains: "They [the rules of *li*] are practiced by means of offerings, acts of strength, words, and postures of courtesy, in eating and drinking, in the observances of capping, marriage, mourning, sacrificing, archery, chariot-driving, audiences, and friendly missions."[19] The practice of *li* inevitably involves a social and political dimension insofar as it places the practitioner in his or her fivefold relationship, namely, those obtained between ruler-subject, husband-wife, parent-child, sibling-sibling, and friend-friend.

With regard to rituals proper, there are two celebrations in which Catholic liturgy needs to be integrated with Confucian rituals: weddings and funerals. There is no doubt that these two moments of the life cycle, more than any other, are deeply marked by Confucian ideas and practices and are most important for East Asians in the Confucian sphere of influence. Unfortunately, East Asian Catholics most often celebrate them in two distinct and parallel ceremonies, one at home (which is very elaborate) and the other in church, according to the Roman ritual (which is required). As a consequence, the "official" liturgical celebration of weddings and funerals is regarded as a canonical requirement but bereft of real significance, whereas the "private" ceremony in the family is invested with greater solemnity and existential meaning. In light of this dichotomy, the Confucian-Catholic dialogue must make ritual and worship two of the most urgent items for consideration. The goal for such dialogue is a harmonious integration of the two rituals, especially for weddings and funerals, in such a way that they can enrich each other.

Prospects

In concluding his comprehensive introduction to Confucianism, Xinzhong Yao discusses its modern relevance. Yao enumerates three values by which Confucianism can be of great significance to contemporary society: an ethic of responsibility, a comprehensive understanding of education, and a humanistic understanding of life.[20]

First, in terms of responsibility, Confucianism places a paramount emphasis on the person's responsibility to self, family, nation, and world. In this respect, says Zao, "Confucianism can make a contribution to a new moral sense, a new ecological view and a new code for the global village."[21] Second, in terms of education, Confucian intellectualism is essentially a tradition based on learning and education. However, learning and education in the Confucian tradition, Zao points out, does not aim at mere accumulation of information and technical skills, though these are not neglected. Rather it aims at self-cultivation:

"Confucian education is designed to penetrate the inner world of a learner, based on the conviction that cultivation of the virtues is more important than adjustment of external behavior."[22] Its goal is to form a "gentleman" (*junzi*), that is, a moral aristocrat, an exemplar of ritually correct behavior, ethical courage, and noble sentiment, a person of *ren*, with "sageliness within" and "kingliness without." Third, in terms of humanism, Confucianism represents an essentially anthropocentric faith. Thus, Zao reminds us, "Confucianism does not lack a transcendental dimension, nor does it want in metaphysical depth. The belief in Heaven and the Heavenly endowed mission underlies Confucian philosophy, politics, and religion."[23]

It is in these three areas that an encounter between Catholicism and Confucianism has very bright prospects. If these prospects are effectively realized, then both Catholicism and Confucianism will be relevant not only in East Asia but also for all the world. Julia Ching puts it best when she describes how Confucianism can be dead or alive:

> And so, is Confucianism relevant? If we mean by the word sterile textual studies, a society of hierarchical human relationships excluding reciprocity, the permanent dominance of parents over children, of men over women, a social order interested only in the past and not in the future, then Confucianism is not relevant, and may as well be dead.
>
> But if we also mean by it a dynamic discovery of the worth of the human person, of his possibilities of moral greatness and even sagehood, of his fundamental relationship to others in a human society based on ethical values, of a metaphysics of the self open to the transcendent, then Confucianism is very relevant, and will always be relevant.[24]

Interestingly, if one substitutes "Confucianism" with "Roman Catholicism," most of the negative characteristics and positive assets apply as well. Consequently, it is in the interest of both religious traditions to engage in a mutual critique and reciprocal learning so as to preserve and enhance their future in the world.

Notes

1 Michael Nylan notes that the expression "Kong Fuzi" apparently first appeared on inscribed spirit tablets dedicated to the Sage during the Yuan period, but it was the Jesuit missionaries of the late sixteenth century who popularized the term in their attempt to elevate Confucius to the status equivalent to that of the fathers of the early church. See Nylan, *The Five "Confucian" Classics* (New Haven, Conn.: Yale University Press, 2001), 363–364.

Lionel Jensen, however, believes that the expression "Kung Fuzi" was invented by the Jesuits themselves. See his *Manufacturing Confucianism: Chinese Traditions and Universal Civilization* (Durham, N.C.: Duke University Press, 1997), 83–86.

2 All the translations of the *Lunyu* are taken from *Confucius Analects, with Selections from Traditional Commentaries*, trans. Edward Slingerland (Indianapolis: Hackett, 2003). The text cited is indicated by the numbers of book and verse. Here 2.4. Other recent important studies of *The Analects* include E. Bruce Brooks and A. Taeko Brooks, *The Original Analects: Sayings of Confucius and His Successors* (New York: Columbia University Press, 1990); and Bryan W. Van Norden, ed., *Confucius and the Analects: New Essays* (Oxford: Oxford University Press, 2002).

3 *Analects* 7.16: "The Master said: 'I transmit rather than innovate. I trust in and love the ancient ways. I might thus humbly compare myself to Old Peng.'"

4 Until the twentieth century, *ru*, Michael Nylan points out, always referred to people, that is, people committed to the study and propagation of the classics (in this sense they are classicists), and never to a set of ideas in contrast to those of Buddhism and Daoism. See Nylan, *The Five "Confucian" Classics*, 2.

5 On the early Confucians primarily as ritual masters, see Robert Eno, *The Confucian Creator of Heaven: Philosophy and the Defense of Ritual Mastery* (Albany: State University of New York Press, 1990).

6 Robert Campany notes that Zhang Binglin's reference to the "way of yin-yang" with regard to early Confucianism is inaccurate since the yin-yang theory has nothing to do with early Confucianism; it did not arise until around 250 B.C.E. Furthermore, according to Kang Youwei (1858–1927) and Hu Shi (1891–1962), *ru* refers not to the government officials of the Zhou Dynasty but to those of the Shang Dynasty (1600?–1100? B.C.E.). Thanks to their knowledge of religious rituals, these professionals were later employed as priests by the succeeding Zhou Dynasty (Western Zhou, 1100?–771 B.C.E., and Eastern Zhou, 770–256 B.C.E.).

7 With regard to Confucius's role in establishing these ancient records, later known as the "Confucian Classics," there are three opinions. A majority of Confucian scholars holds that there had been no "classics" proper before Confucius and that it is Confucius who established what is known as the classics. For other scholars, especially of those of the Old Text School, the classics originated in the early years of the Zhou Dynasty and Confucius's role is essentially limited to arranging them as textbooks for his students. Another group of scholars, while crediting Confucius with a significant role in the formation of the classics by collecting, editing, arranging, and transmitting the ancient records, prefers not to make a generic judgment on Confucius's authorship of these classics as a whole but using the historical and literary method, attempt to determine which parts of these classics were made by Confucius and his disciples and which parts came from later periods. See Xinzhong Yao, *An Introduction to Confucianism* (Cambridge: Cambridge University Press, 2000), 52–54.

8 For a study of the classics, see the very helpful work by Nylan, *The Five "Confucian" Classics*.

9 The "Five Classics" were later expanded to the "Seven Classics" (added were the *Analects* and the *Classic of Filial Piety*). During the Tang Dynasty (618–906) "Nine Classics" were inscribed on stone tablets (the *Classic of Changes*, the *Classic of Documents*), the *Classic of Poetry*, the three commentaries on the *Spring and Autumn Annals*, the *Zhou Ritual* (*zhouli*), the *Book of Etiquette and Ritual* (*yili*), and the *Records of Ritual*. Later, three more books were added to make "Twelve Classics": the *Classic of Filial Piety* (*xiaojing*) and the *Analects*. Finally, in the Song Dynasty (960–1279), the *Book of Mengzi* (*Mencius*) was added to make the "Thirteen Classics."

10 For interpretations of Confucianism and Chinese religious thought in general, see Arthur Waley, *Three Ways of Thought in Ancient China* (London: Allen & Unwin, 1939); Benjamin I. Schwartz, *The World of Thought in Ancient China* (Cambridge, Mass.: Harvard University Press, 1985); and A. C. Graham, *Disputers of Tao: Philosophical Argument in Ancient China* (Chicago: Open Court, 1989); a very accessible history of the development of

Confucianism is John H. Berthrong, *Transformations of the Confucian Way* (Boulder, Colo.: Westview, 1998). For an original exposition of Confucianism in dialogue with Western philosophy, see the three volumes by David L. Hall and Roger T. Ames, all published in Albany by New York State University Press, *Thinking through Confucius* (1987); *Anticipating China: Thinking through the Narratives of Chinese and Western Culture* (1995); and *Thinking from the Han: Self, Truth, and Transcendence in Chinese and Western Culture* (1998). On the history of Chinese philosophy in general, see Wing-Tsit Chan, ed., *A Source Book in Chinese Philosophy* (Princeton: Princeton University Press, 1969); Fung Yu-lan, *A History of Chinese Philosophy*, vols. 1–2, trans. Dek Bodde (Princeton: Princeton University Press, 1952); and Thomé Fang, *Chinese Philosophy: Its Spirit and Its Development* (Taipei: Linking, 1981).

11 Because this school is developed by Lu Jiuyuan and Wang Yangming, it is also known as the School of Lu-Wang. It is also referred to as the Idealistic School in opposition to Cheng-Zhu's rationalism.

12 Tu Wei-ming's most significant works include *Centrality and Commonality: An Essay on Confucian Religiousness* (Albany: State University of New York Press, 1986); *Selfhood as Creative Transformation* (Albany: State University of New York Press, 1985); *China in Transformation* (Cambridge, Mass.: Harvard University Press, 1994); and *Confucian Spirituality*, vols. 1 and 2, ed. Mary Evelyn Tucker (New York: Crossroad, 2003). Also, on Confucianism as a religious way of life, see Rodney Taylor, *The Religious Dimension of Confucianism* (Albany: State University of New York Press, 1990).

13 The religions officially recognized by the Chinese government include Buddhism, Daoism, Roman Catholicism, Protestantism, and Islam.

14 The best one-volume up-to-date history of Christianity in China is Jean-Pierre Charbonnier, *Christians in China*, trans. M. N. L. Couve de Murville (San Francisco: Ignatius, 2007). For a brief historical outline of Christianity in Asia, see Peter C. Phan, *The Blackwell Companion to Catholicism*, ed. James J. Buckley, Frederick Christian Bauerschmidt, and Trent Pomplun (Oxford: Blackwell, 2007), 203–220.

15 For a discussion of the encounter between Catholicism and Confucianism, see John D. Young, *Confucianism and Christianity: The First Encounter* (Hong Kong: Hong Kong University Press, 1983); Julia Ching, *Confucianism and Christianity: A Comparative Study* (Tokyo: Kodansha International, 1977); Stephen Uhalley Jr. and Xiaoxin Wu, eds., *Christianity and China: Burdened Past Hopeful Future* (Armonk, N.Y.: M. E. Sharpe, 2001); Peter K. H. Lee, *Confucian-Christian Encounters in Historical and Contemporary Perspectives* (Lewiston, N.Y.: Edwin Mellen, 1991); and Liam Matthew Brockey, *Journey to the East: The Jesuit Mission to China 1579–1724* (Cambridge, Mass.: Harvard University Press, 2007).

16 Another version of the motto reads: *qinru paifo* (draw close to *ru*/Confucianism, repudiate Buddhism).

17 Ching, *Confucianism and Christianity*, 28.

18 See Ching, *Confucianism and Christianity*, 68–105.

19 *The Li Ki or the Collection of Treatises on the Rules of Propriety or Ceremonial Usages*, trans. James Legge (Oxford: Clarendon, 1885), 388.

20 See Yao, *An Introduction to Confucianism*, 279–286.

21 Ibid., 279.

22 Ibid., 281–282.

23 Ibid., 285.

24 Ching, *Confucianism and Christianity*, 63.

A Response to Peter C. Phan

To Become Good Confucian Catholics

ROBIN R. WANG

The word of God is addressed to all people, in every age and in every
part of the world; and the human being is by nature a philosopher.
—*Fides et ratio, John Paul II*, chapter 6, par. 64

There have been several official statements from Vatican officials, including
Pope John Paul II, that claim that Greek philosophical thought is normative
(i.e., "required") for Christianity. The argument is that God guided Christianity
into the Greek world so that Christianity could articulate itself using Greek
ideas.[1] This "Hellenized" Christianity is now the norm for all Christians, including Christians who come from a Confucian background. Does this then mean
that to be a Christian one has to be, at least, "Western"? Could Catholicism
divorce itself from Greek philosophy and embrace Confucianism as a philosophical heritage? Could Confucianism as a system of philosophical thinking be
embraced for strengthening the Catholic faith?

Fr. Phan's essay helps us to contemplate these questions in a new light.
His essay casts a wide net, producing a series of insights and a nuanced understanding of the history of Confucianism and its encounter with Catholic
Christianity. He views Confucianism as "a philosophical anthropology, an ethical system, a sociopolitical theory, and a religious way of life," and explores the
relationship between Confucianism and Roman Catholicism from the sixteenth
century to the present. This investigation ends with some reflections on the
challenges and prospects for a meaningful intercultural and interreligious
dialogue between Confucianism and Roman Catholicism in a contemporary
globalized world.

After a discussion of the complex history of the Catholic-Confucian encounter, Fr. Phan proposes two possible options: (1) being a Catholic *and* Confucian,
and (2) being Catholic *or* Confucian. In other words, can a Chinese be both
Catholic and Confucian? Must Chinese people abandon their Confucian

heritage in order to be Christians? These questions are about how we are to appreciate this "Confucian heritage." There are many fundamental differences between Catholicism and Confucianism, as Fr. Phan pointed out. However, Fr. Phan also pointed out that there are also "ample opportunities for mutual enrichment." This brief response to Fr. Phan's essay will explore some of the possibilities for how this "mutual enrichment" might take place.

Methodology and the Universality of Human Reasons

In an era that emphasizes the radical difference, Otherness, and incommensurability of different cultures, the first difficulty is grasping some common ground for cultural exchange, some way that would allow us to understand points of intersection between Catholicism and Confucianism. The history of Catholic and Confucian encounters reveals that a meaningful and productive intercultural and interreligious dialogue depends on how we understand diversity. Matteo Ricci demonstrated a fruitful model. According to his understanding, *lumen naturale*, the light of reason, naturally leads to God. This natural light is shared by all human beings. Gottfried Leibniz (1646-1716), a German mathematician and philosopher, follows and refines Ricci's insight by assuming the universality of reason and of natural theology but emphasizes more the various ways that reason is expressed in different cultural contents. These views and practices have laid the groundwork for a significant exchange in history, particularly between the Catholic and Confucian traditions.

In a comparative study of the early Confucian Xunzi (ca. 310–ca. 220 B.C.E.) and early medieval Christian St. Augustine (354–430 C.E.), Aaron Stalnaker develops a conceptual foundation for a comparative study. He makes two important points concerning "vocabulary" and "bridge concepts." The "vocabulary" is a way to get *into* a given cultural and intellectual context and to conceive of different ethical approaches understood as working through different vocabularies.[2] It is a faithful and just way to interpret the primary texts as well as to make an epistemologically neutral interpretation. The "bridge concept" is a way to get *across* different paradigms using a shared theme. These concepts (such as human nature, personhood, spiritual exercises, and will) provide the "bridges" that allow for comparative interpretations of Augustine and Xunzi. The "bridge concepts" approach can be helpful in the Catholic and Confucian dialogue. No doubt, there are many deeply shared concerns in Catholic and Confucian teachings. In the next section, I will turn to some examples of central Confucian concepts that might provide bridges in the contemporary Catholic-Confucian dialogue.

Points of Intersection: To Become a Human Being

Based on a careful reading of classical Confucian texts, we can formulate at least three aspects of a Confucian vision of being a human. These valuable intellectual and practical spaces are inherent and intrinsic to Confucian teaching and provide some basis for dialogue.

1. Ren: The Human Being Is Transformable and Reformable

According to Confucius, a person is not necessarily a human being at birth but rather becomes fully human through a life of cultivation. This conviction presupposes both that human beings are naturally transformable and that they ought to be ethically so transformed. Human beings, therefore, possess inherent natural dignity and moral equality in their ability to complete this lifetime journey. We find this outlook in the *Analects*: The Master said, "Human beings are similar in their natural tendencies, but vary greatly by virtue of their habits" (*Analects* 17.2).[3]

Mencius develops this position further to claim that all human beings have the same nature, which tends toward goodness. Becoming good, however, requires careful cultivation to allow the "sprouts" of virtue to develop into a fully virtuous life. This cultivation requires a person to seek one's heart:

> Mengzi said, "Benevolence is man's heart and appropriateness is man's path. How lamentable it is to abandon the path and not pursue it, to lose this heart and not know to seek it! When men's fowl and dogs are lost, they know to seek for them again, but they lose their heart and do not know to seek for it. The *dao* of learning is nothing else but to seek for the lost heart." (*Mencius* 6A11)

2. Li: A Ritualized Way of Living (Community and the Common Good)

The assumption that a human being is transformable requires that persons direct their lives along a certain path. In this regard, Confucian teaching offers a specific way of living to make the transformation of human beings possible. The Confucian personal reformation takes place through a series of *performative* practices. These practices rest essentially on doing traditional rituals. These rituals contain both specific ceremonial observances and a very wide range of the expectations for daily life, much of which we might now label as matters of "etiquette." In one passage of the *Analects*, for example, Confucius claims that ritual should cover every aspect of our lives, including not only action but also even what we see and hear:

> Yan Hui asks for *ren* (benevolence). Master said, "Self-disciplining and returning to observe the rituals is called *ren*. . . . Do not look at anything that is not ritually proper; do not listen to anything that is not ritually proper; do not speak about anything that is not ritually proper; do not act in any way that is not ritually proper." (*Analects* 12.1)

In *Mencius*, ritual propriety is also seen as having a great importance for being human:

> Mengzi said, "That whereby the superior man is distinguished from other men is what he preserves in his heart—namely, benevolence and ritual propriety. The benevolent man loves others. The man of propriety shows respect to others. He who loves others is constantly loved by them. He who respects others is constantly respected by them." (Mencius 4B28)

One of the many significant functions of ritual is to formulate a common good in the community. Each member of community is bound together through a shared common good. Such Confucian teaching promotes an intrinsic connection between individuals and the community.

3. Xue: Cultivation of the Whole Person through the Love of Learning and Reverence for Traditions

For Confucius, to become human also requires learning, which combines a diligent study of classic texts—a holistic form of study that includes their bodily, emotional, and intellectual appropriation under the guidance of an authoritative teacher. While the love of learning has a primacy, this learning process can only be accomplished through proper guidance from a teacher or master. In the *Analects*, Confucius understands his love of learning as his distinguishing characteristic: "The Master said, 'There are, in a town of ten households, bound to be people who are better than I am in doing their utmost and in making good on their word, but there will be no one who can compare with me in the love of learning'" (*Analects* 5.28).

The *Analects* also illustrates the importance of loving learning and respecting tradition: The Master said, "Make an earnest commitment to the love of learning and be steadfast to the death in service to the efficacious way" (*Analects* 8.13).

The Master said, "Yû, have you heard the six words to which are attached six becloudings?" Yû replied, "I have not." "Sit down, and I will tell them to you.

"There is the love of benevolence without the love of learning—the beclouding here is foolish simplicity. There is the love of wisdom without the love of learning—the beclouding here is dissipation of mind. There is the love of sincerity without the love of learning—the beclouding here is careless disregard of consequences. There is the love of uprightness without the love of learning—the beclouding here is rudeness. There is the love of courage without the love of learning—the beclouding here is insubordination. There is the love of firmness without the love of learning—the beclouding here is extravagant conduct." (*Analects* 17.8)

Love of learning, though, leads to characteristics we would not usually connect with learning, such as moderate desires and carefulness in action:

The Master said, "A *junzi* who eats without seeking fullness, dwells without seeking ease, is earnest in affairs and careful in speech, follows those who have *dao* and rectifies himself, can be said to love learning" (*Analects* 1.14).

This Confucian way of love for learning requires a commitment to *haogu*, reverence for traditions. Confucius points out many times that he is not a creator but a transmitter. He states that he is relying on earlier sages and the classics: The Master said, "A transmitter and not a maker, sincere and loving the ancients, I compare myself to Old Peng" (*Analects* 7.1).

The Master said, "I am not one born knowing it; I love the ancients and earnestly seek it" (*Analects* 7.20).

This respect for tradition remains central throughout the history of Confucianism.

A Puzzle: Confucius's Transcendent Orientation yet This-Worldly Underpinning

These three concepts—the need to transform human beings, the importance of ritual in creating common good, and the centrality of study and tradition—are three points that provide intersection with Catholicism on which further dialogue might be built.

We can now turn in conclusion to one of the main differences between Confucianism and Catholicism. Classical Confucian teachings show that making our current human condition splendid and beautiful must happen through a full-fledged commitment to the Confucian way. However, one may ask whether this process requires divine intervention. In Confucian texts, there is a strong sense of something that has a transcendent existence. Nevertheless, Confucius prefers to keep it at a distance: Fan Chi inquired about wisdom. The Master replied, "To devote yourself to what is appropriate for the people, and show respect to the ghosts and spirits while keeping them at a distance can be called wisdom" (*Analects* 6.22).

The subjects on which the Master did not talk were strange events, feats of strength, chaos, and spirits (*Analects* 7.21).

Zilu asked about serving ghost and spirits. The Master said, "You are not able to serve people—how could you serve ghosts?" "Dare I inquire about death?" "You do not understand life—how could you understand death?" (*Analects* 11.11).

The last passage especially makes clear the source of this distancing from the transcendent: what is most important to Confucius is our actions in this world, serving the living and understanding life. Yet the Confucians do occasionally appeal to the transcendent—in their terms, to *tian* or "heaven." Sometime *tian* simply marks the limits of human control: When Yan Yuan died, the Master said, "Alas! *Tian* is destroying me! *Tian* is destroying me!" (*Analects* 11.9).

More often, appeals to *tian* are meant to give comfort: Si Ma Niu, full of anxiety, said, "Men all have their brothers, only I have not." Zi Xia said to him, "There is the following saying which I have heard: 'Death and life are *ming*; riches and honors are *tian*'" (*Analects* 12.5).

At other times, heaven is the ultimate power in things, and so must be followed: Those who follow heaven are preserved; those who go against heaven are destroyed (*Mencius* 4A7).

According to *Mencius*, the best way to know and to connect with heaven is through one's own heavenly nature.

Mengzi said, "One who exhausts his heart/mind knows his nature. Knowing his nature, he knows heaven. Preserving one's heart/mind and nourishing one's nature is how one serves heaven." (*Mencius* 7A1).

This seed of the unity between human beings and heaven reaches its fruition in the Neo-Confucian teachings during the Song and Ming dynasties. As the above passage from the Mencius makes clear, though, the primary focus is always on the human realm. This humanistic focus combined with a degree of vagueness about the divine leaves space open for incorporating other religious viewpoints, such as Catholicism.

Conclusion

The Confucian texts cited above reveal two things. First, Confucian teaching can supply a rich cultural soil for the growth of Catholicism in China and Asia.

And second, good Confucians are also able to recognize, appreciate, and accept Catholic values through their own philosophical lens. Fr. Phan's essay has demonstrated this valuable opportunity for exchanges and interactions.

Notes

1 "Lecture of the Holy Father: Faith, Reason and the University Memories and Reflections," *Libreria Editrice Vaticana* (September 12, 2006).
2 Aaron Stalnaker, *Overcoming Our Evil: Human Nature and Spiritual Exercises in Xunzi and Augustine* (Washington, D.C.: Georgetown University Press, 2007), 6.
3 All the translations of *Analects* and *Mencius* are my own, based on *Sishu Wujing: Four Books and Five Classics* (Sichuan: Yueling, 1990).

A Response to Peter C. Phan

ROBERT FORD CAMPANY

Let me be clear that I am in some ways the professional mirror opposite of Professor Phan: I am not a theologian, but am rather a historian of Chinese religions and a practitioner of the cross-cultural, comparative study of religions in human history. Our conversation is to a large extent, then, an interdisciplinary dialogue about interreligious dialogue.

The bulk of Professor Phan's remarks concerned the history of the Confucian tradition and, to a lesser extent, the history of the ways in which it was regarded by Westerners. There are a few things in this account with which I disagree, the biggest of which is that we get little sense from it of the extent to which the Confucian tradition has been an elite tradition, with its roots in the aristocracy of the late Zhou era, however much Confucian education may have been open in principle to everyone regardless of birth. But I want to focus on Professor Phan's relatively brief remarks relating directly to the prospects of Catholic-Confucian "dialogue," since that is the theme of this book. I am very sympathetic to Professor Phan's desire for such a "dialogue," although I see rather different prospects for it than he seems to.

There is, first, a distinct oddity noted several times in the talk: that we are trying to imagine a "dialogue" between two traditions, one of which in particular has been and is now many things and no one clear thing, and for which no one in particular can speak authoritatively. It is unclear how, in such a situation, any real "dialogue" is possible. What, in fact, is meant, in quite practical terms, by "dialogue" here? Is it a matter of actual conversations between representatives of distinct traditions, or is it a matter of imagining what such a conversation might look like if it were to occur? To me, this remains unclear.

Second, when Professor Phan discusses the Rites Controversy, he notes that the pope issued in 1742 a "total and absolute prohibition" of the practices of ritually venerating Confucius and one's familial ancestors, whereas in 1939 Rome lifted this ban "on the grounds that they are only of 'civil and political' import"—that is, on the premise that they are now classified not as "religious" at all. Professor Phan concluded this discussion with the statement, "In sum, . . . a Chinese can be both Catholic and Confucian." Well, no, not really, it seems to me, not if the Chinese person in question regards his veneration of Confucius and of his or her ancestors as a religious practice. What we have here is a situation in which one party in the putative interreligious "dialogue" has declared from the start that the other party cannot legitimately conduct its rites as religious at all—that that party must enter the conversation with its core practices understood as differently categorized, hence not on a par. It seems to me that the prospects for a true "dialogue" entered into on this basis are rather dim.

To appreciate the seriousness, and indeed the (as we might even say) spiritual intensity with which offerings to ancestors as understood in the Confucian tradition could be undertaken (or at least imagined), one has only to glance at the chapter "Rightness in Offerings" (Ji yi) chapter of the Records on Rites (Li ji) and read there how, after three days of fasting, the descendant who conducts the ancestral offerings with the proper degree of sincerity will

> think on the places [the departed] frequented, think on how they smiled and spoke, think on what their aims and views were, think on what they delighted in, think on what things they enjoyed. On the third day of such vigil he will come to see those for whom the vigil is employed. On the day of offering, when he enters the chamber [of the ancestral hall] there will seem to be something that he sees [i.e., the deceased] in the place where [his spirit-tablet] is. After he has moved about and is leaving at the door, he will be awestruck upon hearing the sound of [the ancestor's] movements and will sigh as he hears the sound of [the ancestor's] sighing.[1]

It would not be too much to say—despite the passage's characteristic ontological reticence—that the descendant is here enjoined to visualize his ancestors as a sort of spiritual-sensory exercise, and that, having done so with utmost sincerity, he will be granted a multisensory vision of them in the room with him. The psychological weight and practical seriousness with which this duty to remember the ancestors, to actively summon them to mind, is taken can easily be glimpsed today in any culture area where the ancient Chinese early spring festival of Qingming is still celebrated. Whole families turn out to sweep their ancestors' tombs and present food offerings there. The mood is not usually, in my experience, sad, but it may certainly be described as solemn.

Later in his essay, Professor Phan writes that Catholic-Confucian dialogue around the question of what it means to be human is likely to be more fruitful than one that begins with the question of God. If this is true, then I feel it would have been useful to read more about the variety of Confucian views of the nature of humanity than we see in his discussion. There is a lot more to discuss than the question of the "perfectibility" of human nature in the ideal of sagehood—which turns out to have been a surprisingly embodied ideal, as Mark Csikszentmihalyi has recently shown.[2] The Confucian tradition, spurred in part by its ongoing encounters with both Daoist and Buddhist traditions in China and starting quite early,[3] developed extensive practices and understandings of self-cultivation that warrant detailed comparison with Western analogues.

Another suggestion made in the essay that it would have been useful to hear more about is that Catholicism could learn from Confucianism in the area of worship and liturgy. I would agree that the Confucian tradition over many centuries, starting with Xunzi's chapters on rites and music and continuing with segments of the early Han Records of Rites, developed rich, complex reflections on the purposes of ritual and how ritual encodes meaning and shapes human character. These would have been interesting and probably fruitful places to focus attention for a "dialogue" with the equally rich history of liturgical reflections developed in the Catholic tradition.

Toward the end of his remarks Professor Phan used striking phrases to describe the imagined interreligious dialogue that might emerge between Catholicism and Confucianism—phrases that are striking insofar as they suggest parity or equal status, and equal receptivity, between the two parties, such as "enriching and correcting each other" or "a mutual critique and reciprocal learning." I confess I do not see the basis in empirical fact for this optimistic phrasing. Is the Catholic Church open, in principle, to "correction" from any outside entity, especially from any other religious tradition? Does the doctrine of papal infallibility, for example, lend itself to doctrinal or liturgical "correction" on the basis of "dialogue" with others—especially when the church does not even recognize those others as practicing something it is willing to classify as "religious"? If not, with profound respect to the aims evidenced in Professor Phan's enterprise, can talk of "dialogue" between the two, however well intentioned, be anything but rhetoric? Perhaps there are practical uses for such rhetoric, even if that is all it can be, but it would be good to have seen these imagined uses spelled out more explicitly.

Notes

1 Here I have consulted the translation of Irene Bloom in *Sources of Chinese Tradition*, vol. 1, *From Earliest Times to 1600* (New York: Columbia University Press, 1999), 339–340.

2 See Csikszentmihalyi, *Material Virtue: Ethics and the Body in Early China* (Leiden: Brill, 2004).

3 One has only to examine the contents of such texts of late antiquity as the *Guanzi* and the *Huainanzi* to see early evidence of such encounters—or, perhaps more accurately, evidence of the inadequacy of isolating these "-isms" as distinct traditions quite so neatly as we are accustomed to do.

Peter C. Phan Continues the Dialogue

PETER C. PHAN

It is always a great honor to have one's own writings responded to by scholars whose expertise in the field one writes about is greater than one's own. But more than an ego massaging for them, it is a rich learning opportunity for me: errors are corrected, new data discovered, and improvements made. All this has happened, I am very happy to report, as the result of the gracious exchanges, both oral and written, which Professors Robert Ford Campany and Robin R. Wang shared with me, and to them I am deeply grateful. A full response to their learned responses would require another essay, which will abuse the readers' patience. Limited space will allow me only to highlight those aspects that are of greatest interest to the Catholic-Confucian dialogue.

Among Professor Campany's many points, four stand out: the Confucian dialogue partners, the nature of ancestor worship, the role of worship and ritual, and the very nature of dialogue itself. Campany rightly observes that there are no "official" spokespersons for Confucianism with whom Catholics, especially Catholics in the hierarchy, can enter into dialogue. Indeed, Confucianism, in contrast to Buddhism and Daoism, for example, is generally not recognized as an official religion, not even in countries such as China and Vietnam, which are heavily influenced by the Confucian ethos. This is partly a function of the nature of Confucianism itself (is it a "religion"?), as I point out at the beginning of my essay. That does not mean of course that a dialogue between Roman Catholicism and Confucianism is impossible. While Confucianism was "an elite tradition," as Campany rightly notes, it is pervasive in the life of ordinary East Asians whose cultural DNA it is, even though most of them have never read a single line of the so-called Confucian classics. In addition to this dialogue at the level of "life," there is an ongoing dialogue with the Confucian classics themselves and contemporary scholars, both East Asian and Western, who have made Confucian ideas and practices the guide and norm for their lives.

With regard to ancestor worship, Professor Campany is correct in pointing out its deeply religious nature. I have repeatedly argued elsewhere that the Catholic Church has made the veneration of ancestors among Asians theologically acceptable but at an unacceptably heavy price. Instead of recognizing it as an act of religious cult, it has made it into a "political and civil act," thereby emptying its authentic nature and forfeiting the opportunity and challenge to justify its practice on genuinely theological grounds.

Professor Campany has also correctly noted that ritual and worship is a fertile ground for the dialogue between Catholicism and Confucianism. I am grateful to him for the excellent bibliographical references, including his own work on the subject. Once again, may I invoke my own research and publications on a possible enrichment between Confucian and Catholic rites and liturgy, especially mourning and burial rituals.

Finally, with regard to the very possibility of dialogue itself: clearly, dialogue is fruitful only if dialogue partners, Confucian and Catholic, come to the table with sincere humility and a genuine willingness to learn. The point of dialogue is not to score points as in debate; nor is it to convert the other as in evangelization. Rather, it is exclusively for the purpose of sharing with others what one takes to be true and good; to correct one's misunderstandings and errors; to enrich oneself by the truths and values upheld by others; and to work toward a common life, collaboration, and religious sharing for the common good. Professor Campany poses a very challenging question: "Is the Catholic Church open, in principle, to 'correction' from any outside entity, especially from any other religious tradition?" The answer is of course yes, in principle, but whether in fact, the Catholic Church has always been so remains an open question, and I share his pessimism.

Professor Robin Wang highlights three issues. The first is the methodology of dialogue. I agree with her that what brings Catholics and Confucians to dialogue is their profound respect for human reason, what Matteo Ricci calls *lumen naturale*. It is by means of reason that the partners in dialogue can examine together, to use Aaron Stalnaker's terminology, "vocabulary" and "bridge concepts." Of course, the use of reason, at least for Catholics, does not exclude an appeal to divine revelation—an appeal made not as a ground for argument or guarantor of truth, but as a source for knowledge. Such knowledge still requires an explanation, though not a rational demonstration, which must respect the criteria of logical coherence and adequacy to experience, and hence, be open to public reason. Thus, Catholics are not prevented from presenting to their Confucian partners-in-dialogue the truths that come to them from Christian revelation.

Wang next highlights three areas where a Catholic-Confucian dialogue can fruitfully focus, namely, *ren, li,* and *xue*. I agree fully with all three. The first two recall Professor Campany's points, on which I have already made some comments. The third, *xue*, brings up a common feature between Catholicism and Confucianism, namely, the emphasis on self-transformation by means of tradition. Of course, tradition must not be blindly adopted and despotically imposed, a danger to which both religious traditions are prone. Rather, tradition must ever be self-renewing to be authentic and life giving, as Vatican II has reminded us.

Finally, Professor Wang notes the two apparently opposite orientations in Catholicism and Confucianism, the former toward transcendence and the latter toward immanence. Of course, they are not, in principle, mutually contradictory, though in practice one is often tempted to adopt one at the detriment of the other. It is precisely in a dialogue between Catholicism and Confucianism that these two tendencies are held and lived in a fruitful tension rather than annulling their dialectical correlation.

I am most grateful to Professors Campany and Wang for their rich insights from which I, and, I believe, readers of this volume as well, have profited much.

SUGGESTIONS FOR FURTHER READING

1. Liam Matthew Brockey, *Journey to the East: The Jesuit Mission to China: 1579–1724* (Cambridge, Mass.: Harvard University Press, 2007). A well-researched and highly readable account of how the Jesuit missionaries fashioned the Chinese Catholic Church and its religious practices according to the Jesuit ideals of lay piety.
2. Julia Ching, *Confucianism and Christianity: A Comparative Study* (New York: Kodansha International, 1977). Somewhat dated but still very helpful overview of the major theological issues to be discussed between the two religious traditions.
3. Tu Weiming and Mary Evelyn Tucker, eds. *Confucian Spirituality.* 2 vols. (New York: Crossroad, 2003). Excellent collections of studies on various aspects, both historical and systematic, of Confucianism as a way of life.
4. Xinshong Yao, An *Introduction to Confucianism* (Cambridge: Cambridge University Press, 2000). Perhaps the best one-volume introduction to the developments of Confucianism from the beginnings to our time.
5. John D. Young, *Confucianism and Christianity: The First Encounter* (Hong Kong: Hong Kong University Press, 1983). An informative overview of the attempt at "accommodation" or inculturation of Christianity into the Chinese society from Matteo Ricci to Emperor K'ang-hsi.
6. Jean-Pierre Charbonnier, *Christians in China: A.D. 600 to 2000* (San Francisco: Ignatius Press, 2007), trans. M. N. L. Couve de Murville.

INDEX

CPSIA information can be obtained at www.ICGtesting.com
Printed in the USA
BVOW04s0644080115

382423BV00001B/18/P